COOKBOOK
25 YEARS
WOMEN of the FARM BUREAU

Madison County Farm Bureau
Women's Committee
Edwardsville, Illinois

**Recipes compiled by
The Farm Bureau Women's Committee**

**Cover design by Martinko
Submitted by Suzanne Blattner**

This book belongs to_____

APPRECIATION

To all contributors of their favorite recipes and to those who helped with the book and gave of their time, we give our deepest appreciation.

We would have liked to include all recipes, but limited space prevented this. Every effort was made to include a variety of recipes. Extra pages have been left at the end of each chapter for you to add your favorite recipes.

1st printing October, 1981—10,000 copies
2nd printing June, 1986—3,000 copies
3rd printing January, 1992—3,000 copies
4th printing January, 1995—3,000 copies
5th printing October, 1995—4,000 copies
6th printing November, 2000 – 3,000 copies
Special edition BAF, 2001 – 110,000 copies

This edition printed especially for Books Are Fun Limited
International Standard Book Number 0-9644914-0-0

Additional copies may be obtained by
Sending $17.95 plus $3.50 shipping to
Address below.

Published By:
Cookbook Resources, LLC
541 Doubletree Drive
Highland Village, TX 75077
972/317-0245

cookbookresources.com

Printed in China

Farm Bureau Women's Committee has no reason to doubt that recipe ingredients and directions will work successfully. However, the ingredients, instructions, and directions have not necessarily been thoroughly or systematically tested, and the cook should not hesitate to test and question procedures and directions before preparation. The recipes in this book have been collected from various sources, and neither Farm Bureau Women's Committee, nor any contributor, publisher, printer, distributor or seller of this book is responsible for errors or omissions.

MADISON COUNTY FARM BUREAU
WOMEN'S COMMITTEE—1981

COUNTY

Kay Losch, Chairman	Chouteau
Oma Heepke, Co-Chairman	Edwardsville
Carleen Paul, Secretary	Olive
Gracie Koeller	Godfrey
Rose Marie Bauer, Cookbook Chairman	Nameoki-Venice
Lucille Schaefer	Nameoki-Venice

TOWNSHIP

Dorothy Suhre	Alhambra
Karen Mueller	Chouteau
Wilma Willaredt	Collinsville
Myra Campbell	Edwardsville
Genevieve Heepke	Ft. Russell-Wood River
	Foster
	Godfrey
JoAnne Brase	Hamel
Evelyn Keilbach	Helvetia
Sharon Schlaefer	Jarvis
Delores Geiger	Leef
Kathy Hitz	Marine
Wilma Becker	Moro
Mary Jane Gass	Nameoki-Venice
Verna Abert	New Douglas
Norma Hemann	New Douglas
Donna Sievers	Olive
Mildred Dustmann	Omphghent
Donna Koenig	Pin Oak
Sally Raeber	Saline
Beckie Schrumpf	Saline
Dorothy Thurnau	St. Jacob

Program of Work 1956

The proposed 1956 program of work planned by the State Women's committee in January was directed toward understanding and information, coordinating the work of men and women within the framework of Farm Bureau policy. Each county committee plans its own program of work based on the suggested state program and subject to the approval of its county board. The program was based on the five basic areas that are usually present in the Farm Bureau county program.

The following items are what the Women's committee believes to be its accomplishments in Illinois in 1956 in the area of:

I. Organization-Information and Membership

    a. Many more women are attending Farm Bureau district meetings, short courses, annual meetings.

    b. There were 80 counties with a woman representative at the information forum meetings.

Madison County Farm Bureau President Wilbert Engelke discusses women's committee activities with three Madison county women's committee members. Left to right: Mrs. Ed Schillinger, Mrs. Norman Dorsey, chairman; and Mrs. T.E. Albrecht.

1981 Program of Work

The Farm Bureau Women's Committee enables the women of the membership family to take an active and productive part in the Farm Bureau organization. Madison County has had a continuous active Women's Committee for 25 years.

The Women's Committee is a program committee, carrying out programs concerning Health and Safety, Legislation, Community Relations, Commodity Promotion and Special Projects. These programs are carried out to help promote a better understanding between the farmer, the non-farming community and the consumer.

Kay Losch, Womens Committee Chairman
Rose Bauer, Cookbook Chairman

Committee
Working on Cookbook

Kay Losch
Gracie Koeller

Joan Willaredt
Oma Heepke

Standing: Kay Losch, Gracie
Koeller, Joan Willaredt
Seated: (Left to Right) Norma
Hemann, Oma Heepke, Carleen
Paul, and Delores Geiger.

Carleen Paul
Delores Geiger

TABLE OF CONTENTS

V.I.F.
(VERY IMPORTANT
FRIENDS)

These twenty men served as the County Farm Bureau Board of Directors during our 25th year. Seated L to R: Michael Campbell, Secretary; Donald Sievers, Vice-President; Richard Bauer, President; Leroy Brase, Treasurer. Standing L to R: Albert Brandt; Vernon Renken; Wilbur Dustmann; Nick Raeber; Gene Daiber; Keith Koenig; Walter Bohn; Othmar Geiger; Larry Schlaefer; Waldo Keilbach; Robert Thurnau; Louis Koeller; Rex Maxeiner; Russell Abert; Charles Losch; and Fred Heepke.

BAJA CALIFORNIA CHICKEN

8 boned chicken breasts
Seasoning salt and pepper,
  to taste
2 cloves garlic, crushed

4 tablespoons olive oil
4 tablespoons tarragon
  vinegar
⅔ cup dry sherry

Sprinkle chicken with seasoning salt and pepper. Crush garlic into oil and vinegar in a skillet. Sauté chicken pieces until golden brown, turning frequently. Remove; place in a baking dish. Pour sherry over pieces and place in 350° oven for 10 minutes. Yield: 8 servings.

Nancy Reagan (Washington, D.C.)
Wife of President of United States

PUMPKIN PECAN PIE

4 slightly beaten eggs
2 cups canned or mashed
  cooked pumpkin
1 cup sugar
½ cup dark corn syrup

1 teaspoon vanilla
½ teaspoon cinnamon
¼ teaspoon salt
1 unbaked 9-inch pie shell
1 cup chopped pecans

Combine ingredients except pecans. Pour into pie shell—top with pecans. Bake at 350° F. for 40 minutes, or until set.

Nancy Reagan (Washington, D.C.)
Wife of President of United States

United States Senate

MEMORANDUM

IT IS A PLEASURE TO SEND

THE ENCLOSED MATERIAL

IN RESPONSE TO YOUR

RECENT REQUEST.

SAND TARTS

½ cup butter
1 cup sugar
1 egg
1¾ cups flour

2 teaspoons baking powder
Blanched almonds
1 tablespoon sugar
¼ teaspoon cinnamon

Cream butter, add sugar gradually and well beaten egg; add flour mixed and sifted with baking powder. Chill. Toss half of mixture on a floured board and roll ⅛-inch thick, using large round cookie cutter. Sprinkle with sugar mixed with cinnamon (the sand). Split almonds and arrange 3 halves on each at equal intervals. Place on a buttered sheet and bake 8 minutes in a slow oven (or 10 minutes if not brown).

Charles Percy (Washington, D.C.)
United States Senator

HAM & ASPARAGUS ROLL-UPS

Deli sliced ham or leftover
  baked ham thinly sliced can
  be used
Fresh or frozen asparagus
  spears, cooked

2 tablespoons butter
⅛ teaspoon ground cloves
1 teaspoon brown sugar

Cook fresh or frozen asparagus spears to the almost done stage. Drain and set aside. Place two asparagus spears near one edge of the ham slice, roll up and secure with a toothpick. Gently sauté roll-up in butter to which you have added ground cloves and brown sugar. Sauté just enough to heat through. Serve with fresh fruit or salad.

Charles Percy (Washington, D.C.)
United States Senator

WASHINGTON, D.C. ADDRESS:
2110 RAYBURN HOUSE OFFICE BUILDING
(202) 225-5661

HOME ADDRESS:
426 NORTH EIGHTH STREET
EAST ST. LOUIS, ILLINOIS 62201

DISTRICT OFFICE:
FEDERAL BUILDING
EAST ST. LOUIS, ILLINOIS 62201
(618) 274-2200

CHAIRMAN, COMMITTEE ON
ARMED SERVICES

SUBCOMMITTEES:
PROCUREMENT AND MILITARY
NUCLEAR SYSTEMS,
CHAIRMAN

INVESTIGATIONS

Congress of the United States
House of Representatives
Washington, D.C. 20515
MELVIN PRICE
23D ILLINOIS DISTRICT

April 1, 1981

Mrs. Catherine N. Losch
Madison County Farm Bureau Women's Committee
900 Hillsboro Avenue
Edwardsville, Illinois   62025

Dear Mrs. Losch:

With reference to your recent letter, I am pleased to enclose a favorite recipe of mine for use on an outdoor grill.

I can assure you that this is a foolproof method for grilling. I hope your members will enjoy it.

I appreciate your kindness in allowing me to participate in this effort, and I wish you and the ladies of the Women's Committee all good luck as you prepare for another 25 years with the Farm Bureau.

With kindest regards,

Sincerely,

Melvin Price
Member of Congress

MP:dcz
Enclosure

CHUCK WAGON PEPPER STEAK

1 3-pound round bone arm chuck roast (or boneless round roast) cut 2-inches thick
2 teaspoons unseasoned meat tenderizer
2 tablespoons instant minced onion
2 teaspoons thyme

1 teaspoon marjoram
1 bay leaf, crushed
1 cup vinegar
½ cup olive oil (or salad oil)
3 tablespoons lemon juice
¼ cup peppercorns coarsely crushed (or 2 tablespoons bottled cracked pepper)

Sprinkle meat evenly on both sides with meat tenderizer, pierce deeply all over with a fork and place in a shallow baking pan. Mix onion, thyme, marjoram, bay leaf, vinegar, olive oil and lemon juice in a small bowl and pour over and around meat. Marinate at room temperature 2 to 3 hours, turning meat every half hour. When ready to grill, remove meat from marinade; pound half the crushed peppercorns into each side, using a wooden mallet. Grill to a rich brown on rack set about 6 inches above hot coals. Turn and grill until meat is as done as you like it. It should average at least 15 minutes on each side for rare. To serve, place on carving board and cut meat diagonally into ½-inch thick slices. Makes 6 servings.

Hn. Melvin Price (Washington, D.C.)
Congressman

LEMON BREAD

½ cup butter
1 cup sugar
2 eggs
2¼ cups flour

2 teaspoons baking powder
1 lemon rind, grated
½ cup chopped nuts
1 cup milk

Mix all ingredients together and bake at 325° F. for 40 minutes. While still warm, mix and pour over the top:

Juice of lemon

⅓ cup sugar

Paul Findley (Washington, D.C.)
Congressman

Executive Mansion
Springfield, Illinois 62701

March 23, 1981

Dear Ms. Lasch:

Thank you for your kind letter of March 21,
1981, requesting one of my family's favorite
recipes for use in your cookbook. I am pleased
you thought of including us in your project.

Enclosed you will find the recipe for one
of our favorite desserts, Illinois Delicious
Apple Cake. It has been served on several occa-
sions here at the Executive Mansion.

The Governor and Samantha join me in sending
best wishes to you and the Madison County Women's
Committee.

Sincerely,

Mrs. James R. Thompson

Ms. Catherine Lasch, Chairman
Madison County Women's Committee
900 Hillsboro Avenue
Edwardsville, Illinois   62025

Enclosure

Executive Mansion
Springfield, Illinois 62701

ILLINOIS DELICIOUS APPLE CAKE

Grease and lightly flour 9 x 13 pan or two 9 inch pans

3 Eggs
2 cups Sugar
1¼ cups Salad Oil

Use large mixing bowl.   Beat eggs.   Add sugar gradually
then oil.

Add: 3 cups sliced Delicious Apples (use Delicious only)
     1 cup chopped Pecans

Sift together: 3 cups Flour
               1 teaspoon Salt
               1 teaspoon Soda

Add 2 teaspoons Vanilla

Mix well but be careful not to overbeat or apples
will turn into sauce instead of small bits.

Start with cold oven -- bake at 325° for 45 to 60
minutes.   Test with toothpick.

Mrs. James R. Thompson

STATE OF ILLINOIS
STATE SENATE

SAM M. VADALABENE
STATE SENATOR

ROOM 121-B, CAPITOL BUILDING
SPRINGFIELD, ILLINOIS 62706
217/782-5247

April 10, 1981

Ms. Catherine N. Losch, Chairman
Women's Committee
Madison County Farm Bureau
900 Hillsboro Avenue
Edwardsville, Illinois 62025

Dear Ms. Losch:

Enclosed please find two recipes for the Farm
Bureau Cookbook. Our family enjoys these so I hope
others will also.

Sincerely,

"Senator Sam"

SAM M. VADALABENE
State Senator

SMV/m

Enclosure

STATE OF ILLINOIS
STATE SENATE

SAM M. VADALABENE
STATE SENATOR

ROOM 121-B, CAPITOL BUILDING
SPRINGFIELD, ILLINOIS 62706
217/782-5247

 **S** **AM'S PAGHETTI AUCE**

½ pound ground beef	Pinch of oregano
2 12-ounce cans tomato paste	Olive oil
1 can mushrooms (stems &	Salt
pieces)	Pepper
½ teaspoon garlic salt	1 medium onion, diced

Cover bottom of medium size pot with olive oil. Add diced onions. Sauté until transparent. Add ground beef. Stir until ground beef is no longer pink. Add tomato paste, 3 cans of water, mushrooms, ½ teaspoon salt, 1 teaspoon sugar. Sprinkle garlic salt to taste on top; add pinch of oregano. Let come to boil then cook slowly for two hours, stirring frequently so that ingredients do not stick to bottom of pot.

1 pound spaghetti

Let salted water come to a hard boil. Drop in spaghetti so that it is completely submersed. Boil approximately 20 minutes, stirring frequently so that it doesn't stick together. Drain thoroughly in colander (water left in spaghetti will ruin your sauce). Serves 6-8.

Sam M. Vadalabene (Edwardsville)
State Senator, 56th District

STATE OF ILLINOIS
STATE SENATE

SAM M. VADALABENE
STATE SENATOR

ROOM 121-B, CAPITOL BUILDING
SPRINGFIELD, ILLINOIS 62706
217/782-5247

EGGPLANT CASSEROLE

EGGPLANT

Peel and slice eggplant. Salt well on both sides of slices. Place in colander and let drain for four hours. Dry. Put olive oil in skillet. Brown eggplant slices in skillet on both sides (takes about two minutes). Set aside.

SAUCE

Simmer the following together slowly for ½ hour until it is a thick sauce, stirring frequently:

1 quart canned tomatoes, cut up or squeeze until there are no pieces	Garlic salt to taste
	Pepper to taste
	Dash of oregano, sprinkled
1 medium onion, diced	very lightly
1 teaspoon sugar	1 small can tomato paste

Place first layer of sauce mixture in bottom of casserole dish. Add a layer of eggplant, another layer of sauce mixture, sprinkle each layer with grated cheese of your choice (Parmesan preferred). Repeat until all mixtures have been used. This is now ready to eat.

Sam M. Vadalabene (Edwardsville)
State Senator, 56th District

CHEESE AND BACON QUICHE

QUICHE PASTRY:

4 cups unsifted all-purpose
  flour
1 tablespoon sugar
2 teaspoons salt

1¾ cups shortening
1 tablespoon white vinegar
1 large egg
½ cup water

Combine first three ingredients. Add shortening and mix until crumbly. Mix egg, vinegar and water and add to first mixture. Divide dough into 4 balls. Wrap and chill for one hour. Makes two.

QUICHE MIXTURE:

1 pound bacon, fried crisp
  and crumbled
3 tablespoons flour
10 eggs
½ teaspoon nutmeg

½ teaspoon pepper
1½ teaspoons salt
5 cups milk
1 cup half and half
3 cups grated Swiss cheese

Roll out pastry and place in a 15½x10½x1-inch jelly roll pan and bake. Divide bacon and Swiss cheese and cover bottom of pie shell. Add Quiche mixture and bake in 350° F. oven (bottom unit) for approximately one hour or until top is golden.

Mrs. Vince (Deanna) DeMuzio (Carlinville)
Wife of State Senator from 49th District

DRESSING

1 16-ounce loaf bread, toasted
  lightly
2 eggs
¼ cup onions
¼ cup celery
½ cup chicken, cooked and
  ground
¼ cup raisins

1 apple, sliced
1½ teaspoons salt
½ teaspoon pepper
Dash of chili powder
Dash of nutmeg
¼ pound margarine
2 teaspoons sugar

Beat eggs thoroughly and set aside. Cook chicken (save broth). Combine *all* ingredients and mix well. Use broth for liquid. Bake at 350° F. until done. Serves 6-8 people.

Frank C. Watson (Greenville)
State Representative, 55th District

TAGALARINI

¼ pound butter
2 tablespoons minced green
  pepper
2 small cans mushrooms
2 cloves garlic
1 pound or more ground beef
2 small cans tomato paste
1 tall can tomato juice
1 can cream style corn

1 package bread noodles,
  cooked
Pinch cloves
Pinch allspice
Salt
Pepper
American cheese, grated and
  ripe olives

Simmer green pepper, mushrooms and garlic in butter. Add meat, cook for a few minutes. Add tomato paste, tomato juice, corn, noodles, cloves, salt and pepper. Bake, with grated American cheese and ripe olives on top, for 40 minutes or more at 350° F. (Good cooked down in consistency.)

Dwight P. Friedrich (Centralia)
State Representative, 55th District

CHEESECAKE

CRUST:

1 cup flour
¼ cup sugar
1 teaspoon grated lemon peel

½ cup butter
1 slightly beaten egg yolk
¼ teaspoon vanilla

CAKE:

5 8-ounce packages cream
  cheese, soft
¾ teaspoon grated lemon peel
¼ teaspoon vanilla
1¾ cups sugar

3 tablespoons flour
¼ teaspoon salt
4 large eggs
2 egg yolks
¼ cup whipped cream

Crust: Combine flour, sugar, and grated lemon peel. Cut in butter until crumbly. Add egg and vanilla and mix well. Pat ⅓ of the dough on the bottom of 10½-inch springform pan. Bake at 400° F. for 8 minutes. Allow to cool. Butter sides of pan, attach to bottom. Pat dough on sides of pan 1¾ inches high.

Filling: Beat cheese until creamy. Add grated lemon peel and vanilla. Combine sugar, flour and salt separately and gradually blend into cheese mixture. Add eggs and yolks one at a time, mixing after each one. Gently stir in whipped cream. Put in pan. Bake at 450° F. for 12 minutes. Reduce heat to 300° F. and bake approximately one (1) hour or until knife inserted in center comes out clean. Cool thoroughly before removing from pan (or it falls apart).

Topping: (optional): Cherry, blueberry or favorite pie filling. Or garnish with fresh fruit.

Jim McPike (Alton)
State Representative, 56th District

GRATED POTATO PUDDING (KUGELIS)

1 onion	1 slice white bread
½ pound bacon	1 can Milnot milk
1 stick butter (¼ pound)	(evaporated)
½ cup water	5 pounds potatoes

Preheat oven to 400° F. Dice onion and bacon fine. Sauté onion and bacon with water until onion is transparent and water has evaporated. Stir melted butter into this mixture. Soak bread in the Milnot until completely saturated, stirring to break it up. Set aside. Grate potatoes. Add all ingredients and mix well. Pour into a well greased pan and bake ten minutes in 400° F. oven. Lower temperature to 350° F. and continue baking for approximately one hour and 15 minutes.

A. C. 'Junie' Bartulis (Benld)
State Representative, 49th District

CORN BAKE

1 small onion	3 eggs
½ green pepper	1 box Jiffy corn muffin mix
½ cup margarine	1 cup sour cream
1 can cream-style corn	1 cup grated cheese
1 can whole corn	

Sauté onion and green pepper in margarine. Mix together corn, eggs and Jiffy corn muffin mix. Add to cooked vegetables. Pour into large baking dish, top with sour cream and grated cheese. Bake at 350° F. for approximately one hour or until golden brown. Serves 8-10.

Mrs. Everett Steele (Glen Carbon)
Wife of State Representative, 56th District

FRUIT PIZZA

1 14-ounce package Pillsbury cookie roll (sugar or cinnamon)
1 8-ounce package cream cheese

1 cup sifted confectioners powdered sugar
1 cup whipping cream

FRUIT:

3 tangerines, peeled and segmented
1 small apple, cut in slices

5 slices canned pineapple, drained and cut in half
10 maraschino cherries, drained

You may substitute any fresh fruits for many of these canned ones—strawberries, peaches, bananas or grapes. Dip any fresh fruit in pineapple or lemon juice to keep it from discoloring.

Crust: Preheat oven to 350° F. Slice chilled cookie dough in ¼-inch slices and arrange close together on a lightly greased 12½-inch round pizza pan. Press softened dough together to cover pan. Bake 15-18 minutes. Cool completely.

Filling: Soften cream cheese and blend with sugar. Fold in whipped cream. Spread on crust within ½ inch of edge of pan.

Garnish: Arrange fruits in colorful display.

Mrs. Harold (Margery) Steele (Princeton)
Wife of I. A. A. President

STRAWBERRY TARTS

1 package pie crust mix or
  your own pie pastry
24 fresh strawberries, washed
  and hulled
⅓ cup red currant jelly,
  melted

1½ 8-ounce packages
  Philadelphia cream cheese,
  softened
1 teaspoon nutmeg
2 tablespoons milk
3 tablespoons sugar

Cut 2½-inch circles from pie crust. Fit into 1¾-inch muffin pans (mini-muffin pans). Bake 10 minutes at 425° F. Cool tarts. Mix cream cheese, nutmeg, milk and sugar together. Fill tart shells with cheese mixture, dip strawberries into jelly and place on top of tarts. Place in refrigerator until ready to serve. Makes 24 tarts. Tart shells may be made ahead and frozen.

Mrs. Robert (Gracie) Koeller (Godfrey)
Wife of District 15, I. A. A. Director

BACON AND BEEF ROLL UPS

8 to 10 slices of bacon
1 egg
1½ pounds ground beef
¾ teaspoon salt
2 tablespoons Worcestershire
  sauce

¾ cup grated Cheddar cheese
½ teaspoon black pepper
3 tablespoons catsup
¼ cup chopped onion

Combine ground beef and all ingredients (except bacon). Place bacon slices, side by side, on cutting board. Shape ground beef mixture into an oblong roll and lay it across the bacon strips. Draw the bacon strips around the ground beef roll and fasten with toothpicks. Slice the roll between bacon strips. Shape and flatten the patties with your hand. Broil in oven or grill on barbeque grill for approximately 5 to 7 minutes on each side. Makes 8 to 10 patties.

Mrs. Ailene Miller (Danvers), Chairwoman
Illinois Farm Bureau Women's Committee

GIN'S BARBECUE SAUCE

Combine in skillet and cook over medium heat until done but not browned:

3 tablespoons salad oil   **1 small green pepper, minced**
1 medium onion, minced

Add:

¼ cup brown sugar, packed   **1 teaspoon salt**
2 tablespoons prepared   **¾ cup ketchup**
mustard
1 tablespoon Worcestershire
sauce (Lea and Perrins)

Mix together and simmer 15 minutes.

Suggested ways to use:
Place meat (chicken, pork steaks, pork chops, spare ribs, beef ribs, etc.) in shallow pan, salt lightly, cover with aluminum foil and bake in 350° F. oven until almost done. Remove foil and baste generously with barbecue sauce. Replace foil and bake 30 minutes. Remove foil, add more barbecue sauce and bake, uncovered, 15 minutes. Serve with additional barbecue sauce if desired.
When broiling steaks, baste with barbecue sauce when almost done and *reduce* heat.
For sandwich fillings, add barbecue sauce to cooked and drained ground beef or shredded roast beef or roast pork and simmer for 15 minutes.

Virginia Darr (Jerseyville)
District 15 Representative
State Women's Committee

RED SALAD DRESSING

Combine and put into a wide mouth quart jar:

¾ cup white sugar
1 teaspoon salt
2 teaspoons paprika
1 clove garlic (finely minced)

¼ cup vinegar
1 cup salad oil
1 cup catsup

Shake until well mixed. This is good served on lettuce wedge or combination salad. It keeps well in the refrigerator and needs to be shaken every time it is used.

Virginia Darr (Jerseyville)
District 15 Representative
State Women's Committee

BARBECUE SAUCE FOR POULTRY

	NUMBER OF PEOPLE			
	5	10	50	100
Water or tomato juice	½ cup	1 cup	1 quart	2 quarts
Vinegar	1 cup	1 pint	2 quarts	4 quarts
Butter	¼ pound	½ pound	2 pounds	4 pounds
Salt	1 tablespoon	1 ounce	¼ pound	½ pound
Red pepper	½ ounce	¾ ounce	4 ounces	8 ounces

Combine ingredients and heat thoroughly. Dip chicken in sauce. Place skin side up on wire rack. Baste chicken with sauce and turn as needed to avoid burning. Cooking time 25 to 50 minutes, depending on size of chicken.

Frank R. Thomas (Carlinville)
Manager, Madison County Farm Bureau

PORTUGUESE RED BEAN SOUP

3 ham shanks
1 linguesa (sausage)
1 large soup bone, 1½ pounds
2 cups dried, red beans,
    soaked overnight
1 can tomato sauce

¼ teaspoon ground allspice
2 tablespoons oil
1 medium-sized round onion,
    sliced
3 tablespoons minced parsley
2 large potatoes, diced

Boil ham shanks, linguesa and soup bone in enough water to cover. When meat is almost done, add beans and cook until done. Add tomato sauce and spice. In oil, fry onion slices and parsley until tender. Add to soup stock. Add potatoes and cook until done. Salt to taste. Other vegetables, such as cabbage, watercress, carrots, etc. may be added to this soup.

Kay Losch (East Alton)
Co-Chairman, Women's Committee

CHINESE RICE

2 tablespoons butter
1 pound ground beef
1 medium onion, chopped
⅔ cup long grain rice

2 cups chopped celery
2 cups boiling water
4 tablespoons soy sauce
1 can cream of chicken soup

Brown ground beef and onion in 2 tablespoons butter. Add soy sauce and simmer. While meat is cooking, boil water and add celery and rice. Reduce heat and cook until celery and rice are tender and all water is absorbed. In a casserole, alternate layers of meat, vegetables and soup. Bake at 350° F. for ½ hour.

Oma Heepke (Edwardsville)
Co-Chairman, Women's Committee

CHEESABUTTER

½ cup butter
¾ teaspoon Italian seasoning
⅛ teaspoon garlic powder
Black pepper to taste

1 cup (4 ounces) shredded
  Cheddar cheese
1 teaspoon lemon juice

Beat butter, seasoning, garlic powder and pepper. Blend in cheese and lemon juice. Form into log shape on waxed paper and refrigerate until ready to use. Serve with warm bread.

Carleen Paul (Worden)
County Committee Secretary

CHERRY TOPPED CHEESECAKE

1 box Duncan Hines yellow
  cake mix
2 tablespoons oil
2 8-ounce packages cream
  cheese, softened
½ cup sugar

4 eggs
1½ cups milk
3 tablespoons lemon juice
3 teaspoons vanilla
1 1-pound 5-ounce can cherry
  pie filling

Preheat oven to 300° F. Reserve 1 cup dry cake mix. In large mixing bowl, combine remaining cake mix, 1 egg and oil (mixture will be crumbly). Press crust mixture evenly into bottom and ¾ way up the sides of a greased 13x9x2-inch pan*. In same bowl, blend cream cheese and sugar. Add 3 eggs and reserved cake mix; beat 1 minute at medium speed. At low speed, slowly add milk and flavorings; mix until smooth. Pour onto crust. Bake at 300° F. for 45 to 55 minutes or until center is firm. When cool, top with pie filling; chill before serving. Store in refrigerator; freeze covered with foil.
* Cheesecake can also bake in 2 9-inch pans for 40 to 50 minutes.

Mrs. James (Sharon) Ewen (Kampsville)
Wife of President of Calhoun County

NEVER FAIL SUGAR COOKIES

3 cups flour
1 cup sugar
1 teaspoon baking soda
½ teaspoon salt
1 teaspoon vanilla

1¼ cups shortening
3 tablespoons milk
2 eggs
1 teaspoon cream of tartar

Sift all dry ingredients together. Cut in shortening with pastry blender until consistency of corn meal. Add flavoring to milk. Work eggs and milk, flavoring in like pie dough. Chill thoroughly. Roll out and cut. Bake at 360° F. until golden brown. This is an old recipe that David's mother, Louise Meyer, has given me. It probably is 75 to 100 years old. The boys helped make this recipe at Christmas for many years and is a favorite cookie at our house.

Mrs. Dave (Verna) Meyer (Keyesport)
Wife of President of Bond County

CHICKEN BROCCOLI CASSEROLE

3 whole chicken breasts
2 packages frozen chopped
   broccoli
4 tablespoons butter
4 tablespoons flour
2 cups milk

Salt
Pepper
5 slices American cheese
Pepperidge Farm stuffing
Butter

Boil chicken breasts (with carrot, celery, onion or whatever you have on hand) until done. Drain and cut into pieces. Cook the broccoli according to directions on package. Drain. Make cheese sauce. Melt 4 tablespoons butter in bottom of double boiler. Stir in flour. Blend well over low heat. Stir in, slowly, the milk and bring mixture slowly to the boiling point and cook 2 minutes. Add salt and pepper to taste and cheese. Alternate in buttered casserole: chicken, broccoli, cheese sauce, then again. Top with stuffing. Enough to cover the top. Dot with butter. Bake in 350° F. oven about 30 minutes until bubbly.

Mrs. Mike (Pam) Painter (White Hall)
Wife of President of Greene County

CHERRY WINKS

¾ cup shortening
1 cup sugar
2 eggs
3 tablespoons milk
1 teaspoon vanilla

2¼ cups all-purpose flour
1 teaspoon baking powder
½ teaspoon soda
½ teaspoon salt
Maraschino cherries

Combine shortening and sugar and cream well. Blend in eggs and add milk and vanilla. Blend in dry ingredients and mix well. Drop by teaspoonful onto greased cookie sheet. Top each cookie with ⅙ Maraschino cherry. Bake in moderate oven, 375° F., for 10 to 12 minutes.

Mrs. Ralph (Irene) Downey (Jerseyville)
Wife of President of Jersey County

ALMA'S APRICOT DIAMONDS

3 cups sifted flour
1 cup sugar
1 cup finely chopped nuts,
  pecans (reserve ¼ cup for
  top)
1 teaspoon baking powder

Grated rind of one lemon
1¼ cups butter
4 egg yolks
1 pound dried apricots,
  soaked in water 1 hour
1 cup sugar to taste

Combine sugar, flour, baking powder, grated lemon rind and ¾ of the nuts. Work in butter as for pie crust, then add egg yolks to make crumbly mixture. Measure ⅔ cup of crumbly mixture and set aside. Apricots, soaked in water for 1 hour, are cooked until tender. Sugar is added and cooking is continued 10 minutes more. Apricots are put through a blender to make a puree that is allowed to cool slightly. The crumb mixture is spread into a greased jelly roll pan, 10 by 15 inches, and pressed lightly to make an even base but with the sides slightly higher. The apricot puree is spread evenly over the crumb base and reserved crumbs and nuts are sprinkled on the top. The dessert is then baked in a 350° F. oven for 45 minutes.

Mrs. Richard (Rose) Bauer (Granite City)
Wife of President of Madison County

V.I.F. (VERY IMPORTANT FRIENDS)

V.I.F. (VERY IMPORTANT FRIENDS)

APPETIZERS AND BEVERAGES

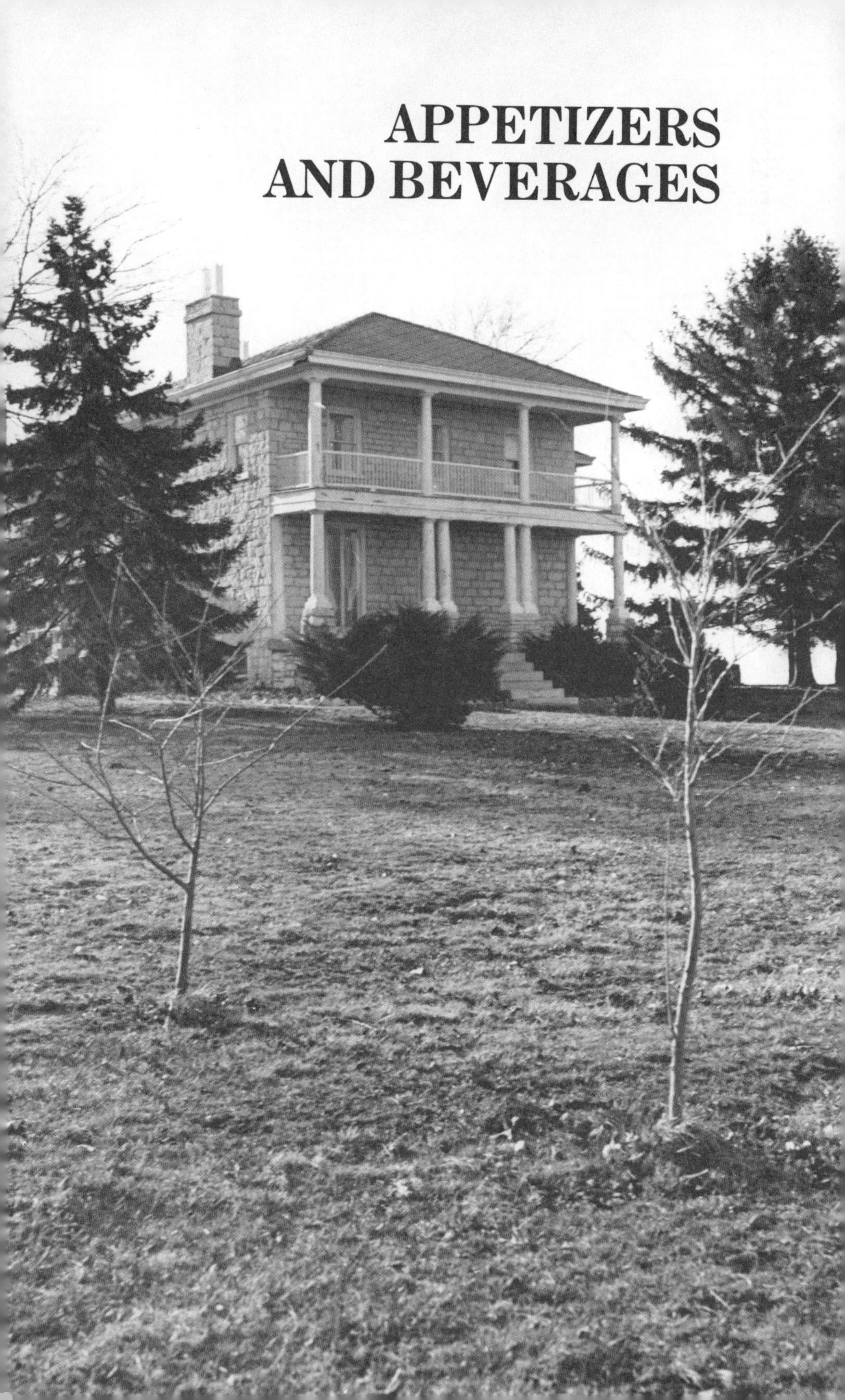

The Godfrey House, home of Captain Benjamin Godfrey, was built in the early 1830's. Godfrey, founder of Monticello Female Seminary and builder of the Alton, Springfield Railroad, was one of the County's most noted residents.

APPETIZER MEATBALLS

MEATBALLS:

1 pound hamburger   1 envelope dry onion soup
                             mix

SAUCE:

½ cup chili sauce   ⅛ teaspoon garlic salt
½ cup grape jelly

Mix hamburger and dry soup mix together. Form into small balls and bake in a 350° F. oven for 15 to 20 minutes. While meatballs are baking, blend chili sauce, jelly and garlic salt together. Put meatballs in an ovenproof serving dish, pour sauce over meatballs and warm for another 15 minutes. These meatballs are easy to freeze. After forming balls, place on a cookie sheet, freeze through and then bag for future use.

Beckie Schrumpf (Highland)

BRAUNSCHWEIGER SPREAD

1 8-ounce package Oscar   1 tablespoon chopped onion
   Mayer braunschweiger liver 2 tablespoons lemon juice
   sausage   1 teaspoon Worcestershire
1 8-ounce package   sauce
   Philadelphia cream cheese

Combine softened cream cheese and sausage. Mix well and add onion, lemon juice and Worcestershire sauce and seasonings and mix well again. Mold into a ball shape or put in a serving bowl. Chill. It's best to make the day before serving as it gives the onion, etc. time to draw through. Serve on party rye bread or crackers of your choice.

VARIATION: A small jar of sweet pickle relish, drained, can be substituted for the chopped onion, lemon juice and Worcestershire sauce.

Melba Helmkamp (East Alton)
Beverly Dustmann (Dorsey)

BETTY TOSOVSKY'S CHEESE DIP

1 8-ounce package
  Philadelphia cream cheese
⅓ cup Wish Bone deluxe
  French dressing

2 tablespoons catsup
2 teaspoons finely chopped
  onion

Let cream cheese come to room temperature and mix with the other three ingredients. Serve with raw vegetables.

Virginia Herrmann (Edwardsville)

CHAFING DISH MEATBALLS

1 pound ground beef
½ cup dry bread crumbs
⅓ cup minced onion
¼ cup milk
1 egg
1 tablespoon snipped parsley
1 teaspoon salt

⅛ teaspoon pepper
½ teaspoon Worcestershire
  sauce
¼ cup shortening
1 12-ounce bottle chili sauce
1 10-ounce jar grape jelly

Mix ground beef, crumbs, onion, milk, egg and next 4 seasonings. Gently shape into 1-inch balls. Melt shortening in large skillet; brown meatballs. Remove meatballs and drain on paper towels. Drain fat from skillet. Heat jelly and chili sauce until jelly is melted, stirring constantly. Add meatballs and stir until coated. Simmer 30 minutes, serve hot in chafing dish. Makes 5 dozen meatballs.

NOTE: These meatballs freeze well. After balls are browned and drained, put them in plastic freezer bags and into the freezer. When ready to use, make the sauce and finish cooking. This recipe also works well in a crock-pot.

June Launhardt (Collinsville)
Carol Russell (Bethalto)

CHEESE BALL

1 8-ounce Philadelphia cream
cheese
1 6-ounce jar Old English
cheese

1 small package Roquefort
cheese
½-1 cup pecans, chopped

Place cream cheese, Old English cheese and Roquefort cheese into a mixer or food processor, mix until creamy. Place on waxed paper and chill until it can be rolled into a ball. When ball is chilled enough to handle, roll it in chopped nuts.

Kathryn Cook (Marine)

CHEESE BALL

2 8-ounce packages cream
cheese
1 teaspoon celery salt
½ teaspoon onion salt

1 cup chopped beef
1 tablespoon Worcestershire
sauce
Parsley flakes

Beat cheese and other ingredients together, except parsley flakes. Roll into ball and roll in parsley flakes. Serve with crackers.

Charlene Bandy (Moro)

DEVILED HAM AND CHEESE LOAF

1 can deviled ham
1 8-ounce package cream
cheese (room temperature)

2 tablespoons milk
1 package shredded Cheddar
cheese

Place deviled ham on a plate. Stir milk into softened cream cheese and form around deviled ham. Press shredded cheese around cream cheese. Mixture should have the shape of a dome. Chill in refrigerator and serve with crackers.

Suzanne Blattner (Madison)

EMERGENCY HORS D'OEUVRES

Cheddar cheese, sharp or mild

Stuffed olives

Stick a toothpick through the side of the olive and into ½ inch cube of cheese. These look great and taste delicious.

Abby Daugherty (Granite City)

IZZIE'S ZUCCHINI MUNCHIES

3 cups thinly sliced zucchini
1 cup Bisquick
½ cup chopped green onion
½ cup grated Parmesan cheese
2 tablespoons chopped parsley
½ teaspoon pepper

½ teaspoon salt
½ teaspoon Italian herb seasoning
¼ teaspoon garlic powder
Dash tabasco sauce
½ cup oil
4 eggs, slightly beaten

Mix all together and spread in a greased and floured glass baking dish 13x9x2-inches. Bake at 350° F. for 25 to 30 minutes. Cool and cut into squares. Serve hot or cold.

Gracie Koeller (Godfrey)

PASTRAMI CHEESE BALL

1 8-ounce package cream cheese
2 tablespoons Bacos
2 tablespoons dried onion flakes
2 tablespoons Worcestershire sauce

2 tablespoons margarine, softened
1 3-ounce package pastrami, save some to roll ball in

Dice pastrami. Mix all ingredients together. Roll into a ball; then roll ball into remaining pastrami.

Lela Voigt (Collinsville)

42

DIP

1 round loaf German rye
  bread
1 cup sour cream
1 cup real mayonnaise

1 teaspoon parsley flakes
1 teaspoon onion flakes
1 teaspoon Beau Monde

Hollow out bread to put the dip in. Tear the bread into pieces big enough to dip.

Melba Helmkamp (East Alton)

RUSSIAN BREAD WITH DIP

2 loaves Russian round rye bread

FILLING:

2 cups sour cream
1¼ cups Hellmanns
  mayonnaise (you must
  use Hellmanns)

2 teaspoons dill weed
2 teaspoons Beau Monde
2 tablespoons dry onions
2 tablespoons parsley flakes

Cut circle in top of 1 loaf of bread and scrape inside out of bread. Fill with filling, store in container and refrigerate overnight. Can be wrapped in foil or Saran Wrap.

Beverly Dustmann (Dorsey)
Pam Maxiener (Godfrey)

SHRIMP CHEESE BALL

2 3-ounce packages cream
  cheese
1½ teaspoons prepared
  mustard
1 teaspoon grated onion

1 teaspoon lemon juice
Dash pepper
Dash salt
1 4½-ounce can shrimp
⅔ cup chopped nuts

Combine cream cheese, mustard, onion, lemon juice, pepper and salt; blend well. Drain shrimp. Stir shrimp into cheese mixture. Chill. Form into ball. Roll in nuts. Serve with assorted crackers.

Judy Ernst (Alhambra)

EASY GARLIC DIP

1 cup real mayonnaise
1 cup sour cream

1 package powdered Good
Seasons salad dressing mix

Mix thoroughly. Serve with chips, crackers or fresh vegetables.

Barbara Floyd (East Alton)

HOT BROCCOLI DIP

½ cup chopped onions
½ cup chopped celery
½ cup chopped mushrooms
1 10-ounce package frozen
broccoli, chopped

1 6-ounce package garlic
cheese, diced
1 can mushroom soup
3 tablespoons butter

Sauté onion and celery in butter until golden. Add mushrooms and sauté until light brown. Keep warm. Cook broccoli and drain thoroughly. While hot, stir in cheese and mushroom soup. Add other ingredients and serve hot.

Ruth Becker (Edwardsville)

HOT BROCCOLI DIP

2 5-ounce jars pasteurized
processed cheese spread
with garlic, melted
1 package onion soup mix
1 can mushroom soup
1 4-ounce can sliced
mushrooms, drained

2 10-ounce packages frozen
chopped broccoli or
spinach
½ cup butter or margarine,
melted
1 tablespoon instant minced
onion

Combine cheese spread, soup mix, mushroom soup and sliced mushrooms. Cook broccoli or spinach in unsalted water and drain thoroughly. (Squeeze excess moisture from spinach, if used.) Add to cheese mixture along with butter and onions and heat to serving temperature. Serve warm with chips.

Peggy Torrence (Highland)

PARTY MIX

1½ cups Kix cereal
1 cup Cheerios cereal
2 cups small cheese crackers
2 cups thin pretzel sticks
½ pound can mixed nuts

¼ cup melted butter
½ teaspoon Worcestershire
 sauce
¼ teaspoon celery salt
¼ teaspoon garlic salt

Preheat oven to 250° F. Combine cereals, crackers, pretzels and nuts in a 9x13-inch pan. Blend butter and seasonings. Pour over cereal mixture. Stir thoroughly. Bake for 30 minutes, stirring with wooden spoon after 15 minutes. Makes six cups.

Esther Schuette (Staunton)

FANCY CHICKEN LOG

2 8-ounce packages
 cream cheese
1 tablespoon bottled steak
 sauce
½ teaspoon curry powder
1½ cups minced cooked
 chicken

⅓ cup minced celery
¼ cup chopped parsley
¼ cup chopped toasted
 almonds
Ritz crackers

Beat together first three ingredients. Blend in next two ingredients and 2 tablespoons parsley; refrigerate remaining parsley. Shape mixture into a 9-inch log. Wrap in plastic wrap and chill 4 hours or overnight. Toss together remaining parsley and almonds. Use to coat log. Serve with Ritz crackers. Makes about 3 cups.

Ruth Keller (Edwardsville)

FLORENCE'S DIP

1 cup mayonnaise
1 teaspoon horseradish
1 teaspoon vinegar

1 teaspoon curry powder
1 teaspoon onion salt
1 teaspoon garlic salt

Mix all ingredients together. May be used with all fresh raw vegetables.

Dorothy Westerholt (Edwardsville)

DILL WEED DIP

1 round loaf black rye bread
1 cup sour cream
1 cup Hellmann's mayonnaise
1 tablespoon dill weed

1 teaspoon dried minced
  onion
1 tablespoon parsley flakes
Season salt to taste

Combine all ingredients, except bread. Season to taste with season salt. Chill several hours before serving. Serving suggestion: Cut out a hole in center of a loaf or round black rye bread. Fill hole with dill weed dip. Serve with remaining bread.

Darlene Stille (Alhambra)

POLISH MISTAKES

1 pound ground chuck
1 pound Italian sausage
1 pound Velveeta cheese
1 teaspoon garlic powder

1 teaspoon oregano
1 to 1½ loaves party rye
  bread

Brown meats and drain grease. Return meat to pan and add cheese. Cook until cheese is melted and mixed. Add seasonings. Spread on rye bread. These can be frozen. When ready to serve heat for 15 minutes at 350°.

Frances Runyon (Wood River)

PORKY PARTY TREATS

3 cups buttermilk biscuit mix
  or Bisquick
8 ounces grated Cheddar
  cheese

12 to 16 ounces bulk pork
  sausage
¼ cup water

Mix above ingredients together, may mix better with hands. Form into small balls ¾ to 1-inch in diameter. Bake at 375° F. for 15 minutes. Serve warm. These little treats freeze well. If freezing for future use, reduce baking time to 10 minutes before freezing and bake another 10 minutes just before serving.

Delores Geiger (Alhambra)

SHRIMP CHIP DIP

1 5-ounce can shrimp, drained
  and chopped
1 cup dairy sour cream
¼ cup chili sauce
2 teaspoons lemon juice

½ teaspoon salt
½ teaspoon pepper
1 teaspoon prepared
  horseradish
Dash Tabasco sauce

Combine all ingredients and refrigerate. Use as a dip or spread for potato chips or crackers.

Jacqueline Thomas (Carlinville)

SMOKY CHEESE BALL

2 8-ounce packages cream
  cheese, softened
1 8-ounce package smoky
  Cheddar cheese, shredded
  (2 cups)

½ cup butter or margarine,
  softened
2 tablespoons milk
2 teaspoons steak sauce

Combine ingredients and beat until fluffy. Chill. Shape into ball and roll in chopped nuts.

Cheryll Sievers (Staunton)

SWEDISH MEAT BALLS

2 eggs, slightly beaten
½ cup milk
⅓ cup dry bread crumbs
4 teaspoons minced onion
1 tablespoon melted butter
1 teaspoon salt

½ to 1 teaspoon nutmeg
Dash pepper
1 pound ground beef
1 can consommé soup
2 tablespoons cornstarch
¼ cup cold water

Combine egg, milk, and bread crumbs; let stand until bread is moist. Add onion (browned if desired in butter), seasonings, and meat. Mix well. Shape into small balls. Fry on both sides about 5 minutes each side. Drain on paper towels. Add one can of consommé soup and 2 tablespoons cornstarch which have been mixed with cold water. Stir gently until thickened. Serve as an appetizer or as a meal with noodles.

Doris Lacy (Collinsville)

SHRIMP DIP

¼ cup milk
1 8-ounce package cream
cheese, softened
1 4½-ounce can shrimp,
rinsed, drained and
chopped

1 teaspoon lemon juice
1 teaspoon Worcestershire
sauce
½ teaspoon garlic salt
¼ teaspoon dill weed

Blend milk gradually into cream cheese. Stir in shrimp, lemon juice, Worcestershire sauce, garlic salt and dill weed. Cover. Refrigerate for 1 hour before serving.

Virginia Schuette (Staunton)

SPINACH DIP

1 cup parsley, chopped
1 cup green onions, chopped
1 10-ounce package frozen
spinach, chopped, thawed
and drained thoroughly

1 quart Hellmann's
mayonnaise

Mix all together thoroughly. Good with carrot sticks, celery sticks, broccoli and cauliflower flowerlets.

Idell Bright (Edwardsville)

PARTY CANAPÉS

2 pounds pork sausage
2 pounds Velveeta spread

Party rye bread, about 1½
loaves

Cut Velveeta in squares, melt in double boiler. Fry bulk pork sausage in skillet and drain. Mix into Velveeta. Spread on party rye bread. Can be made ahead and frozen on cookie sheets. Take out and put under broiler a few minutes and serve when needed. Very good.

Mae Grapperhaus (Troy)

SWEET-SOUR MEAT BALLS

5 slices dry bread	¼ teaspoon pepper
2 pounds ground beef	1 teaspoon salt
½ cup onion, grated	2 eggs, slightly beaten
½ teaspoon garlic salt	

Cut bread into cubes. Soak in a little water until soft. Squeeze out water. Combine with remaining ingredients, shape into balls the size of walnuts; place in 15½x10½x1-inch jelly roll pan. (Or brown in skillet.) Bake in very hot oven, 450° F. for 15 to 18 minutes. Place balls in sweet-sour sauce and simmer 10 minutes. Makes 36 meat balls.

SWEET-SOUR SAUCE:

1 1-pound 12-ounce can	½ teaspoon salt
tomatoes (3½ cups)	1 teaspoon onion, grated
1 cup brown sugar, packed	10 gingersnaps
¼ cup vinegar	

Combine all ingredients. Cook to boiling. Makes sauce for 36 meat balls.

Janice Bradley (Marine)

LIGHT EGG NOG

3 fresh eggs	3 cups whole milk
3 tablespoons sugar	1 teaspoon rum flavor
¾ teaspoon vanilla	Dash of nutmeg

Mix the ingredients well in a blender. Other flavors may be added to taste.

THICK EGG NOG

5 eggs	1 teaspoon rum flavoring
3 tablespoons sugar	1½ cups vanilla ice cream
1½ cups whole milk	Dash of nutmeg

Mix the ingredients well in blender. Other flavors may be added to taste.

Norma Hemann (New Douglas)

CRANBERRY SLUSH

1 quart cranberry juice
1 can frozen lemonade (small)

1 lemonade can bourbon

Mix together and place in freezer. Serve in glass as a cocktail.

Gracie Koeller (Godfrey)

HOLIDAY CRANBERRY PUNCH

1 32-ounce bottle orange-
  pineapple juice
1 32-ounce bottle cranberry
  juice cocktail

¼ cup sugar
3 whole cloves
2 cinnamon sticks
Orange slices (optional)

Combine ingredients. Heat in crock pot. Remove cloves and cinnamon sticks before serving. Top with thin orange slices if desired. Yield 2 quarts.

Frances Runyon (Wood River)

GOLDEN PUNCH

1 12-ounce can frozen
  lemonade
1 16-ounce can frozen orange
  juice

2 cups sugar
2 cups cold water
4 quarts chilled ginger ale

Combine lemonade, orange juice, sugar and water. Stir until sugar is dissolved. Just before serving, add ginger ale and stir gently.

Diane L. Martin (Edwardsville)

LIME PUNCH

½ gallon lime sherbet
2 liters Mountain Dew

46 ounces pineapple juice

Place sherbet in punch bowl. Stir in chilled Mountain Dew. Add cold pineapple juice and stir.

Darlene Stille (Alhambra)

MILK PUNCH

1 gallon milk
1 gallon sherbet (recommend
   pineapple flavor)

2 quarts ginger ale

Mix milk and sherbet together. Add ginger ale before serving.

Carleen Paul (Worden)

BANANA PUNCH

4 cups sugar
6 cups water
1 12-ounce can frozen orange
   juice plus 1 can water
1 6-ounce can frozen
   lemonade plus 1 can water

1 46-ounce can pineapple
   juice
5 bananas, mashed

Combine sugar and water. Bring to a boil, stirring until sugar is dissolved. Cool. Add remaining ingredients and mix well. Freeze in three half-gallon cartons. To serve, partially thaw one carton, and add 1 28-ounce bottle ginger ale.

Jacqueline Thomas (Carlinville)

ORANGE JULIUS

⅓ cup condensed orange juice
½ cup milk
¼ cup water

¼ cup sugar
½ teaspoon vanilla
6 ice cubes

Put all ingredients in blender until ice cubes are well crushed. Serve fast. Serves two.

Helen Eich (Edwardsville)

51

HOT CHOCOLATE DRINK MIX

1 box non-fat dry milk for
  16 quarts
2 pounds Nestles Quick

1 12-ounce jar dry coffee
  creamer
2 cups powdered sugar

To make hot chocolate, use ½ cup dry mix and ½ cup hot water for each cup of drink.

Reita Sparrowk (Bethalto)

MIKE'S HOT FUDGE SAUCE

1 stick butter
2¼ cups powdered sugar

⅔ cup evaporated milk
6 ounces chocolate (squares)

Melt butter, mix in sugar. Add milk and chocolate. DO NOT STIR. Cook 30 minutes in double boiler. Remove from heat. Beat with spoon until smooth. Can be kept in refrigerator and reheated.

Helen Eich (Edwardsville)

MULLED CIDER

4 quarts apple cider
1 cup orange juice
1 cup sugar
1 teaspoon whole allspice
½ teaspoon mace

2 teaspoons whole cloves
6 sticks cinnamon
Orange slices and lemon
  slices

Combine all ingredients except fruit slices in a large saucepan. Cover. Bring to a boil and simmer for 30 minutes. Strain. Garnish with fruit slices. Delicious hot or may be served as a cold cider punch.

Carol Russell (Bethalto)

QUANTITY PUNCH

1 48-ounce can pineapple
   juice
4 packages raspberry Kool
   Aid

8 quarts water
4 cups sugar
1 quart white soda

Chill all ingredients before mixing. Mix first 4 ingredients and add soda just before serving.

Cheryll Sievers (Staunton)

PUNCH

4 cups sugar
6 cups water
1 small can frozen orange
   juice

1 small can frozen lemonade
48 ounce can pineapple juice
5 bananas
2 quarts ginger ale

Bring sugar and water to a boil and let cool. Add bananas mashed in blender to sugar mixture. Add juices. Freeze mixture. Then an hour before serving, place in punch bowl and add ginger ale.

Dorothy Marti (Pocahontas)

RUSSIAN SPICED TEA

1½ cups Tang
1 cup instant Nestea
1½ cups sugar
3 teaspoons cinnamon

1 teaspoon cloves
¼ teaspoon nutmeg
1 3-ounce envelope Wyler's
   lemonade

Mix all ingredients well and store in jar. To serve, add boiling water to 1 to 2 teaspoons of mixture in cup or mug.

Mrs. Aletha A. Schmidt (Edwardsville)

SLUSH

1 12-ounce can frozen
  lemonade
1 6-ounce can frozen orange
  juice
1 46-ounce can pineapple
  juice

1½ cups whiskey
2 cups water
2 teaspoons instant tea (put in
  water and dissolve)
1½ cups sugar
White soda

Mix above ingredients together except for soda and freeze. Add about ½ cup of slush to white soda per drink.

VARIATION:

2 cups water
2 cups sugar dissolved in
  above water
8 cups water
2 6-ounce or 1 12-ounce can
  frozen orange juice

2 6-ounce or 1 12-ounce can
  frozen lemonade
2 cups vodka

Mix and put in freezer. When you use it, put a few tablespoonsful in glass and fill with white soda and stir.

M. L. Maedge (Highland)
Vera Mae Henschen (Alhambra)

VARIATION:

Liquor may be eliminated.

Joan Thurmond (Highland)

VODKA SLUSH

1 quart 7-Up soda
1 cup Vodka

1 small can lemonade, frozen
3 cans water

Stir together and place in covered container. Freeze. Let set out for few minutes before spooning into cocktail glasses.

Donna Sievers (Staunton)

APPETIZERS AND BEVERAGES

APPETIZERS AND BEVERAGES

APPETIZERS AND BEVERAGES

APPETIZERS AND BEVERAGES

SOUPS

Monticello Female Seminary, founded by Benjamin Godfrey, opened on April 11, 1838 with 16 students. First building was erected in 1837 on 16 acres donated by Godfrey. Today, the buildings and campus are utilized by Lewis and Clark Junior College.

AUNT MI'S TURKEY-NOODLE SOUP

Carcass from 15-20 pound
  turkey
5 quarts water
1 cup chopped celery
½ cup chopped celery leaves
1 cup onions, chopped
7 chicken bouillon cubes
1 tablespoon salt
¼ teaspoon pepper
1 small bay leaf

½ cup chopped parsley
1 cup fresh or frozen green
  peas
1 cup sliced carrots
1 cup cut green beans
4 cups (8 ounces) fine egg
  noodles
¼ cup butter or margarine
¼ cup flour

Place carcass, water, celery, celery leaves, onions, bouillon, salt, pepper and bay leaf in 8-quart saucepan. Heat to boiling, lower heat, cover, and simmer 1 hour. Remove carcass and let cool. Add parsley, peas, carrots, green beans to soup; heat to boiling, reduce heat, cook 10 minutes, or until vegetables barely tender. Remove meat from carcass and return meat to soup—discard carcass. Again heat soup to boiling, add noodles, cook uncovered 10 minutes. Melt butter in small frying pan, stir in flour; cook over low heat, stirring constantly until mixture is browned—stir into boiling soup. Simmer 5 minutes. Makes 5 quarts soup.

Carolyn Losch (East Alton)

CARAWAY SOUP

2 tablespoons flour
2 tablespoons shortening
1 onion, chopped
2 teaspoons caraway seed
1 teaspoon paprika

8 cups water
1 cup sour cream
2 eggs
1 medium potato, grated or
  finely shredded

Sauté onion in shortening, add flour, and brown very lightly. Add paprika and caraway seed and sauté for about 5 minutes more on low heat. Add water and potato. Bring to boil and cook until potato is done. Have sour cream in bowl and add a small amount of soup and stir well. Add sour cream mixture to soup. Beat eggs in small bowl and add to soup in a thin stream, stirring vigorously while pouring. Serve with croutons if desired.

Suzanne Blattner (Madison)

AUTUMN SOUP

1 pound ground beef
1 cup chopped onion
4 cups water
1 cup cut-up carrots
1 cup diced celery
1 cup cubed, pared potatoes
2 teaspoons salt

1 teaspoon bottled Brown
 Bouquet sauce
¼ teaspoon pepper
1 bay leaf
⅛ teaspoon basil
6 tomatoes*

In a large saucepan, cook and stir meat until brown. Drain off fat. Cook and stir onions with meat until onions are tender, about 5 minutes. Stir in remaining ingredients, except tomatoes; heat to boiling. Reduce heat; cover and simmer 20 minutes. Add tomatoes; cover and simmer 10 minutes longer or until vegetables are tender. Makes 6 servings.

*1 28-ounce can tomatoes, with liquid, can be substituted for the fresh tomatoes. Reduce water to 3 cups. Stir in tomatoes with remaining ingredients; heat to boiling. Reduce heat, cover and simmer 20 minutes. The canned tomatoes break apart and give a rosy color.

Louise Eckert (Collinsville)

GREEN BEAN SOUP

2 pounds green beans, cut
4 medium potatoes, cut in
 bite-size pieces
2 large onions, chopped
4 cloves garlic, chopped
1 stick butter or margarine

2 tablespoons paprika
½ cup flour, or more
1 8-ounce carton Smetina
 sour cream, room
 temperature
Salt and pepper to taste

In large pot, put green beans and potatoes with water to cover and cook. In skillet, sauté onions and garlic in butter or margarine. Add paprika and enough flour to make a paste and add to beans. In medium saucepan, heat Smetina over medium to high heat, slowly add some soup to Smetina so it does not curdle. Turn up heat to boil, then add Smetina mixture to beans and let cook ½ hour or more. Salt and pepper to taste. Serve with fried pork chops with caraway seeds sprinkled on top and cream bread and butter.

Brenda Norwood Dusek (Collinsville)

LOUISE'S CLAM CHOWDER

1 10¾-ounce can cream of
  celery soup
1 10¾-ounce can cream of
  potato soup

1 10¾-ounce can milk
1 can clams with juice
Salt and pepper

Combine all ingredients and heat to boiling. Season with salt and pepper to taste.

Gracie Koeller (Godfrey)

NOAH'S CLAM CHOWDER

1 can cream of potato soup
1 can cream of celery soup
1 can New England style clam
  chowder

1 pint half and half cream
1 small can clams, minced
1 teaspoon butter

Mix potato soup, celery soup, New England style clam chowder, half and half and clams. Simmer—the longer the better. May be put in crock pot for 3 hours. Add butter if desired.

Kathryn Cook (Marine)

NOAH'S ARK CLAM CHOWDER

1 stick butter
1 large or 2 small onions
2 cans Doxee minced clams
  (drain and save juice)

3 cans Campbell's New
  England clam chowder
6 cans cream of potato soup
½ gallon half and half cream

Mix all ingredients together in large pot, cover and bake at 200° F. for 4 hours or simmer in deep fryer 4 hours. Stir every hour. If it gets too thick, add extra clam juice. Freezes well.

Evelyn Keilbach (Highland)

CHILI

1 pound hamburger
1 onion, chopped
1 16-ounce can red kidney
  beans
1 can or 1 pint tomato juice

1 can water
1 tablespoon chili powder, or
  to suit taste
2 tablespoons sugar, or less to
  suit taste

Fry and stir to crumble hamburger. Sprinkle salt in pan to start instead of oil. Add onion to hamburger before it is finished cooking so onion can cook a little. Combine next five ingredients in saucepan and add hamburger and onion and cook ½ hour or so.

Florence Rapp (Edwardsville)

COUNTRY SUPPER SOUP

2 pounds chuck, cut in six
  pieces
Salt
Pepper
2 tablespoons oil
2½ quarts water
1 onion, chopped
1 cup sliced celery

½ cup chopped parsley
1 10-ounce package frozen
  mixed vegetables
½ small head of cabbage,
  shredded
4 to 6 medium potatoes,
  peeled and cut in half
1 6-ounce can tomato paste

Sprinkle chuck with salt and pepper; in Dutch oven, brown in oil at medium heat. Add water, onion, celery, parsley and 1½ teaspoons salt. Bring to boil—simmer 1½ hours. Add vegetables and tomato paste— simmer 45 minutes longer or until potatoes are tender.

Louise Eckert (Collinsville)

CREAM OF MUSHROOM SOUP

¼ cup butter or margarine
1 small onion, chopped
1 stalk celery, chopped
3 tablespoons flour
3 cups milk
1 teaspoon salt

⅛ teaspoon pepper
1 pint sliced fresh mushrooms
  or 1 cup drained canned
  mushrooms
2 cubes chicken bouillon

Boil fresh mushrooms until done. In saucepan, cook onion and celery in butter until tender. Stir in flour. Add milk; cook until mixture boils and thickens, stirring constantly. Season with salt and pepper. Add 2 cubes or teaspoons chicken bouillon to soup and let dissolve.

Beverly Dustmann (Dorsey)

CREAMY POTATO SOUP

6 cups potatoes, pared and
  cubed
2 cups celery, diced
1 cup onion, chopped fine
3 tablespoons butter

Salt and pepper to taste
1½ cups evaporated milk
1½ cups water
1 teaspoon Worcestershire
  sauce

Cook potatoes, celery, and onions in 2-quart saucepan until potatoes are done. Add butter, salt, pepper, milk, water and sauce. Place over low heat. Heat just to the boiling point. Serve hot. May be garnished with shredded cheese.

Mary Jane Gass (Granite City)

POTATO SOUP

4 potatoes, diced
1 onion, chopped

2 cups water, more or less

Combine ingredients and cook until tender, either in pressure pan or in saucepan. When done, add:

1 cup milk or more

Little butter

Heat.

Florence Rapp (Edwardsville)

65

FAMOUS-BARR'S FRENCH ONION SOUP

3 pounds peeled onions (5
pound bag of onions peeled
equals 3 pounds)
¼ pound butter or margarine
1½ teaspoons freshly ground
pepper

2 tablespoons paprika
1 bay leaf
¾ cup flour
3 quarts canned beef bouillon
1 cup white wine, optional
2 teaspoons salt

Slice onions ⅛ inch thick. Melt butter, place onions in it, sauté slowly for 1½ hours in a large soup pot. Add all other ingredients except bouillon, sauté over low heat 10 minutes more. Add bouillon and simmer for 2 hours. Adjust color to a rich brown with carmel coloring or kitchen bouquet. Season with salt to taste. Put in refrigerator overnight. This recipe yields 2 quarts finished soup.

Proper serving:
Heat soup in fireproof casserole or individual fireproof bowls. Using 8-ounces soup topped with three 1½ inch slices of Famous-Barr French bread and topped with 1½ ounces imported Swiss cheese. Place under broiler until brown, approximately 5 minutes at 550° F.

Gracie Koeller (Godfrey)

HAMBURGER SOUP

1 pound ground beef
1 16-ounce can tomatoes, cut
up
2 medium onions, chopped
2 medium carrots, sliced
2 stalks celery, chopped
⅓ cup pearl barley

¼ cup catsup
1 tablespoon instant beef
bouillon granules
2 teaspoons seasoned salt
1 teaspoon dried basil,
crushed
1 bay leaf

In a large saucepan, cook ground beef until browned. Drain off fat. Stir in remaining ingredients and 5 cups water. Bring to a boil. Reduce heat; cover and simmer for one hour. Season to taste with salt and pepper. Remove bay leaf. Serves six.

Betsy Knezevich (Godfrey)

HAMBURGER VEGETABLE SOUP

1 pound ground beef
1 cup chopped onion
1 cup diced potatoes
1 cup shredded cabbage
1 cup sliced celery
½ cup rice

2 cans tomatoes
4 cups water
½ teaspoon basil
¼ teaspoon thyme
1 bay leaf
Salt to taste

Brown meat and onion. Add remaining ingredients. Mix well. Bring to boil. Cover and simmer for one hour or more. Add noodles if so desired.

Louise Eckert (Collinsville)

CREAMY VEGETABLE SOUP

1 10-ounce can condensed
  beef broth
1 cup thinly sliced carrots
1 9-ounce package frozen
  green beans
1½ cups small pasta shells,
  uncooked
1 10-ounce can tomato soup
6 ounce can tomato paste
3 cups milk

1½ cups sliced zucchini
1½ teaspoons Italian
  seasoning
¼ teaspoon garlic powder
¼ teaspoon pepper
1½ cups shredded Provolone
  cheese
¼ cup grated Parmesan
  cheese

Place beef broth, carrots and frozen beans in a 4-quart Dutch oven. Bring to a boil; reduce heat; cover and simmer until vegetables are tender, about 10 minutes. Meanwhile, cook pasta according to package directions; rinse and drain. Add shells, tomato soup, tomato paste, milk, zucchini and seasonings to broth mixture. Bring to a boil; reduce heat; cover and simmer 10 minutes. Remove from heat and stir in cheeses until melted. If necessary, return to low heat and finish melting cheese. Do not boil. Yield: 11 cups.

Marina Brugger (East Alton)

CHILLED PEA SOUP

2 cups fresh or 1 10-ounce
package frozen peas
2 cups shredded lettuce
1 13¾-ounce can chicken
broth
⅓ cup water
¼ cup tomato juice

¼ cup finely chopped green
onion
1 tablespoon chopped parsley
½ teaspoon salt
¼ teaspoon white pepper
¼ teaspoon thyme, crushed
½ cup whipping cream

In a two-quart saucepan, combine peas, lettuce, chicken broth, water, tomato juice, onion, parsley, salt, white pepper and thyme. Bring to boiling. Reduce heat; cover and simmer 20 minutes. Turn into blender; cover and blend until smooth. Cool slightly, stir in whipping cream. Cover and chill. If desired, garnish with sour cream and fresh mint. Makes 4 servings.

Betsy Knezevich (Godfrey)

MICHIGAN PORK AND BEAN SOUP

3 cups chicken broth
1 pound potatoes, peeled and
cut in ½ inch cubes (about
3 medium sized potatoes)
1 small onion, chopped fine
½ cup thinly sliced celery
1 clove garlic, crushed

1 small bay leaf
2 1-pound cans beans in
tomato sauce
2 cups diced cooked ham
Salt to taste
Fresh ground pepper to taste

In a saucepan, bring broth to boil. Add potatoes, onion, celery and bay leaf. Cover and simmer until potatoes are tender, about 10 minutes. Add beans and diced ham. Stir and simmer 10 minutes more. Season with salt and pepper to taste. Serve in large bowls. 6 to 8 servings. Makes about two quarts.

VARIATION: May be made with roast pork, cooked chicken or turkey.

MICROWAVE: In a two-quart glass or porcelain casserole, mix all ingredients except salt and pepper. Cover with plastic wrap and cook in microwave oven ten minutes. Season with salt and pepper to taste.

Mrs. George P. Eckert (Collinsville)

TOMATO SOUP

1 quart canned tomatoes or
  1 quart cooked fresh
  tomatoes with salt added

¾ quart milk
1 tablespoon sugar
1 teaspoon baking soda

In separate pans, heat the tomatoes and milk to the same temperature. Add the baking soda to the tomatoes, stirring until done fizzing. Then pour the tomatoes into the milk, stirring while combining. Add the sugar. Serve with crackers immediately.

Nellie Dauderman (Alhambra)

TOMATO SOUP

1 pint tomato juice
¼ teaspoon baking soda (or a
  pinch to sweeten—add to
  tomato juice)

1 pint milk
Butter or margarine

Heat tomato juice and baking soda before adding milk; then heat after adding milk and little butter or margarine. Add broken crackers, about 4 or 5 or more and serve. (Mom's recipe)

Florence Rapp (Edwardsville)

SOUPS

SOUPS

DAIRY

DAIRY

Shurtleff College gained area wide respect as the Alton Seminary, founded June 4, 1832. Today, Shurtleff is part of the College of Medicine (Dentistry) of Southern Illinois University-Edwardsville.

HOMEMADE BUTTER

2 quarts cream = 1 pound butter

Use either sweet or sour cream. Use a churn or mixer to churn the cream (this should be around 60° F.) until the butter "comes" or until buttermilk separates. Pour off buttermilk (save for cooking—it makes great biscuits or pancakes). Wash butter. To do this, add cold water and work butter with a wooden spoon or butter paddle. Repeat, adding fresh water and work until the milk is out of the butter. To the butter, add ½ to 1 teaspoon salt per pound. Press into dish.

Carleen Paul (Worden)

BUTTERMILCHSUPPE (BUTTERMILK SOUP)

3 tablespoons cornstarch	1 teaspoon salt
4 cups buttermilk	1 egg yolk, beaten
1 tablespoon chives	1 hard cooked egg, chopped

Stir cornstarch into buttermilk until smooth. Cook over medium heat, stirring constantly, until thick. Stir in salt and chives. Beat a small amount of hot mixture into egg; return to buttermilk mixture, stir well. Serve hot. Garnish with chopped egg.

Florence Dinwiddie

You can double the volume of butter by simply whipping 1 pound with a cup of cold water. Beat butter, at room temperature, with electric mixer.

BUTTERMILK BISCUITS

2 cups flour	½ cup shortening
2 teaspoons baking powder	Pinch of salt
¼ teaspoon baking soda	¾ cup buttermilk

Mix together all ingredients and roll so that biscuits can be cut ½-inch to ¾-inch thick with cutter. Bake at 450° F. for about 15 minutes.

Charline Rehberger Tucker (Highland)

CHEESE ROLLS

4 tubes buttermilk biscuits   ¼ pound butter
½ pound grated Cheddar
   cheese

Melt butter and cheese together. Place rolls side by side in buttered pan and pour cheese and butter mixture over top with spoon. Spread over all the rolls. Bake 20 minutes in 400° F. oven.

Mrs. Louis A. Schmidt (Edwardsville)

BROCCOLI SOUFFLE

2 cartons (12-ounces) cottage   1 package frozen chopped
   cheese (small curd)   broccoli
6 eggs   6 tablespoons flour
¼ pound butter
½ pound American cheese,
   cut into cubes

Beat eggs slightly, put all ingredients into large bowl, mix until blended. Pour into greased pan, bake at 350° F. for 1 hour. Makes 12 servings.

Helen Miller (Granite City)

Use sweet butter when baking. If you must use salted butter, cut down or eliminate the salt called for in the recipe.

MACARONI AND CHEESE

1 7-ounce package macaroni   1 stick butter or margarine
1 11-ounce can cheese soup   2½ soup cans of milk
½ package Cheddar cheese,
   cut in pieces

Cook macaroni as per directions. In saucepan, put soup and Cheddar cheese and stir until melted. Add butter and milk. Pour over macaroni and stir. Put mixture in 9x13-inch glass pan. Bake at 400° F. for 30 minutes or until top is golden.

Donna Price (Granite City)

COTTAGE CHEESE SALAD

2 cups small curd cottage
  cheese
1 8-ounce carton Cool Whip

1 16-ounce can crushed
  pineapple, well drained
1 3-ounce box orange Jello

Mix cottage cheese, Cool Whip and pineapple. Then add dry Jello. Mix well and refrigerate until ready to serve. Cannot be cut. Serve with a spoon. Note: Quick and easy to make. Serves 8.

Louise M. Kipp (Edwardsville)

VEGETABLE DIP

1 cup cottage cheese
1 package Ranch salad
  dressing mix

1 tablespoon milk

Place cheese and milk in blender. Then add dry salad dressing mix. (Sour cream can be used in place of cottage cheese.)

Mrs. Louvain Vieth (Edwardsville)

FROZEN POTATO CASSEROLE

Preheat oven to 350° F.

1 2-pound 8-ounce package
  frozen hash brown potatoes
4 ounces grated Cheddar
  cheese
½ cup chopped onion
1 can cream of chicken soup,
  undiluted

1 12-ounce carton sour cream
½ stick (¼ cup) margarine,
  softened
1 teaspoon salt
1 teaspoon pepper

TOPPING:

1 cup corn flakes

½ cup margarine

Mix partially thawed potatoes with next 7 ingredients. Pour into large greased casserole. Combine margarine and corn flakes and cover potato mixture. Bake 1 hour.

Ruth Brave (Granite City)
Sheila Schrumpf (Highland)

CHEDDAR COTTAGE DIP

2 cups cottage cheese
2 teaspoons grated onion
1 teaspoon celery salt
¼ teaspoon Worcestershire
sauce

2 cups shredded Cheddar
cheese

In a small mixing bowl, beat together cottage cheese, onion, celery salt and Worcestershire sauce, at highest speed of mixer, until fairly smooth. Gradually add 1 cup cheese and continue beating at high speed until smooth. Fold in remaining cup of cheese. Serve immediately, or if refrigerated, allow to come to room temperature before serving.

JoAnn Brase (Edwardsville)

CHEESE MEAT LOAF

1½ pounds ground beef
1 egg
½ cup cracker crumbs
½ cup chopped onion
2 8-ounce cans tomato sauce

1 teaspoon salt
½ teaspoon oregano
⅛ teaspoon pepper
2 cups shredded Mozzarella
cheese

Combine beef, egg, cracker crumbs, onion, ⅓ cup tomato sauce (save remaining sauce for later), salt, oregano and pepper. Mix well and shape into flat rectangle about 10x12-inches on wax paper. Sprinkle cheese over meat mixture. Roll like jelly roll and press ends to seal the meat loaf. Bake in shallow dish at 350° F. for 1 hour. Drain off excess fat. Bake 15 minutes more, pouring remaining tomato sauce over meat loaf.

Beverly Dustmann (Dorsey)

VARIATION: 2 8-ounce cans of tomato sauce with cheese may be substituted for the plain tomato sauce in the above recipe.

Donna Price (Granite City)

Take butter directly from the refrigerator and cream it after cutting the stick into about eight pieces. Keep mixer speed low when you start creaming. This method is better for most types of cookies than allowing it to soften. If butter softens too much, it means you have to add extra flour and that cuts down on the shortness or tenderness of the cookies.

CHEESE BALL

2 8-ounce packages
  Philadelphia cream cheese
1 3-ounce jar English cheese

1 wedge Roquefort cheese
1 onion, cut fine
1 cup pecans, cut fine

Combine first 4 ingredients and roll in ball, then roll in finely chopped pecans. Refrigerate and serve with your choice of crackers.

Lois Beckmann (Granite City)

CHEESE CAKE

1 cup graham cracker crumbs
¼ cup light brown sugar
¼ cup melted butter
5 packages, 8-ounce size,
  cream cheese (room
  temperature)

1¼ cups sugar
3 tablespoons flour
1½ teaspoons vanilla
¼ cup milk
6 eggs (room temperature)

1. Preheat oven to 375° F. In large bowl, toss cracker crumbs, brown sugar and butter. Press into bottom of 9-inch spring form pan. Bake for 10 minutes. Cool in pan on rack.
2. FILLING: Preheat oven to 500° F. In large bowl, beat cheese and sugar with electric mixer at high speed until light and fluffy.
3. Blend in flour, vanilla, and milk until mixture is smooth. Beat in eggs, one at a time, beating thoroughly after each addition.
4. Pour mixture over baked crumb crust in pan. Bake in preheated oven for 15 minutes. Reduce heat to 250° F. Bake 1 hour longer.
5. Leave cake in oven, with heat turned off and door shut for 20 minutes. Remove from oven.
6. Cool on rack until room temperature, then refrigerate cake 3 hours longer. Remove from spring type pan.
7. STRAWBERRY TOPPING: Slice berries in half and place cut side down around edge of cake. Place several whole berries in center.
8. GLAZE: Combine ⅔ cup strawberry or red currant jelly (melted) with one tablespoon rum. Cool slightly. Brush berries with glaze. Refrigerate until ready to serve.
If desired, you may add ¼ teaspoon nutmeg and 1½ teaspoons grated orange rind to the cheese filling mixture. If you like a thicker crust, you may double crust ingredients.

Dottie Suhre (Alhambra)

BAKED CUSTARD

2 eggs or 4 egg yolks
⅓ cup sugar
¼ teaspoon salt

2 cups milk, scalded
½ teaspoon vanilla, if desired

Heat oven to 350° F. Beat eggs, sugar and salt slightly to mix. Stir in scalded milk. Add vanilla. Pour into 6 custard cups or a 1½-quart baking dish and set in pan of hot water 1 inch deep. Sprinkle a little nutmeg over top. Bake 45 to 50 minutes or just until a silver knife inserted 1 inch from edge comes out clean, soft center sets as it stands. Immediately remove from oven. Serve cool or chilled in same cups on dessert plates or unmold and serve. Serves 6.

Carleen Paul (Worden)

BLACK FOREST ICE CREAM

3 cans (large) evaporated milk
2½ ounces unsweetened
  chocolate
2 eggs

1 cup sugar
1 17-ounce can dark
  sweetened pitted cherries,
  drained and quartered

Melt the chocolate in 1 can milk. Beat the eggs and sugar together. Stir into hot mix. Stir together all ingredients. Chill. Freeze in ice cream freezer. Cherries can be added after 10 to 15 minutes so they don't freeze too hard. Makes 2 quarts.

Reita Sparrowk (Bethalto)

HOMEMADE ICE CREAM

2 cups sugar
4 eggs
½ gallon milk
1 can Pet evaporated milk or
  1 can Eagle Brand
  condensed milk

1 tablespoon vanilla

Beat eggs until thick. Slowly beat in sugar until very thick. Add milk and vanilla. Pour into freezer and turn until stiff. Makes 1 gallon.

VARIATION: For flavored ice cream, add crushed fruit when almost frozen. To make chocolate, use chocolate milk.

Sheila Schrumpf (Highland)

PINEAPPLE CHERRY ICE CREAM

1 quart milk
1 cup sugar
1 can crushed pineapple,
  drained

1 jar Maraschino cherries

Cut up cherries. Add all other ingredients. Pour in ice cube trays and put in freezer.

Pat Bojkovsky (Glen Carbon)

MY DAD'S FAVORITE CHOCOLATE CREAM PIE

1½ cups sugar
3 tablespoons cornstarch
½ teaspoon salt
3 cups milk
3 egg yolks, slightly beaten

1 tablespoon butter
1½ teaspoons vanilla
½ cup cocoa
1 prepared 9-inch pie crust
  shell

Mix sugar, cornstarch, salt and cocoa in saucepan. Stir in the milk. Cook over medium heat, stirring constantly, until mixture thickens and boils. Boil 1 minute and remove from the heat. Stir at least half of the hot mixture into egg yolks. Blend into hot mixture in the sauce-pan. Boil 1 minute more, stirring constantly. Remove from the heat and blend in the butter and vanilla. Pour immediately into the baked pie shell. Finish with pie meringue. Let cool at room temperature, or pie may be chilled thoroughly and top with whipped cream.

Carleen Paul (Worden)

EGGNOG

2 eggs, well beaten
4 tablespoons sugar
2 cups milk

½ teaspoon vanilla
Dash nutmeg

Beat eggs and sugar together. Beat milk with eggs and sugar. Serve cold, sprinkled lightly with nutmeg. One tablespoon either brandy or rum flavoring may be substituted for vanilla.

Verna Kasubke (New Douglas)

PARTY PINK JELLO

1 cup milk
¼ pound marshmallows
  (½ of a 10-ounce package)
1 3-ounce package strawberry
  Jello
1 6-ounce package cream
  cheese

1 #2 can undrained crushed
  pineapple
1 cup whipped cream
1 tablespoon mayonnaise

Melt marshmallows on low heat with milk. Pour hot mixture over Jello. Blend in cheese into Jello mixture. Add pineapple. Cool. Fold in whipped cream and mayonnaise. Chill until firm.

Mary Jane Gass (Granite City)

1-2-3 CHEESECAKE

CRUST:

24 graham crackers (crushed)   1 stick melted oleo

Mix together and put into 9 x 13-inch pan.

FILLING:

2 8-ounce packages cream
  cheese
1 pound box powdered sugar

1 12-ounce carton whipped
  topping (Cool Whip)

In a large bowl, blend the cream cheese and the powdered sugar with an electric mixer. Add the whipped topping and blend. Pour over graham cracker crust.

TOPPING:

1 can Thank You cherry pie
  filling

Pour over the top of filling. Refrigerate 2 hours and serve.

June Launhardt (Collinsville)

DAIRY

DAIRY

DAIRY

SALADS AND
SALAD DRESSINGS

Lock and Dam 26, downtown Alton, is south of the confluence of the Mississippi and Illinois Rivers. The replacement for Lock and Dam 26 will be located downstream. This navigational and flood control Lock and Dam provides an important link in the river traffic of Mid-America.

APPLE SALAD

6 medium apples, diced
2 tablespoons lemon juice
1 20-ounce can diced
   pineapple
½ pound white grapes

18 large marshmallows
½ cup nuts
Maraschino cherries for
   decoration

Pour lemon juice over apples. Combine with drained pineapple, grapes, marshmallows and nuts. Serve with dressing.

DRESSING FOR APPLE SALAD:

Drain pineapple to make one cup of juice, add

2 slightly beaten eggs
2 tablespoons flour

1 cup sugar
2 tablespoons butter

Combine all ingredients and cook until thick. Cool. Pour over fruit. Refrigerate several hours.

Brenda Keck (St. Jacob)

APPLE SALAD

½ dozen or more apples
   (depends on size)
1 dozen marshmallows, cut
   or use miniature
½ cup walnuts or pecans
1 small can crushed
   pineapple, drained
   (reserve juice)

1 or 2 small eggs
½ cup sugar
2 tablespoons flour
Grapes or white cherries may
   be added also for variation

Peel and dice apples, add a little lemon juice to prevent darkening. Add marshmallows, nuts and drained pineapple. Take reserved juice and heat. Mix eggs, sugar and flour together and blend into heated juice. Cook until thick. Cool and pour over mixture of apples.

Rose Schrage (Edwardsville)

APPLESAUCE SALAD

1 3-ounce package strawberry
   or cherry gelatin
1 cup boiling water

1 cup applesauce
1 cup miniature
   marshmallows

Combine boiling water with gelatin. Stir in applesauce and marshmallows. Chill until firm in refrigerator.

Darlene Stille (Alhambra)

APRICOT CHEESE DELIGHT

1 29-ounce can apricots,
   drained and cut fine
1 29-ounce can crushed
   pineapple, drained
1 cup miniature
   marshmallows

2 3-ounce packages orange
   Jello
2 cups boiling water
1 cup fruit juice, apricot and
   pineapple combined

Chill the drained fruit and reserve the juice. Dissolve the Jello in the boiling water and add the fruit juice. Chill until slightly congealed. Fold in fruit and miniature marshmallows. Pour into an 11x7x2-inch glass dish. Chill until firm. Spread with topping.

TOPPING:

½ cup sugar
3 tablespoons flour
1 egg, slightly beaten
1 cup combined juices
2 tablespoons butter

1 package whipped Dream
   Whip, prepared according
   to directions
¼ cup grated cheese of your
   choice

Combine sugar and flour, blend in beaten egg and juice. Cook over low heat until thickened, stirring constantly. Remove from heat, stir in butter, let cool. Fold in beaten Dream Whip and spread over Jello mixture. Sprinkle top with grated cheese. Cut in squares and serve on lettuce.

Mrs. Edward Barth (Brighton)

APRICOT JELLO SALAD

2 3-ounce boxes apricot Jello
2 cups boiling water
2 cups cold water
1 20-ounce can crushed
  pineapple
1 egg
1 tablespoon butter or
  margarine

½ cup sugar
1 tablespoon flour
1 3½-ounce package
  Philadelphia cream cheese
1 5-ounce carton Cool Whip

In 9x13x2-inch pan (glass), prepare Jello according to directions. Add crushed pineapple that has been drained (should have one cup or a little less juice). Let set until firm. In a small saucepan, combine the cup of pineapple juice with the egg, butter, sugar and flour. Cook until thick like pudding. Cool. Add Philadelphia cream cheese and Cool Whip, spread on the firm Jello.

Lois Beckmann (Granite City)

BEAN AND CABBAGE SALAD

1 15-ounce can large red
  kidney beans, drained
1 15-ounce can garbanzo
  beans, drained
½ small head cabbage, cut
  fine
1 small onion, finely chopped
1 small clove garlic, finely
  chopped
½ cup coarsely chopped
  green and red peppers

¼ cup vinegar
¼ cup oil
1½ teaspoons salt
½ teaspoon dry mustard
½ teaspoon sugar or a little
  more
Dash of pepper
1 teaspoon celery seed
5 slices bacon

Place beans, cabbage, onion and peppers in a large bowl. Mix well. Combine oil, vinegar, garlic, salt, dry mustard, sugar, pepper and celery seed. Pour dressing over bean mixture. Toss lightly to combine. Cover and chill 4 to 6 hours, stirring occasionally. Cut bacon into ½ to 1-inch pieces and cook in a large frying pan until crisp. Remove to absorbent paper towel. Toss vegetables before serving. Garnish with bacon. Serves 6.

Mrs. George P. Eckert (Collinsville)

ROBIN'S BROCCOLI SALAD

2 pounds fresh broccoli
4 hard-cooked eggs, cubed
8 radishes, sliced
1 small onion, cut very thin
  rings

½ cup mayonnaise
4 tablespoons plain yogurt
4 teaspoons Dijon or Guldens
  mustard
½ teaspoon salt or garlic salt

Clean broccoli, cut flowerettes from stems. Peel stems and halve or quarter as necessary for even cooking. Add stems to flowerettes. Cook in small amount of water in large pot for 7 to 10 minutes. Don't overcook. Drain and chill. To the chilled broccoli add eggs, radishes and onions. For salad dressing, mix together mayonnaise, yogurt, mustard and salt. Pour dressing over salad. Toss lightly just before serving. (Dressing is also good over hot broccoli or cauliflower. Sprinkle lightly with croutons as garnish on hot dish.)

Mildred Urban (Highland)

GREEN BEAN SALAD

1 can green beans (drained)
1 can peas (drained, save 1
  teaspoon juice)
1 small can pimentos

1 small onion (cut fine)
1 green pepper (cut fine)
4 stalks celery (cut fine)

BRINE INGREDIENTS:

1½ cups sugar
1 teaspoon juice from peas
½ cup corn oil

1 cup vinegar
Dash of paprika

Drain the vegetables, reserving the 1 teaspoon pea juice; cut the onion, green pepper and celery fine. Mix the brine ingredients in a large bowl and add all the vegetables, mix all together and chill overnight and then drain off the brine, and serve cold.

Mary Jane Koeller (Godfrey)

92

FRESH CRANBERRY SAUCE

1 pound fresh whole
  cranberries
1½ cups sugar

2 boxes raspberry gelatin
1 cup boiling water

Wash cranberries and place in a saucepan. Cover with water. Cook until they are all broken and then add the sugar and let it come to a boil, stirring often. Dissolve the gelatin in the boiling water and add to the cranberries, that have cooked, and stir.

VARIATION: You may add chopped celery and apples to the salad. As it cools, it will set and be ready to serve in 4 to 5 hours.

Frieda Paul (Staunton)

CRANBERRY SALAD

1 4-ounce box strawberry
  Jello
1 4-ounce box orange Jello
3 cups hot water
1 cup sugar
½ package cranberries

1 orange
1 small apple, peeled
1 small can crushed
  pineapple
½ cup chopped nuts

Dissolve Jello in 3 cups hot water, add sugar. Grind cranberries, orange (juice and rind), and apple. Add to congealed Jello with crushed pineapple and nuts. Refrigerate.

Viola Huebener (Alton)

CRANAPPLE SALAD

2 cups fresh cranberries
⅔ cup sugar
3 cups miniature
  marshmallows

2 cups fresh chopped apples
½ cup chopped walnuts
1 cup whipped whipping
  cream

Combine ground cranberries, sugar and marshmallows. Cover and refrigerate overnight. Combine other ingredients before serving. (Best to double recipe) Option—green grapes.

Diane Mindrup (Edwardsville)

CRANBERRY JELLO SALAD

Grind together (fine):

1 package (4 cups)
cranberries
2 peeled apples

2 small or 1 large orange
(seeded and peeled)
3 stalks celery

Add:

1 cup miniature
marshmallows
1¼ cups sugar (optional)

1 8-ounce can crushed
pineapple and juice

(Marshmallows can be omitted, then more sugar is needed—¼ to ½ cup) Mix well and let stand overnight or several hours to season. Dissolve one 3-ounce box orange Jello in one cup boiling water. Let cool until jell stage, then add previously prepared mixture. Refrigerate until firm.

Irma Henkhaus (Alhambra)

MARINATED CARROTS

5 cups carrots (sliced, cooked
and drained)

Mix together:

1 can tomato soup
¾ cup sugar
½ cup salad oil
⅓ cup vinegar
2 medium onions, chopped
fine
1 green pepper, chopped fine

1 teaspoon mustard
1 teaspoon salt
1 teaspoon pepper
1 teaspoon celery seed
1 teaspoon Worcestershire
sauce
1 teaspoon basil leaves

and pour over cooked carrots. Let stand 12 hours before serving. Keeps up to 3 weeks in refrigerator.

Melba Helmkamp (East Alton)

CRANBERRY-PINEAPPLE SALAD

1 can Eagle Brand milk
¼ cup lemon juice
1 can crushed pineapple
(drained)

1 can whole cranberry sauce
1 pint Cool Whip
1 cup chopped nuts

Mix Eagle Brand milk and lemon juice thoroughly. Add the remaining ingredients and mix well. Pour into a pan and freeze for 5 hours or longer.

Gracie Koeller (Godfrey)

CARROT SALAD

Mix and chill:

2 pounds carrots peeled and
grated
1 8-ounce can undrained
crushed pineapple
1 cup miniature
marshmallows

1 cup flaked coconut
1 cup sour cream (or little
more)
½ cup raisins

Brenda Norwood Dusek (Collinsville)

COPPER PENNIES

2 pounds carrots, sliced
2 medium onions, sliced thin
1 medium green pepper, cut
in thin strips
¾ cup vinegar
⅔ cup sugar

½ cup oil
1 10¾-ounce can tomato soup
1 teaspoon Worcestershire
sauce
¾ teaspoon salt

Cook carrots until tender, 8 to 10 minutes. In the meantime, combine last 6 ingredients for dressing. Drain carrots. Mix all together. Cover and chill overnight. May be kept several days in refrigerator.

Evelyn Keilbach (Highland)

GREEN CHEESE SALAD

1 box lime Jello
2 cups boiling water
1 small package cream cheese
18 large or 2 cups small
   marshmallows
1 small can crushed
   pineapple

½ cup whipping cream
½ cup pecans
Few drops green food
   coloring

Dissolve Jello in 1 cup hot water. Dissolve cheese and marshmallows in other cup hot water. Stir in small pan over low heat until dissolved. Chill until partly set, add well drained pineapple, whipped cream and nuts. Pour into mold.

Mildred Roemelin (Moro)

FRUIT SALAD

1 large can chunk pineapple,
   reserve juice
1 cup miniature
   marshmallows
1 cup nut halves
2 bananas, sliced

Chopped maraschino
   cherries (8)
½ cup sugar
1 egg, beaten
2½ tablespoons cornstarch

Boil sugar, cornstarch and pineapple juice. Add egg. Cook until thickened. Let cool. Stir in pineapple, marshmallows, nuts, bananas and cherries.

Edna Suessen (Edwardsville)

FRUIT SALAD

1 3-ounce package cherry
   Jello
1 #3 can fruit cocktail
1 11-ounce can Mandarin
   oranges

1 20-ounce can pineapple
   tidbits
½ cup miniature
   marshmallows
3 bananas, sliced

Prepare the Jello the day before. Cut Jello in cubes. Add to fruit cocktail, oranges, pineapple tidbits, miniature marshmallows and bananas.

Bernice Willaredt (Granite City)

GUMDROP SALAD

½ cup sugar
4 tablespoons flour
1 tablespoon vinegar
Juice of 1½ lemons
⅛ teaspoon salt
¾ cup pineapple juice
1 pint whipping cream
1 20-ounce can pineapple
tidbits or crushed

1 pound white grapes, halved
and seeded
1 small bottle red or green
cherries
½ cup nutmeats
½ pound miniature
marshmallows
½ pound gumdrops, assorted
flavors

Blend ½ cup sugar and flour. Add vinegar, lemon juice, salt and pineapple juice, drained from pineapple. Cook in double boiler until smooth and thick, stirring constantly. Cool. Whip cream and fold into mixture. Combine drained pineapple tidbits, grapes, cherries, nutmeats and add to cooled mixture. Add marshmallows and gumdrops. Let stand in refrigerator 12 to 24 hours to blend flavors. Serves 12 to 14 persons.

Mildred Urban (Highland)

FINGER JELLO

3 small packages of any
flavor Jello

3 envelopes Knox gelatin
4 cups boiling water

Mix Jello and gelatin together. Pour boiling water over mixture and stir until mixture is dissolved. Pour into a 9x12-inch pan and chill. Cut into shapes after mixture is well chilled.

Ruth Ann Henke (Staunton)

JELLO SALAD

1 small can crushed
pineapple
1 3-ounce package strawberry
Jello

1 pound cottage cheese
1 envelope Dream Whip,
prepared

Soften Jello in pineapple, heat until dissolved. Let stand until cool. When it begins to jell, fold in cottage cheese and whipped Dream Whip. Jell and serve.

Mrs. Ella Bentrup (Staunton)

BUTTER MINT SALAD

1 3-ounce box lime or lemon
  gelatin
1 16-ounce can crushed
  pineapple
½ 10-ounce bag miniature
  marshmallows

1 9-ounce carton Cool Whip
1 8-ounce bag yellow butter
  mints, crushed

Pour dry gelatin into pineapple. Add marshmallows and let set overnight. Combine the Cool Whip and crushed butter mints. Fold this into
the gelatin mixture. Spread in a 9x13-inch pan. Refrigerate until
served.

Judy Ernst (New Douglas)

ITALIAN SLAW

1 head cabbage, shredded
1 onion, thinly sliced
⅞ cup sugar
1 cup vinegar

¾ cup salad oil
2 teaspoons sugar
1 teaspoon dry mustard
1 teaspoon celery salt

Place shredded cabbage in bowl in layers of cabbage and onion rings.
Pour ⅞ cup of sugar over the top of cabbage. Mix the remaining ingredients and bring to a boil. Pour over cabbage while still hot. Cover
and let stand overnight. Mix and serve.

Shirley Beck (Pocahontas)

JELLO FRUIT SALAD

1 8-ounce container cottage
  cheese
1 large container Cool Whip
1 small can crushed
  pineapple, drained

½ cup cut up maraschino
  cherries, drained
½ cup chopped nuts
1 3-ounce package Jello, any
  flavor, dry

Mix together all ingredients and chill. May substitute 1 can drained
fruit cocktail for pineapple-cherries.

Cheryll Sievers (Staunton)

FROZEN FRUIT SALAD

4 1-pound 4-ounce cans
   crushed pineapple
2 1-pound cans sliced peaches
2 cups fresh white seedless
   grapes, halved or (2
   1-pound 4-ounce cans)
1½ cups maraschino cherries,
   cut in eighths or (3 1-pound
   packages frozen
   strawberries)
½ pound marshmallows,
   quartered (30)

2 teaspoons ginger,
   crystallized, finely chopped
1 envelope unflavored gelatin
¼ cup cold water
1 cup orange juice
¼ cup lemon juice
2½ cups sugar
2 cups coarsely chopped
   pecans
2 quarts heavy cream,
   whipped

Drain fruit, save 1½ cups pineapple juice. Cut peaches in cubes, ½ inch. Combine fruit, marshmallows and ginger. Soften gelatin in cold water. Heat pineapple juice to boiling, add gelatin; stir to dissolve. Add orange and lemon juices, sugar and stir to dissolve. Chill. When mixture starts to thicken, add fruit and nuts. Fold in whipped cream. Spoon into quart cylinders such as cottage cheese cartons. Cover and freeze. Makes 9 quarts to freeze ahead for holidays or busy times. To serve, remove from freezer and thaw enough to slip out of carton and cut in 1-inch slices. Serve on lettuce as salad or serve as dessert topped with whipped cream.

Mrs. Wilma Becker (Moro)

HEAVENLY FRUIT SALAD

1 large package vanilla
   instant pudding

1½ cups milk

Mix. Chill for 10 minutes.

Fold in small container of Cool Whip.

1 large can fruit cocktail,
   drained
2 bananas, sliced

½ cup cut cherries
1 cup miniature
   marshmallows

Fold together and chill.

Peggy Torrence (Highland)

LUNCHEON TUNA SALAD

1 3-ounce box lemon Jello
½ cup salad dressing
½ cup whipped Milnot
½ cup pecans
1 cup diced cheese
1 cup drained tuna

½ cup chopped green pepper
½ teaspoon salt
1 tablespoon finely chopped
  onion
1½ cups chopped celery
3 boiled eggs, diced

Dissolve Jello in 1 cup boiling water. Add salt when dissolved. When Jello starts to set, add salad dressing and Milnot. Add other ingredients. Mix and pour into loaf pan. Place in refrigerator at least 3 hours before serving. Unmold and slice. Will serve 8 to 10.

Mrs. Virginia Plegge (Bethalto)

MACARONI SALAD

1 7-ounce package macaroni
½ cup sugar
Salt to taste
Pepper to taste
1 medium green pepper,
  chopped

½ onion, chopped
1 2-ounce jar pimento
½ cup vinegar
4 tablespoons salad dressing
¾ head cabbage, chopped

Cook macaroni according to directions on package. Drain and cool. Add remaining ingredients and mix. Let set in refrigerator 1 day before serving.

Janice Bradley (Marine)

MARSHMALLOW PINEAPPLE JELLO

1 10-ounce package miniature
  marshmallows
2 boxes lemon Jello
1 large can crushed pineapple

3 cups water
¼ pint whipping cream
2 tablespoons mayonnaise
¼ cup Cheddar cheese, grated

Cover bottom of 9x13-inch pan with miniature marshmallows. Boil together 2 boxes lemon Jello, crushed pineapple and 3 cups water. Pour over marshmallows and stir until dissolved. Chill until set in refrigerator. Whip cream, add mayonnaise. Spread on Jello. Sprinkle with grated Cheddar cheese.

Joan Willaredt (Edwardsville)

ORANGE JELLO SALAD

1 3-ounce package vanilla
  pudding
1 3-ounce package orange
  gelatin
1 11-ounce can Mandarin
  orange sections, drained

2 cups Dream Whip or Cool
  Whip
3 cups fluid (orange juice and
  water)

Mix pudding, gelatin and liquid. Cook until it boils, then cool thoroughly. Fold in whipped topping; add oranges. Chill in refrigerator until ready to serve. Serves 6 to 8.

Pauline Shafer (East Alton)

PARTY CHERRY SALAD

1 #2 can pineapple
1 16-ounce can bing cherries,
  pitted
⅓ cup lemon juice
Water
Pineapple syrup
Cherry syrup

2 3-ounce packages cherry
  Jello
1 8-ounce package cream
  cheese
3 tablespoons light cream
½ cup chopped nuts

Drain pineapple and cherries. Add lemon juice and water to syrups to make 3½ cups; heat to boiling and dissolve Jello in hot liquid. Divide into equal portions. Chill one portion until partially set and add pineapple. Pour into 6x9½x2½-inch pan. Chill until firm. Add cream to soft cheese and spread over Jello. Chill until firm. Chill remaining Jello until thick, add nuts and cherries. Pour over cream cheese mixture and chill.

Wilma Willaredt (Collinsville)

PINK SALAD

1 9-ounce carton Cool Whip
1 can Eagle Brand milk
1 can cherry pie filling
3 tablespoons Realemon

1 cup pecans, chopped
1 can crushed pineapple,
  drained

Mix all ingredients with spoon and chill.

Janice Bradley (Marine)

PEA SALAD

1 large can peas, drained
2 hard boiled eggs, chopped
1 stalk celery, diced
¼ cup relish or pickles,
  chopped

½ onion, chopped
2 slices cheese, chopped
2 tablespoons salad dressing

Combine all ingredients and refrigerate until ready to serve.

Janice Bradley (Marine)

GERMAN POTATO SALAD

6 cups sliced cooked potatoes
6 slices crisp fried bacon,
  crumbled
2 hard-boiled eggs, chopped
1 tablespoon salt

Pepper to taste
¾ cup diced green pepper
½ cup chopped onion
½ teaspoon celery seed

Mix or toss together the above ingredients. Then cook until thick and pour over potato mixture the following:

½ cup sugar
¾ cup water
½ cup vinegar

1 rounded tablespoon
  cornstarch
½ the bacon grease

Blend well and let stand for a few hours before serving.

Amy Ellen Schaefer (Staunton)

PICNIC POTATO SALAD

6 large potatoes, cubed
3 tablespoons sugar
1 teaspoon salt
1 teaspoon dry mustard
2 teaspoons minced onion
⅛ cup vinegar

1 cup mayonnaise
3 hard boiled eggs, separate
  yolks from whites
1 green pepper, diced
1 red pepper, diced
1 cup celery, diced

Cook potatoes with skins on and cool (cook to firm stage). Peel and cube. Put in bowl with sugar, salt, dry mustard and minced onion and vinegar. Then add mashed egg yolks which has been mixed well with mayonnaise. Lastly add peppers, celery and chopped egg whites.

Rhoda Brandt (Worden)

HOT MASHED POTATO SALAD

1 quart mashed potatoes
1 teaspoon or more sugar
1 teaspoon vinegar
½ to ¾ teaspoon mustard
3 boiled eggs, sliced
1 teaspoon sweet relish if
  desired or 1 teaspoon
  minced onion

3 tablespoons mayonnaise or
  salad dressing
Salt and pepper to taste

Mix all the above with mashed potatoes and sprinkle with paprika. Serve warm or cold. Good for rush.

Florence Rapp (Edwardsville)

PATIO POTATO SALAD

½ cup milk
⅓ cup sugar
¼ cup vinegar
1 egg
4 tablespoons margarine
1 tablespoon cornstarch
¾ teaspoon salt

¾ teaspoon celery seed
¼ teaspoon dry mustard
¼ cup chopped onion
¼ cup mayonnaise
7 medium potatoes, cooked,
  peeled, diced and chilled
3 hard boiled eggs, chilled

In medium saucepan combine milk, sugar, vinegar, egg, margarine, cornstarch, salt, celery seed and dry mustard. Cook and stir over low heat until thickened. Remove from heat, blend in onion and mayonnaise. Cool. Combine potatoes and eggs, fold in dressing. Chill. Just before serving, sprinkle with paprika. 6 to 8 servings.

Delores Geiger (Alhambra)

SAUERKRAUT SALAD

1 can sauerkraut, large
1 cup sugar
½ cup vinegar
1 cup green pepper, chopped

½ cup onion, chopped
½ cup celery, chopped
¼ cup salad oil
1 small jar pimento

Mix all ingredients and chill several hours before serving.

Suzanne Blattner (Madison)

7-UP SALAD

1 3-ounce package lime Jello
1 3-ounce package lemon
  Jello
2 cups hot water
2 cups chilled 7-Up

2 cups miniature
  marshmallows
2 bananas, sliced
1 #2 can crushed pineapple,
  drained, save juice

Combine Jellos with hot water to dissolve. Add chilled 7-Up and pineapple. Set aside. Then add marshmallows and bananas and refrigerate until thick.

TOPPING:

Pineapple juice
2 tablespoons flour
½ cup sugar
1 egg

1 package Dream Whip,
  prepared
½ cup nuts (optional)

Cook pineapple juice, flour, sugar, egg until thick, cool. Whip Dream Whip according to directions on package and combine with cooled thickened juice. Spread over Jello mixture and sprinkle with nuts.

Donna Price (Granite City)

CAROLYN'S TACO SALAD

1 29-ounce can peach slices,
  drained and halved
1 15¼-ounce can dark red
  kidney beans, drained
3 cups lettuce, shredded or
  torn in small pieces

¼ cup green onions, sliced
¾ cup shredded Cheddar
  cheese
½ cup sliced ripe olives
1 cup broken Nacho cheese-
  flavored corn chips

DRESSING:

¼ cup cooking oil
2 tablespoons cider vinegar
¼ teaspoon dry mustard

1 teaspoon salt
½ teaspoon chili powder

Combine peaches, beans, lettuce, onions, cheese and olives. Chill thoroughly. Combine oil, vinegar and spices. Pour over salad ingredients when ready to serve. Top with corn chips.

Kay Losch (East Alton)

SWEET POTATO SALAD

2 cups sweet potatoes, cooked
   and sliced
3 stalks celery, cut fine
½ medium onion, chopped
6 hard-cooked eggs, chopped

Pinch garlic salt
Salt and pepper to taste
4 tablespoons mayonnaise or
   enough to moisten it well

Place all ingredients in bowl. Toss together lightly, chill and serve.

Mrs. Louvain Veith (Edwardsville)

MARINATED VEGETABLE SALAD

½ head cauliflower
3 carrots, scraped and cut
   into thin sticks
1 small bunch broccoli
1 onion, peeled and sliced

½ cup vegetable oil
2 tablespoons vinegar (wine)
2 tablespoons prepared
   mustard

Separate cauliflower into flowerets, combine with carrot sticks in saucepan with ½ inch salted water. Add broccoli (save stems, use later in soup, etc.) buds, onions. Boil 5 minutes, drain. Mix oil, wine vinegar, mustard. Pour over cooled vegetables. Serves 4-6. Will stay fresh in refrigerator up to a week.

Mrs. Ronnie Sommers (Godfrey)

MIXED VEGETABLE SALAD

2 10-ounce packages mixed
   vegetables, cooked
   according to directions
1 onion, diced
1 green pepper, chopped
1 cup celery, chopped

1 cup sugar
½ cup vinegar
2 teaspoons prepared
   mustard
2-3 tablespoons flour

Add onion, green pepper and celery to cooked vegetables. In small saucepan, cook sugar, vinegar, mustard and flour until thick. Cool and pour over vegetables and marinate 24 hours in refrigerator.

Lois Beckmann (Granite City)

VEGETABLE SALAD

1 15-ounce can small peas
1 15-ounce can white corn
1 cup chopped celery
1 cup chopped green pepper
1 15½-ounce can French style green beans

¼ cup chopped pimentos
1 cup chopped onion
1 cup sugar
½ cup vinegar
½ cup oil

Drain vegetables before combining them in a salad bowl. Bring sugar, vinegar and oil to a boil. Cool. Pour liquid over vegetables. Stir thoroughly. Let stand at least 12 hours before serving. Will keep for a week in refrigerator.

Verna Abert (New Douglas)

VEGETABLE SALAD

1 medium head lettuce, broken into pieces
1 cup celery, chopped
1 medium onion, sliced and broken into rings
1 package frozen peas, raw

2 cups mayonnaise
2 tablespoons sugar
4 ounces Cheddar cheese, shredded
8 slices bacon, fried crisp and broken

Layer in order given. Do not mix. Make at least one day ahead, cover. Use 9x13-inch pan. Layer each separate ingredient in order given. Start with lettuce and end with bacon. Will stay crisp several days if you do not mix.

VARIATIONS:
Any of the following may be added:

½ cup green pepper
6-8 thinly sliced water chestnuts
3 hard cooked eggs

3 tomatoes, cut in bite-size pieces
½ cup cauliflower flowerettes
Parmesan cheese

Mary Lou Sutton (Alton)
Norma Meyer (Edwardsville)
Ginger Schuette (Staunton)

PEACHY FRUIT SALAD

1 20-ounce can peach pie
  filling
1 20-ounce can pineapple
  chunks, drained
1 11-ounce can mandarin
  oranges, drained

1 8-ounce jar maraschino
  cherries, drained
2 medium bananas, sliced
1 cup miniature
  marshmallows

Slice bananas into drained pineapple juice and let set for five minutes. Combine the rest of ingredients by folding them in gently. Chill.

Ruth Ann Henke (Staunton)

SALAD OF GOLD

1 3-ounce package lemon
  Jello
⅔ cup boiling water
⅔ cup syrup from pineapple
⅔ cup evaporated milk
2 tablespoons vinegar

2 3-ounce packages cream
  cheese
1 cup carrot pieces
⅔ cup crushed pineapple,
  drained

Put Jello and water in blender and dissolve. Add syrup, milk, vinegar and cream cheese. Process until smooth. Add carrots and pineapple. Process on grind. Pour into a 2-quart mold and chill. Serves 6-8.

Lois Beckmann (Granite City)

UNDER THE SEA SALAD

1 cup crushed pineapple
1 8-ounce package cream
  cheese
⅓ cup sugar
2 tablespoons lemon juice

1 cup cold water
2 packages unflavored gelatin
1 package Dream Whip
2 3-ounce packages lemon or
  lime Jello

Combine pineapple, cream cheese, sugar and lemon juice. Heat until cheese is melted. Combine water and unflavored gelatin and add to above mixture. Let cool. Then add Dream Whip, prepared as directed on box. Pour into loaf cake pan and let set until hard in refrigerator. When set, prepare lemon or lime Jello as directed on box, and pour over first layer. Refrigerate until Jello is set.

Louise Eckert (Collinsville)

STRAWBERRY ORANGE JELLO

1 envelope plain gelatin
1¼ cups water
1 6-ounce can concentrated
  orange juice

1 pint fresh strawberries
1 banana

Sprinkle gelatin on cold water in small saucepan, wait 1 minute to soften, then heat, stirring frequently until gelatin dissolves. Stir in orange juice until defrosted and thoroughly blended. Chill in refrigerator until syrupy. Fold in sliced berries and banana. Spoon into 6 dessert cups. 75 calories in each serving.

Beverly Meyer (Edwardsville)

WATERGATE SALAD

1 small box pistachio instant
  pudding mix
1 20-ounce can crushed
  pineapple
1 cup marshmallows
  (miniature)

1 cup coconut, shredded*
1 cup chopped nuts
1 9-ounce carton whipped
  topping

Mix pudding with crushed pineapple. Add the marshmallows, coconut and nuts and stir. Then mix in the whipped topping. Chill and serve. Makes 8 servings. *Coconut may be omitted.

Eileen Becker (Moro)
Mildred Dustman (Dorsey)

FRESH REFRIGERATOR PICKLES

3 large cucumbers 1-1½ inch
  in diameter sliced ¹⁄₁₆ inch
  thick
1 medium onion, sliced

1 tablespoon salt
2 teaspoons celery seed
¼ cup sugar
½ cup vinegar

Combine cucumbers and onion in bowl. Sprinkle with salt and celery seed. Stir gently and let stand 1 hour. Combine sugar and vinegar. Stir until dissolved. Pour over cucumbers, stir, cover and refrigerate. Ready to eat in about 1 day.

Mrs. Ella Bentrup (Staunton)

FRESH SPINACH SALAD

1½ pounds fresh spinach
1 head lettuce
1 bunch green onions

6 hard boiled eggs
1 pound bacon fried
1 package frozen peas

DRESSING:

1 package Hidden Valley
Ranch
1 16-ounce jar Real
mayonnaise

1 12-ounce carton sour cream

Cut up and combine salad ingredients. Pour dressing over salad. Refrigerate 24 hours.

Ruth Keller (Edwardsville)

SPINACH SALAD WITH DRESSING

10 ounces or 1 pound fresh
spinach
½ head lettuce
4 hard boiled eggs, cut up

8 slices crisp fried bacon,
crumbled
½ or ¾ can water chestnuts,
sliced

DRESSING:

1 medium onion, chopped
1 cup Wesson oil
¼ cup vinegar

½ cup catsup
⅓ cup sugar
½ teaspoon salt

Mix all ingredients in blender. Pour dressing over salad and toss when ready to serve.

Virginia Herrmann (Edwardsville)

QUICK SALAD DRESSING

Take 2 or 3 bunches of garlic, clean buttons. Put in pint jar and add oil (olive is best), salt and pepper. You always have a tasty dressing on hand that keeps well. May add vinegar also to the jar. Let set on your counter, looks neat. Use sparingly.

Lillian Brokaw (Granite City)

BLENDER DRESSING FOR SPINACH SALAD

⅔ cup sugar
1 medium onion, chopped
1 teaspoon salt
1 teaspoon prepared mustard

1 teaspoon celery salt
⅓ cup vinegar
1 cup oil

Blend all ingredients in blender until smooth. Pour over spinach or leaf lettuce topped with hard boiled eggs and bacon pieces if desired.

Ruth Becker (Edwardsville)

BLENDER MAYONNAISE

1 egg
½ teaspoon salt
½ teaspoon dry mustard
¼ teaspoon paprika

2 tablespoons vinegar or
lemon juice
1 cup vegetable oil

Put egg, salt, dry mustard, paprika, vinegar and 4 tablespoons vegetable oil in blender. Blend 30 seconds on low speed. Gradually and very slowly add rest of the vegetable oil. Blend 30 seconds or until thick. If it does not emulsify, pour mixture into another container. Clean blender well, beat 1 egg then slowly pour mixture into beaten egg, beat until thick.

Kay Losch (East Alton)

COOKED SALAD DRESSING

½ cup sugar
1 tablespoon flour
2 eggs
¼ teaspoon salt

1 teaspoon prepared mustard
½ cup water
½ cup vinegar

Mix together sugar, flour, salt; beat in eggs, add mustard and mix well. Add water and vinegar and mix well again. Cook over low heat, stirring constantly until thickened or until it bubbles; or cook in double boiler to prevent scorching.
NOTE: Be sure to mix in order given to prevent lumps.

Eva Koeller (Godfrey)

FRENCH DRESSING

2 cans tomato soup
1¼ cups sugar
1 cup vinegar
1 teaspoon paprika
1 teaspoon pepper
3 teaspoons salt

2 tablespoons Worcestershire
   sauce
1 tablespoon mustard
1 dash garlic powder
1½ cups oil

Blend together all ingredients and beat until well mixed. Keeps in refrigerator for a long time.

Sharon Schlaefer (St. Jacob)

POPPY SEED DRESSING

1½ cups sugar
1 cup vinegar
2 tablespoons grated onion
   (optional)

2 cups Wesson oil
¼ teaspoon dry mustard
1½ teaspoons poppy seed

Combine sugar, vinegar and onion and beat 5 minutes. Then add Wesson oil and mustard and beat 5 minutes more. Add poppy seed and stir well. Keeps well in the refrigerator. Makes 1 quart of dressing.

Mrs. Raymond Schrage (Edwardsville)

VARIATION: 1 teaspoon onion juice may be added.

Joan Thurmond (Highland)

TEXAS CELERY SEED FRENCH DRESSING

1 cup plus 2 tablespoons
   sugar
2¼ teaspoons salt
2 teaspoons paprika
1 teaspoon dry mustard
2 teaspoons celery seed

⅚ cup cider vinegar
⅔ cup tomato catsup
1 small onion, chopped
¾ cup vegetable oil
Small clove garlic

Put all the above in blender and mix thoroughly. Store in covered container in refrigerator.

Lucille Brase (Edwardsville)
Florence Rapp (Edwardsville)

KAY'S SALAD DRESSING

1½ cups vinegar
½ cup salad oil
1½ cups sugar
¼ cup water

1 garlic button
1 tablespoon Worcestershire
sauce
2 tablespoons salt

Put all in quart jar and shake to mix. Make ahead and chill in refrigerator. Shake when ready to use on salad.

Debra Losch (East Alton)

MARSHMALLOW DRESSING

2 tablespoons vinegar
1 egg, well beaten
2 tablespoons sugar

6 marshmallows
1 cup Cool Whip or whipped
cream

Cook in top of double boiler, the vinegar, egg and sugar until thick. Add marshmallows and beat until melted. Cool. Add Cool Whip. Serve on molded or fruit salads.

Suzanne Blattner (Madison)

SLAW DRESSING

2 tablespoons sugar, add
enough vinegar to make it
wet
½ teaspoon mustard

2 heaping tablespoons
mayonnaise or Miracle
Whip

Add enough milk to make it creamy.

Donna Sievers (Staunton)

112

SALADS AND SALAD DRESSINGS

SALADS AND SALAD DRESSINGS

SALADS AND SALAD DRESSINGS

SALADS AND SALAD DRESSINGS

BREADS

The Chain of Rocks stretch of the Mississippi was a barrier to early river traffic. The bridge in the foreground (owned by Venice, IL) has been replaced by the I-270 bridge seen in the background. An early pumping station of St. Louis is seen at the brink of the rapids.

ANGEL BISCUITS

5 cups flour (sifted)
¾ cup Crisco
3 teaspoons baking powder
1 teaspoon baking soda
1 teaspoon salt

3 tablespoons sugar
1 package dry yeast
½ cup lukewarm water
2 cups buttermilk

Sift dry ingredients together. Cut in shortening (well). Add buttermilk and yeast (which has been dissolved in ½ cup lukewarm water). Mix with spoon until flour is moistened. DO NOT OVERMIX. Place in greased covered bowl and keep in refrigerator (for weeks). To use, roll dough on floured board ½ to ¾-inch thick and cut. Let rise in warm place about 2 hours. Bake 400° F. for 12 minutes on lightly greased sheet.

Nellie Dauderman (Alhambra)

SWEET ANISE BREAD

1 cup milk
1 cup sugar
1 teaspoon salt
½ cup margarine or butter
1 cup very warm water
3 packages or cakes yeast
   (active dry or compressed)

6½ cups sifted flour (about)
1 tablespoon Anise seed
1 cup light or dark seedless
   raisins
½ cup chopped pecans

Scald milk; stir in sugar, salt and margarine; cool to lukewarm. Measure water into large bowl. Sprinkle or crumble in yeast; stir until dissolved. Stir in lukewarm milk mixture and three cups of the flour; beat smooth. Cover; let rise in warm place, free from draft, until doubled in bulk, about 1 hour. Stir dough down; stir in anise seed, raisins, pecans and remaining flour to make soft dough. Turn out onto floured board; knead until smooth and elastic, about 10 minutes. Place in greased bowl, turning to grease all sides. Cover; let rise in warm place until doubled in bulk, about 45 minutes. Punch dough down; divide in half. Cover and let rise on floured board 10 minutes. Shape into loaves; place in greased 9x5x3-inch pans. Cover; let rise in warm place, until centers of loaves are slightly rounded above tops of pans, about 1 hour. Bake in a moderate oven 375° F., about 45 minutes, or until done. Remove from pans; cool on wire racks. If desired, sprinkle loaves thickly with sifted confectioners sugar. Yield: 2 loaves.

Alberta Brandt (Worden)

BOSTON BROWN BREAD

Mix and let stand until cold:

1 pound raisins	2 tablespoons butter
2 teaspoons baking soda	2 cups boiling water

Add together:

2 cups sugar	2 eggs
1 teaspoon salt	1 cup nuts
4 cups flour	

Mix all together. Grease several vegetable cans. Fill half full. Bake at 350° F. for one hour.

Pat Bojkovsky (Glen Carbon)

BUTTER PECAN ROLLS

1 package dry yeast	¼ cup sugar
¼ cup water	1 teaspoon salt
1 cup milk, scalded	3¼-3½ cups sifted all-purpose
¼ cup shortening	flour
1 egg, beaten	

Soften yeast in lukewarm water. Combine hot milk, shortening, sugar and salt; cool to lukewarm. Add one cup of flour, beat well. Beat in softened yeast and egg. Gradually add remaining flour to form soft dough; knead. Let rise in warm place until double (about 1½ hours) punch down, turn out on lightly floured surface and divide dough in half. Roll each piece in 12x8-inch rectangle; brush with 2 tablespoons melted butter, sprinkle with sugar cinnamon (½ cup sugar and 2 teaspoons cinnamon). Beginning with long side, roll each jelly roll fashion, seal edge. Cut each roll in 8-1½-inch slices.

TOPPING—BUTTER PECAN ROLLS

In each of two 9½x5x3-inch loaf pans, mix ½ cup brown sugar, ¼ cup butter and 1 tablespoon light corn syrup. Heat slowly, stirring until blended. Remove from heat; sprinkle ⅓ cup pecans in each pan and top with 8 rolls, cut side down. Let rise in warm place until double, 35 to 45 minutes. Bake in moderate oven 375° F. about 25 minutes. Invert on rack and remove from pans while hot. Recipe can be doubled.

Mrs. Wilma Becker (Moro)

QUICK BROWN BREAD

2 cups whole wheat flour
1 teaspoon salt
½ teaspoon baking soda
1½ teaspoons baking powder
1 egg

1 cup buttermilk or sour milk
½ cup molasses
¼ cup melted shortening or
  cooking oil

Mix flour, salt, soda, baking powder, thoroughly in mixing bowl. Beat egg, add buttermilk or sour milk, molasses, shortening and mix. Add liquid mixture to dry ingredients and stir, barely mixing. Pour into oiled 8-inch square pan. Bake 30 minutes at 350° F. Serve warm. Yield 12 to 16 servings.

Frances Runyon (Wood River)

MINNIE'S BOSTON BROWN BREAD

2 cups raisins
2 cups water
1 teaspoon salt
1 teaspoon baking soda
2¼ tablespoons butter

2 eggs
1 cup sugar
1 teaspoon vanilla
2¾ cups flour

Preheat oven to 350° F. Simmer the raisins, water and salt for 15 minutes. While still hot add baking soda and butter, stirring well. Set aside. Beat eggs, sugar and vanilla until well blended. As the flour is being added to the egg mixture, start pouring in the raisin mixture, stirring this addition by hand. Do not overmix. Bake in 3 well greased and floured No. 2 size cans. Fill about ¾ full and bake 35-40 minutes or until inserted straw comes out clean.

Norma Hemann (New Douglas)

BEER BISCUITS OR MUFFINS

4½ cups Bisquick
1 can beer (warm)

3½ tablespoons sugar

Mix Bisquick, beer and sugar until smooth. Grease muffin pans and fill half full. Bake at 375° F. for 12 minutes.

Gracie Koeller (Godfrey)

CAN CAN DATE-NUT BREAD

1 cup chopped dates
¾ cup raisins
1 teaspoon baking soda
1 cup boiling water
2 tablespoons soft butter

1 cup sugar
1 teaspoon vanilla
1 egg
1⅓ cups flour
¾ cup chopped pecans

Place dates and raisins in covered bowl. Add soda and boiling water. Cover and let stand. Cream butter and sugar. Add vanilla and egg and beat well. Add flour, mix until moistened. Pour in fruit mixture, including liquid and pecans, and mix gently to prevent crushing the fruits. Before filling cans, melt a small amount of butter in each can in the oven. Then fill cans ⅔ full. Bake at 325° F. for 45 minutes. Remove from cans while warm. (Use greased #2 cans)

Mildred Roemelin (Moro)

RAISED POTATO DOUGHNUTS

1 13-ounce can Pet milk with
   same amount of potato
   water
1 cup sugar
1 cup shortening
1 tablespoon salt
1 cake or package dry yeast
2 eggs

1 cup mashed potatoes
9-10 cups flour (measure only
   8 cups with baking powder
   and soda. Enough for soft
   dough only)
½ teaspoon baking powder
½ teaspoon baking soda

Cook potatoes and mash, save the potato water, cool. Scald milk. Add potato water, sugar, shortening and salt; cool to lukewarm. Dissolve yeast in milk and slightly beaten eggs, add mashed potatoes, then beat in flour which was sifted with baking powder and baking soda. Place on board. Knead until smooth. Put dough in greased bowl to rise until double in bulk. Knead down again. Let rise. Roll and cut doughnuts. Let rise again. Fry in deep fat at 375° F. Brown on one side and turn only once, drain on paper towels. Fry about 4 to 5 minutes. If you desire to ice them, make icing and put on while hot. I use chocolate powdered sugar icing. Put on cookie sheet to freeze. Then wrap and store extra doughnuts in freezer. Makes 5 to 6 dozen.

Mrs. Earl Grotefendt (Highland)

CARAMEL PECAN ROLLS

1 package Fleischmann's
active dry yeast
1 cup warm water, 105° to
115° F.
¼ cup granulated sugar
1 teaspoon salt

2 tablespoons Fleischmann's
margarine, softened
1 egg
3¼ to 3½ cups Gold Medal
flour

In mixing bowl, dissolve yeast in warm water. Stir in sugar, salt, margarine, egg and 2 cups of flour; beat until smooth. With spoon or hand, work in enough remaining flour until dough is easy to handle. Place greased-side-up in greased bowl; cover tightly. Refrigerate overnight or up to 4 or 5 days.

⅓ cup Fleischmann's
margarine, melted
½ cup brown sugar, packed
1 tablespoon corn syrup

⅔ cup pecan halves
½ cup granulated sugar
2 teaspoons cinnamon

Combine melted margarine, brown sugar, corn syrup and pecan halves. Pour into greased oblong pan, 13x9½x2-inches. Combine sugar and cinnamon. On floured board, roll dough into 15x9-inch oblong. Spread with melted margarine and sprinkle with sugar-cinnamon mixture. Roll up tightly, beginning at wide side. Seal edge well. Cut into 1-inch slices and place in prepared pan. Cover; let rise in warm place (85°) until double, about 1½ hours. (If kitchen is cool, place dough on a rack over a bowl of hot water and cover completely with towel.) Heat oven to 375° F. Bake 25 to 30 minutes. Makes 15 rolls.

Ruth R. Rogier (Highland)

COCONUT BREAD

2 sticks butter
2 cups sugar
6 eggs
1 12-ounce box vanilla wafers,
crushed

1 7-ounce package flaked
coconut
1 cup nuts, chopped

Cream butter and sugar. Add eggs, one at a time and mix well. Add crumbs, coconut and nuts. Bake at 350° F. for 1 hour in 2 greased and floured loaf pans. VERY GOOD!

Judy Ernst (Pocahontas)

CRANBERRY FRUIT NUT BREAD

2 cups sifted all-purpose flour
1 cup sugar
1½ teaspoons baking powder
1 teaspoon salt
½ teaspoon baking soda
¼ cup shortening

1 teaspoon grated orange peel
¾ cup orange juice
1 egg, well beaten
1 cup fresh cranberries,
   coarsely chopped
½ cup chopped nuts

Preheat oven to 350° F. Sift together dry ingredients. Cut in shortening. Combine orange peel, juice and egg. Add to dry ingredients, mixing just to moisten. Fold in cranberries and nuts. Turn into greased 9x5x3-inch pan. Bake for 60 minutes. Cool. Wrap and store overnight.

Rhoda Brandt (Worden)

CRESCENT ROLLS

1¾ cups lukewarm water
1 package dry yeast
½ cup sugar
½ cup shortening, melted and
   cooled

3 eggs, beaten
1 teaspoon salt
5 cups flour (may use little
   more)

Mix first three ingredients and let stand for five minutes. Add remaining ingredients. Mix well. Turn into a greased bowl and let rise until double in bulk. Punch down; divide into eight parts. Roll each part into a circle and divide into eighths or sixths. Brush with melted butter; starting with wide end roll into crescents. Let rise again until doubled in bulk. Bake in 400° F. oven for 12 minutes or until golden brown.
NOTE: May leave dough in refrigerator for 3 to 4 days.

VARIATION: Mix 1 cup ground nuts, ¼ cup sugar and enough milk to make a paste. Cook over medium heat to scalding, simmer until pasty. Spread over triangles and roll into crescents. Let rise and bake as above.

Norma Lesko (Granite City)

DATE & NUT BREAD

1 cup dates, cut up
½ cup chopped nuts
2 tablespoons shortening
2 teaspoons baking soda
2 cups hot coffee
3 cups sifted flour

1½ cups sugar
1 egg, beaten
1 teaspoon baking powder
1 teaspoon vanilla
½ teaspoon salt

Preheat oven to 350° F. Mix dates, nuts, shortening, baking soda and hot coffee. Set aside to cool. Mix together flour, sugar, egg, baking powder, vanilla and salt. Add to above mixture and blend thoroughly. Put in #2 size greased tin cans. Fill only about ½ to ⅔ of can. Bake at 350° F. for about 40 minutes.

Barbara Krohne (Granite City)

GARDENER'S BREAD

Yield 2 loaves.

2 medium size fresh pears
⅓ cup finely grated unpared zucchini
⅓ cup finely grated carrot
3 cups flour, sifted
1½ teaspoons salt
1 teaspoon baking soda
¾ teaspoon cinnamon

¼ teaspoon baking powder
¼ teaspoon ground ginger
3 large eggs
1½ cups sugar
1 cup oil
1½ teaspoons vanilla
½ teaspoon grated lemon peel
½ cup chopped nuts

Grate pears to measure 1½ cups. Grate zucchini and carrot, one at a time, and press out excess liquid in a strainer. Combine flour with salt, soda, cinnamon, baking powder and ginger. Beat eggs. Gradually beat in sugar, then oil. Add vanilla and lemon peel. Blend in flour mixture. Add the pear, zucchini, carrot and nuts and mix well. Divide mixture into 2 loaf pans. Let stand 5 minutes. Bake below center of moderate oven at 350° F. about 55 to 65 minutes. Remove bread from oven and let stand in pans 10 minutes. Turn out onto wire racks to cool.

Celeste Erb (Edwardsville)

EASY ROLLS

1 9-ounce box Jiffy white
  cake mix
1 package dry yeast

1¼ cups warm water
½ teaspoon salt
2½ to 3 cups flour

Mix the cake mix and dry yeast. Then combine the warm water and salt and stir into the dry mix. Gradually, work in flour. You need more or less flour to make soft dough that can be handled. Mix well with hands. Put in bowl. Cover with towel, set in warm place for one hour. Punch down and shape into rolls of your choice. Brush with oil or margarine. Place on greased cookie sheet or cake pans. Let rise once more about two hours. Bake 400° F. until golden brown. Leftover rolls could be wrapped in foil, reheated at 350° F. These rolls stay fresh for days.

Mildred Urban (Highland)

EGG BREAD

½ cup warm water
¼ cup margarine, melted
2 packages dry yeast
1½ cups lukewarm milk

¼ cup sugar
1 tablespoon salt
3 eggs
7¼ to 7½ cups sifted flour

In mixing bowl, dissolve yeast in water. Stir in milk, sugar and salt. Add eggs, margarine and half the flour. Mix with spoon. Add rest of flour, mixing with hands. Turn onto lightly floured surface and knead until smooth and blistery. Round up in greased bowl; bring greased side up. Cover with damp cloth. Rise until double in bulk. Punch down; round up. Let rise again. Divide dough into three 14-inch long rolls and three 10-inch rolls. Make an oval with the three braided 14-inch rolls. Put the other three braided rolls on top. Let rise. Brush top with glaze of one egg yolk and tablespoon water. Sprinkle sesame seeds on top. Bake in 425° F. oven for about 30 minutes or until it sounds hollow when tapped.

Nellie Dauderman (Alhambra)

OUR AUNT ANNIE'S FILLED COFFEE CAKE

¾ cup white sugar
¼ cup shortening or
  margarine
1 egg
1 teaspoon vanilla

½ cup milk
1½ cups flour
2 teaspoons baking powder
½ teaspoon salt

Mix all ingredients together.

TOPPING:

½ cup brown sugar
¼ cup flour
½ teaspoon cinnamon
½ teaspoon nutmeg

¼ cup nuts, chopped
2 tablespoons soft margarine
  or butter

Mix all ingredients together. Take ½ of the dough and put into a pan, then put ½ of the topping mixture on the dough. Put the other half of the dough on the topping and then add the remaining half of the topping on the dough. Bake at 325° F. for 20 to 30 minutes.

Mrs. Verna Kasubke (New Douglas)

HOT ROLLS
(Made with Mashed Potatoes)

¾ cup sugar
6 cups flour (takes a little
  more)
1 package dry yeast
3 eggs

1 teaspoon salt
½ cup Spry or Crisco
1 cup mashed potatoes
1 cup potato water
1 cup milk, scalded

Put shortening in scalded milk to melt, add potatoes and let cool. Mix sugar, flour, yeast and salt together. When milk and potatoes and water are mostly cooled, mix all ingredients together. Let stand ½ hour; then work down and let rise about 3 hours. This can then be put in the refrigerator with a cover. You may use from it each day or you can put it in muffin pans or shape into rolls and place in an 8½x13-inch pan. This makes about two 8½x13-inch pans of rolls. These are easy to make and very good. If refrigerated, they take 4 to 5 hours to rise before baking. Bake in 350° F. oven for 15 to 20 minutes or until lightly browned.

Ruth R. Rogier (Highland)

EGGNOG-CHERRY NUT BREAD

2½ cups flour
¾ cup sugar
1 tablespoon baking powder
1 teaspoon salt

1¼ cups eggnog
⅓ cup oil
½ cup walnuts, chopped
½ cup maraschino cherries

In a mixing bowl, stir together flour, sugar, baking powder and salt. Mix eggnog, egg and oil, stir into dry ingredients, mixing well. Fold in nuts and cherries. Turn into greased loaf pan. Bake at 350° F. for 1 hour and 10 minutes. Cool 10 minutes before removing from pan. Preparation time is 1½ hours. Serves 10.

Peggy Torrence (Highland)

ONION POPOVERS

2 eggs, beaten
1 cup milk
1 tablespoon oil

½ teaspoon salt
½ teaspoon onion powder
1 cup flour

Preheat oven to 425° F. Combine first five ingredients. Blend in flour until smooth. Beat 1 minute with electric mixer or 3 minutes with rotary beater. Fill greased muffin pans half full. Bake 20 minutes and reduce heat to 350° F. and bake 25 minutes more or until brown and firm to touch.

Suzanne Blattner (Madison)

QUICK BREAD

1 cup warm water
2 tablespoons sugar
1 package dry yeast

1½ teaspoons salt
2 tablespoons oil
3-3½ cups flour

Put water and sugar in a bowl. Stir in yeast and wait five minutes or until it gets foamy. Stir salt and oil into yeast mixture. Add flour one half cup at a time. Beat until almost impossible to move spoon. Knead the dough. Put in a greased bowl and cover. Let rise until dough doubles in size. Knead again, cover, let rise ten minutes. Flatten dough, roll up, pinch ends and put in pan. Oil top of bread, cover, let rise 30 minutes. Bake at 375° F. for 30 minutes.

Pat Bojkovsky (Glen Carbon)

GERMAN STREUSEL COFFEE CAKE & GLAZE

1 or ½ package dry yeast
2 cups flour
2 tablespoons sugar
1 teaspoon salt

¼ cup butter, soft
3 eggs, beaten
⅔ cup hot milk

First warm your beaten eggs, milk and butter. Mix this with all dry ingredients. Beat for 3 minutes. Pour into greased 9x13-inch cake pan. Sprinkle with crumbly topping, and let rise for ½ hour. Bake in hot oven 350° F. until done. Remove from oven and glaze while still warm.

CRUMBLY TOPPING:

Mix together:
½ cup sugar
⅔ cup flour

¼ cup butter
½ teaspoon cinnamon

VANILLA GLAZE:

Mix together:
1 cup powdered sugar
1 tablespoon butter, melted

¼ teaspoon vanilla
1 or 2 tablespoons milk

JoAnn Brase (Edwardsville)

CARROT PINEAPPLE BREAD

3 cups flour
1 teaspoon baking soda
2 teaspoons cinnamon
3 eggs
2 cups sugar
1 cup salad oil

3 teaspoons vanilla
2 cups grated carrots
1 small can crushed
pineapple with juice
1 cup chopped pecans

Sift dry ingredients together. Beat in eggs, sugar, oil and vanilla. Add grated carrots and pineapple with juice. Beat well, add dry ingredients and stir in nuts. Pour into two greased and floured 9x5-inch bread pans and bake 1 hour at 350° F.

Diane Mindrup (Edwardsville)

MOLASSES APPLE BREAD

2¼ cups flour
1 teaspoon baking soda
½ teaspoon salt
1½ teaspoons cinnamon
½ teaspoon nutmeg
⅛ teaspoon cloves
⅓ cup shortening
⅔ cup brown sugar

2 eggs
½ cup dark molasses
⅔ cup milk
2 cups diced apples (2 large apples)
½ cup chopped walnuts or pecans

Sift together flour, baking soda, salt, and spices. Set aside. Cream together shortening and sugar, add eggs, one at a time, beating well. Add molasses, mix well. Add flour mixture alternately with milk. Fold in apples and nuts. Pour into greased and floured 9x5-inch pan and bake at 350° F. for 1 hour. Cool on rack for ten minutes and remove from pan. Cool thoroughly on rack. Wrap in foil and store overnight before slicing.

Mrs. Elizabeth S. Knezevich (Godfrey)

MOLASSES OATMEAL BREAD

2 cups boiling water
2 cups quick-cooking oats
¼ cup margarine
½ cup light molasses
1 tablespoon salt

2 packages active dry yeast
1 cup warm water, 105°-115° F.
6 cups flour

Add quick-cooking oats to boiling water, cook until thick, about 1 minute. Remove from heat and add margarine, molasses and salt. Stir until margarine is melted. Cool to lukewarm. In a large bowl, mix yeast and warm water. Add the lukewarm molasses mixture and 3 cups flour and beat until smooth, about 2 minutes. Gradually add the remaining 3 cups of flour and knead until smooth, about 10 minutes. Place in a greased bowl and let rise until double, about 1 hour at 85°. Divide. Place in two 9x5x2¾-inch pans. Let rise at 85° for 1 hour. Bake at 375° F. for 55 to 60 minutes. Turn out on wire racks to cool. Makes 2 loaves, about 2 pounds each.

Cornelia Parrill (Edwardsville)

PARKER HOUSE ROLLS

6 to 6½ cups all-purpose flour
½ cup sugar
2 teaspoons salt
2 packages active dry yeast

1 cup butter or margarine,
  softened, divided
1 egg
2 cups hot tap water

About 3½ hours before serving: In large bowl, combine 2¼ cups flour, sugar, salt and yeast; add ½ cup butter or margarine. With mixer set on low speed, gradually pour 2 cups hot tap water (120° to 130° F.) into dry ingredients. Add egg; increase speed to medium; beat 2 minutes, occasionally scraping bowl with rubber spatula. Beat in ¾ cup flour or enough to make a thick batter; continue beating 2 minutes, occasionally scraping bowl. With spoon, stir in enough additional flour (about 2½ cups) to make soft dough. Turn dough onto lightly floured board and knead until smooth and elastic, about 10 minutes. Shape dough into a ball and place in greased large bowl, turning to coat top with grease. Cover with towel and set in warm place, 80°-85° until doubled, about 1½ hours. Punch dough down by pushing center of dough with fist. Turn onto lightly floured board; knead lightly to make smooth ball, cover with bowl and let rest 15 minutes. In 17¼x11½-inch roasting pan, over low heat, melt remaining butter or margarine; tilt to grease bottom of pan.

On lightly floured surface with floured rolling pin, roll dough ½-inch thick. With floured 2¾-inch round cutter, cut dough in circles. Fold cut circle in half and arrange in buttered pan, each nearly touching each other. Knead trimmings together and cut more rolls. Cover pan with towel; let rise in warm place until doubled, about 40 minutes. Meanwhile, preheat oven to 425° F. Bake rolls 18 to 20 minutes until golden brown. Makes 3½ dozen rolls.

Irene H. Weder (Highland)

MY MOM'S GERMAN STOLLEN

2½ cups milk, scalded
1½ cups sugar, dissolved in
    warm milk
1 pound butter or margarine,
    creamed with sugar

3 packages dry yeast,
    dissolved in ¼ cup warm
    water (not too hot)
4 eggs, well beaten
5 cups all-purpose flour

Mix all ingredients, well, with a spoon. Set in a warm place to rise until light.

5 or 6 cups flour
2 ounces chopped almonds
6 or 8 candied cherries, cut
    small

½ lemon rind, grated
Some citron, grated

When light add the other 5 or more cups flour, fruit, nuts, lemon rind and citron. The dough should be a little sticky. Mix and knead well. Then mold into stollen and let rise 2 to 3 hours. Be sure the pans are well buttered. Use margarine for this. Brush plenty of good butter on top of the stollen and sugar to taste. If you prefer icing, then only brush top with butter (no sugar). Let rise until double in bulk. When ready to bake, put into the oven at 300° F. for 20 minutes. Then turn the oven down to 250° F. Small stollen should bake 1 hour; large stollen should bake 1¼ to 1½ hours, according to taste.

Verna Kasubke (New Douglas)

RAISIN BRAN MUFFINS

1 15-ounce box of raisin bran
    cereal
3 cups sugar
5 cups flour
2 teaspoons salt

5 teaspoons baking soda
1 quart buttermilk
4 eggs, beaten
1 cup vegetable oil

Use a large bowl and mix all dry ingredients well. Then add the buttermilk, beaten eggs and oil. Mix well, making sure all dry ingredients are moistened. Store mix in airtight container for up to six weeks in refrigerator. For baking, preheat oven to 400° F. Stir mixture and fill muffin tins ⅔ full and bake for 15 minutes, or until golden brown.

Beckie Schrumpf (Highland)

QUICK PRALINE ROLLS

1 package yeast
¼ cup warm water
2 tablespoons sugar
2 teaspoons baking powder
1 teaspoon salt

2¼ cups flour
⅓ cup butter
⅓ cup milk
1 beaten egg

SUGAR FILLING:

⅓ cup butter
¾ cup brown sugar

½ cup nuts
Powdered sugar icing

Dissolve yeast in warm water. Mix sugar, baking powder, salt and flour. Cut in butter until fine. Stir in milk, beaten egg and dissolved yeast. Beat well. Roll dough into a 10x15-inch rectangle and spread with sugar mixture. Roll and slice. Place on cookie sheet and flatten. Let rise until double in bulk. Bake at 425° F. for 10 to 12 minutes. Spread with icing.

Dorothy Marti (Pocahontas)

PUMPKIN BREAD

3 cups sugar
1 cup oil
4 eggs
2 cups pumpkin
⅔ cup water
3½ cups flour
½ teaspoon baking powder

2 teaspoons baking soda
1 teaspoon salt
1½ teaspoons cinnamon
1½ teaspoons cloves
1½ teaspoons allspice
1 cup nuts, chopped

Combine sugar, oil, eggs, pumpkin and mix thoroughly. Add water and mix. Sift together dry ingredients. Slowly add to mixture. Mix well, add nuts and mix. Bake in 2 well greased loaf pans for 1 hour at 350° F.

Mildred Dustmann (Dorsey)

VARIATION: Use 1 teaspoon of spices instead of 1½ teaspoons, 1 teaspoon of baking soda, ½ teaspoon salt, 3 cups flour, 3 eggs and omit water and nuts. Bake at 350° F. for 1½ hours.

Joan Thurmond (Highland)

YEAST NUT TORTE

1 package dry yeast
¼ cup lukewarm water
1 cup milk, scalded and
   cooled
1 cup butter, melted

3 egg yolks, slightly beaten
1 teaspoon salt
⅓ cup sugar
4 cups flour

FILLING:

3 egg whites
1 cup sugar

1 cup pecans, finely ground

Dissolve yeast in warm water. Mix milk, butter, egg yolks, salt and sugar in a large bowl. Add yeast mixture, then flour and beat thoroughly with a spoon. Cover tightly with waxed paper and place in refrigerator overnight. The next day, roll out on floured pastry cloth into a rectangle 12x18 inches. For filling, beat sugar gradually into egg whites, which have been beaten to a soft peak. Fold in nuts. Spread filling on dough; roll up, starting with the narrow edge, as you would a jelly roll. Place in a greased, 10-inch tube pan. Pinch edges together to form the circle. Before baking, place pan in a warm place and let rise about 45 minutes. Bake in a moderate oven at 350° F. for 1 hour.

Alternate method: Make two loaves of bread by cutting dough in half after rolling into a 12x18-inch rectangle. Spread ½ the filling on each half of dough and roll along length of dough. Place in prepared bread pan (9x5-inch), seam side down. Let rise 1 hour in warm place after covering bread. Bake 45 minutes.

Doris Lacy (Collinsville)

MARY ANN'S OATMEAL PANCAKES

2 cups milk
2 cups quick oats
2 eggs, separated
⅓ cup cooking oil

⅓ cup flour
2½ teaspoons baking powder
1 teaspoon salt

Scald milk; pour over oats; let cool. Sift together flour, baking powder and salt. Beat egg yolks and add them to oat mixture; add oil and stir in flour mixture. Beat egg whites until stiff but not dry; fold into oat mixture. Fry on lightly greased griddle or skillet.

Carolyn Losch (East Alton)

REFRIGERATOR ROLLS

1 cake (½-ounce) yeast
¼ cup lukewarm water
⅝ cup shortening or lard
½ cup sugar

2 cups scalded milk
8 cups all-purpose flour,
  sifted
2 teaspoons salt

Soften the yeast in the lukewarm water. Add the shortening and sugar to the hot milk, cool and combine with the yeast and water. Stir in the sifted flour and salt until the dough is stiff enough to knead. Follow the straight dough method for making bread at the end of the second kneading, cut off as much as needed. Shape as desired and put in a warm place to double in bulk, then bake in a hot oven, 375° F., for 15 to 20 minutes. Grease the surface of the remaining dough. Cover and put in the refrigerator. This dough can be kept satisfactorily for rolls for at least a week.

Mildred Dustmann (Dorsey)

ROLLS

¾ cup shortening
1 cup boiling water
1 cup cold water
2 eggs
7 cups flour

¾ cup sugar
2 teaspoons salt
1 yeast cake dissolved in 3
  tablespoons warm water

Add cold water to the shortening dissolved in boiling water. Beat eggs, sugar and salt together, add to previous ingredients. Add the yeast cake dissolved in warm water. Add flour, let rise once, knead down, let rise again. Then make into rolls and let rise. Be sure to grease pans and bake at 375° F. 12 to 15 minutes. If you do not want to use all the dough, you can store it in the refrigerator and use later.

Mrs. Don Wilkening (Edwardsville)

RICH REFRIGERATOR DOUGH

¾ cup milk
½ cup sugar
2 teaspoons salt
½ cup melted butter

2 packages dry yeast
½ cup warm water
2 eggs, beaten
6 cups sifted flour

Scald milk, stir in sugar, salt, butter and cool to lukewarm. Dissolve yeast in warm water. Add lukewarm milk mixture, eggs and half the flour. Beat until smooth. Stir in remaining flour to make stiff dough. Cover and refrigerate for several hours or overnight. Use dough for bread, rolls or coffee cake with your favorite filling. Bake rolls in 375° F. oven for 15 minutes or until light brown. Bake bread in 375° F. oven for 30 minutes or until brown.

Ella Bentrup (Staunton)

STRAWBERRY BREAD

3 cups flour
2 cups sugar
1 teaspoon baking soda
1 teaspoon salt
1½ teaspoons cinnamon

1 3-ounce package strawberry
  Jello
4 eggs, beaten
1 cup oil
2 cups strawberries, mashed

Stir all dry ingredients together and put into large bowl. Make a "well" and add eggs, oil and strawberries. Mix. Preheat oven to 350° F. Bake in two 9x5-inch pans for 1 hour.

Charlene Bandy (Moro)

SWEET POTATO BREAD

7 cups flour
4 teaspoons baking soda
2 teaspoons salt
2 teaspoons cinnamon
2 teaspoons nutmeg
6 cups sugar

4 cups mashed sweet potatoes
2 cups corn oil
1⅓ cups water
8 eggs

Grease and flour four loaf pans. Preheat oven to 350° F. In a large bowl, mix first six ingredients. In another bowl, mix sweet potatoes, oil, water and eggs and mix well. Add this mixture to dry ingredients and stir just until flour is moistened. Turn into prepared pans and bake for one hour or until cake tester comes out clean.

Carol Roseberry (Alton)

RHUBARB NUT BREAD

1½ cups brown sugar, packed
⅔ cup cooking oil
1 egg
1 teaspoon vanilla
1 cup sour milk or buttermilk

1 teaspoon salt
1 teaspoon baking soda
2½ cups flour
1½ cups diced fresh rhubarb
½ cup chopped nuts

Preheat oven to 350° F. Mix sugar and oil, add egg, vanilla, milk and sifted dry ingredients. Fold in diced rhubarb and nuts. Divide batter and pour into two well-greased and floured bread pans.

TOPPING:

¼ to ½ cup sugar   1 tablespoon butter

Mix and sprinkle over top of batter. Bake at 350° F. for 55 to 60 minutes.

Evelyn Keilbach (Highland)

WHOLE WHEAT NUT BREAD

1½ cups flour
3 teaspoons baking powder
½ teaspoon salt
1 cup unsifted whole wheat
   flour
1 egg, beaten

1 teaspoon vanilla
¾ cup sugar
¼ cup melted butter or salad
   oil
1¼ cups milk
1 cup chopped nuts

Preheat oven to 350° F. Sift flour with baking powder and salt. Stir in whole wheat flour. In a bowl combine egg, vanilla, sugar and butter. Beat well and add milk. Blend in flour mixture, being careful not to over blend. Stir in nuts and pour in greased loaf pan. Bake for 60 to 65 minutes.

Ella Bentrup (Staunton)

WHOLE WHEAT ROLLS

1 cup milk	½ cup warm water
3 tablespoons molasses	2 packages yeast
2 tablespoons sugar	2¼ cups whole wheat flour
2½ teaspoons salt	(about)
¼ cup butter	2¼ cups white flour (about)

Scald milk, stir in molasses, sugar, salt and butter. Cool to lukewarm. Measure warm water into large bowl. Sprinkle in yeast, stir until dissolved. Stir in lukewarm milk mixture. Add 1 cup whole wheat and 1 cup white flour and stir until smooth. Add enough of each flour to make soft dough. Knead until smooth and elastic about 8 to 10 minutes. Place in greased bowl, cover and let rise until double in bulk, about 45 minutes. Punch down, shape into rolls. Brush lightly with melted butter. Let rise until doubled, about 30 minutes. Bake 400° F. oven for 15 minutes.

Wilma Becker (Moro)

ZUCCHINI BREAD

3 eggs, beaten	1 teaspoon baking soda
1 cup cooking oil	½ teaspoon baking powder
2 cups sugar	1 teaspoon salt
2 cups grated zucchini	1 teaspoon cinnamon
2 teaspoons vanilla	½ cup chopped nuts
3 cups flour	

Preheat oven to 325° F. Grease and flour two loaf pans. Beat eggs, then add oil, sugar, grated zucchini and vanilla and cream together. Sift and measure flour, baking soda, baking powder, salt and cinnamon. Add sifted ingredients to creamed mixture and mix well. Bake for 1 hour.

Mildred Dustmann (Dorsey)
JoAnn Brase (Edwardsville)
Alberta Brandt (Worden)

VARIATION: Use all above ingredients except fold in 1 cup drained crushed pineapple with zucchini. Use 2 teaspoons baking soda, 1½ teaspoons cinnamon and ¾ teaspoon nutmeg. Add 1 cup raisins with 1 cup nuts. Bake at 350° F. for one hour. Use 2 greased and floured 5x9-inch loaf pans.

Louise M. Kipp (Edwardsville)

VARIETY BREAD

3½ cups flour
3 cups sugar
2 teaspoons baking soda
2 teaspoons baking powder
½ teaspoon salt
½ cup oil

⅔ cup water
4 eggs
½ cup chopped nuts
1 teaspoon cinnamon
2 cups solid pack pumpkin

Mix dry ingredients in a large bowl. Make a well. Add rest of the ingredients. Mix by hand. Grease and flour four 1-pound coffee cans (fill to second ring). Bake at 325° F. for 1 hour and 15 minutes or until toothpick comes out clean. You may use a bundt pan or an angelfood cake pan or three 5x8-inch loaf pans. Good spread with cream cheese. Keeps well frozen.

VARIATIONS: May substitute 2 cups of mashed bananas, grated apples, peaches, applesauce or 1 cup raisins and 1 cup nuts and 2 cups applesauce. Eliminate cinnamon and try strawberries or blackberries or apricots. (2 cups of almost any fruit will work—grated or mashed.)

Norma Lesko (Granite City)

BREADS

BREADS

BREADS

MAIN DISH

A petroleum tow is seen traversing the Chain of Rocks Canal. This canal enables river traffic to navigate without fear of the rapids a mile to the west.

ALL IN ONE CASSEROLE

2¼ cups thinly sliced potatoes
1 pound ground beef,
  browned
Salt and pepper to taste
1 medium onion, diced

2 cups cooked macaroni
1 can cream style corn
1 green pepper, diced
1 10¾-ounce can tomato soup

Grease large two-quart casserole with margarine, layer ingredients in above order. Bake ½ hour at 350° F.

Irma Henkhaus (Alhambra)

ALL IN ONE SKILLET DINNER

2 tablespoons oil
1 cup chopped onion
½ pound ground beef
1½ cups sliced carrots
4 ounces medium noodles
1 quart water

2 teaspoons Worcestershire
  sauce
1 teaspoon salt
⅛ teaspoon pepper
Parsley for garnish

Brown onion and beef in melted fat about 10 minutes. Add carrots, noodles and water. Cover and simmer over low heat about 30 minutes. Add Worcestershire sauce, salt and pepper. Mix lightly, arrange on hot platter. Garnish with parsley.

Olga Blom (Alhambra)

BRUNCH CASSEROLE

8 slices bread, cubed
2 cups grated, sharp Cheddar
  cheese
1½ pounds link sausage, cut
  in thirds

6 eggs
2¼ cups milk
¾ tablespoon dry mustard
1 can mushroom soup
½ cup milk

Place bread in greased 9x13-inch casserole. Spread with cheese. Brown sausage, drain and place on cheese. Beat eggs with milk and mustard. Pour over mixture in baking pan, cover and refrigerate overnight. Next day dilute soup with milk and pour over casserole and bake 40-45 minutes at 350° F.

Virginia Herrmann (Edwardsville)
Gracie Koeller (Godfrey)

BRUNCH SOUFFLE

5-6 pieces dried white bread
(dry in oven if fresh)
6 eggs
2 cups half-and-half
1 pound fried sausage (half
hot and half mild)

¼ cup onion
10 ounces or more shredded
Swiss cheese
Cayenne pepper

Line a buttered 9x13-inch baking dish with dried bread. Beat 6 eggs. Add half-n-half to eggs and beat. Fry 1 pound sausage and onions together. Drain well. Place sausage on top of bread. Top sausage with shredded cheese. Pour egg and cream mixture over cheese and sprinkle top with cayenne pepper. Let set in refrigerator 3 hours. Bake at 350° F. for 45-50 minutes. Serves 6.

Cindy Hemann (New Douglas)

CHEESE 'N BEEF CORNBREAD

2 tablespoons butter
1½ pounds ground beef
1 cup chopped onion
1 6-ounce can tomato paste
1 teaspoon salt
1 teaspoon chili powder
⅛ teaspoon pepper

1 tablespoon flour
1 cup (4 ounces) cubed or
   shredded Cheddar cheese
½ cup sliced pitted ripe olives
1 18-ounce package corn
   muffin mix

In a large skillet melt the butter; add the beef and onion and cook until the beef is lightly browned. Stir in the flour, tomato paste, salt, chili powder and pepper. Remove from heat and add the cheese and olives. Spread evenly over the bottom of a 9-inch square pan (or in a 10-inch iron skillet). Prepare the muffin mix according to package directions (or use any cornbread recipe) and spread over the beef mixture. Bake at 400° F. for 30 to 40 minutes, or until cornbread is done. Let stand 5 minutes, then loosen around the edges and invert onto a serving platter. Makes 8 servings.

Reita Sparrowk (Bethalto)

CHEESE HAM STRATA

12 slices white bread
¾ pound sharp processed
   American cheese, sliced
1 10-ounce package frozen,
   chopped broccoli, cooked
   and drained

2 cups diced, cooked ham
6 eggs, slightly beaten
3½ cups milk
2 tablespoons onion
½ teaspoon salt
½ teaspoon dry mustard

Cut 12 doughnut circles from bread and set aside. Fit scraps of bread in bottom of 13x9x2-inch pan. Place cheese in layer over bread. Add layer of broccoli, then a layer of ham. Arrange doughnuts on top. Combine remaining ingredients and pour over bread. Cover and refrigerate at least 6 hours or overnight. Bake uncovered at 325° F. for 55 minutes. Let stand 10 minutes before serving.

VARIATION: Velveeta cheese and potato chips may be added just before baking.

Dottie Suhre (Alhambra)

DINNER IN A PUMPKIN

1 pumpkin, 10 inches in
  diameter
4 cups hamburger
¼ cup soy sauce
2 tablespoons brown sugar
1 4-ounce can mushrooms,
  drained

1 10-ounce can cream of
  chicken soup
2 cups rice, cooked
2 cups chopped celery
2 cups chopped onions
1 cup chopped green peppers

Brown hamburger, then drain well. Add the onion, celery, and peppers. Cook rice according to directions on box. Add all to meat. Mix well. Clean pumpkin and add all the mixture to pumpkin. Put lid on and bake at 375° F. for 1 to 2 hours.

Viola Huebener (Alton)

5 HOUR STEW

2 pounds beef stew meat,
  cubed
4 medium potatoes, diced
6 carrots, diced
1 cup chopped onion
1 cup chopped celery
3 tablespoons minute tapioca

1 12-ounce can V-8 cocktail
  juice
1 teaspoon salt
⅓ teaspoon pepper
⅓ teaspoon garlic salt
⅓ teaspoon seasoning salt

Put in pan as listed. Do not mix. Put in oven at 250° F. for 5 hours.

Mrs. Leslie J. Cooper (Dorsey)

GROUND BEEF AND RICE CASSEROLE

1 pound hamburger
2 small onions
1 can chicken noodle soup

1 can mushroom soup
1 soup can of water
½ cup uncooked rice

Brown meat and onions, add soup, water and rice. Mix well. Pour in greased casserole. Bake 1½ hours at 350° F.

Mildred Roemelin (Moro)

HAMBURGER AND POTATO CASSEROLE

1 pound ground beef
½ cup fine cracker crumbs
¼ cup ketchup
¼ cup chopped onion

1 teaspoon salt
⅛ teaspoon pepper
¾ cup evaporated milk

Mix above ingredients together.

4 cups raw potatoes, sliced
1 teaspoon onion, chopped
1 teaspoon salt

⅛ teaspoon pepper
Parsley flakes

Arrange sliced potatoes and onion in a 2-quart baking dish. Sprinkle salt, pepper and parsley flakes over all. Add hamburger mixture, bake in open baking dish at 350° F. to 375° F. for 1 hour. I bake it at 350° F. for 1¼ hours.

Ruth R. Rogier (Highland)

HAMBURGER CORN BAKE

1½ pounds ground beef
1 cup chopped onion
1 12-ounce can whole kernel
  corn, drained
1 10-ounce can cream of
  chicken soup
1 10-ounce can cream of
  mushroom soup

1 cup sour cream
¾ teaspoon salt
¼ teaspoon pepper
4 cups medium noodles,
  cooked and drained
1 cup soft bread crumbs
2 tablespoons butter, melted

In large skillet, brown meat and onion. Stir in corn, soups, sour cream, salt and pepper and mix well. Stir in noodles. Turn into 2½-quart casserole. Mix bread crumbs and melted butter. Sprinkle on top. Bake at 350° F. for 45 minutes or until hot. Serves 8 to 10.
Note: You may substitute cream of celery soup for the cream of mushroom soup.

Judy Ernst (Alhambra)

MINIATURE MEAT LOAVES

2 pounds ground chuck
4 slices soft bread crumbs
¾ cup chopped onion
1 teaspoon salt
¼ teaspoon pepper

1 10-ounce can condensed
  vegetarian soup
¼ cup milk
½ cup cubed Swiss cheese or
  Kraft pimento

Mix together lightly all ingredients except cheese. Shape into 8 small loaves and place in a 15½x10½x1-inch glass utility dish. Press cheese cubes into each, *covering* with meat mixture. Bake for 35 minutes in a 375° F. oven.

Mary Jane Koeller (Godfrey)

NORMA'S ONE DISH MEAL

½ cup uncooked rice
1 pound ground beef
½ cup chopped onion
1 pint stewed tomatoes

1 16-ounce can cream corn
Flour
Salt and pepper to taste

Cook rice as directed on package and set aside. Fry ground beef and onion. Grease 2-quart baking dish. Layer rice, ground beef, tomatoes with a little flour, salt and pepper and corn. Cover and bake at 350° F. for 45 to 50 minutes.

Norma Albrecht (Worden)

HAMBURGER PIE

1 chopped onion, small
1 tablespoon oil
1 pound hamburger
1 teaspoon salt

2 cups green beans, drained
1 can tomato soup
Mounds of mashed potato

Preheat oven to 350° F. Brown onion in oil, add hamburger and salt; brown slightly. Place in 2-quart baking dish. Layer the green beans, then tomato soup. Top with mounds of mashed potato. Bake for 20 minutes or until potatoes are brown tipped. May add 1 tablespoon steak sauce to hamburger for a spiced flavor.

Donna Sievers (Staunton)

HAMBURGER NOODLE BAKE

1½ pounds ground beef
1 clove garlic
Salt and pepper to taste
1 teaspoon sugar
6 green onions, tops and all
2 8-ounce cans tomato sauce
3 ounces cream cheese

1 cup sour cream
1 16-ounce package elbow
  macaroni noodles (cooked
  as directed on package)
½ cup shredded sharp
  Cheddar cheese

Sauté ground beef. Add garlic, salt, pepper, sugar and onions. Cook 20 minutes. Combine tomato sauce, cream cheese, sour cream. Place noodles in casserole in 3 layers with sauce between. Sprinkle ½ cup Cheddar cheese over top and bake at 350° F. until bubbly, about 30 minutes.

Sharon Schlaefer (St. Jacob)

HAMBURGER SPECIAL

1 pound hamburger
½ cup chopped onion
2 teaspoons salt
½ teaspoon pepper
1 4-ounce can drained
  mushrooms

2 cups Skroodles
1 10-ounce package frozen
  mixed vegetables
3 cups water

Brown hamburger with onion, salt and pepper in electric skillet at 350° F. When hamburger is well browned, add mushrooms, Skroodles, mixed vegetables and water. Stir mixture and cover with lid. Reduce temperature to simmer for 20 minutes. Serves 4 to 6.

Janice Nagel (Alhambra)

PINEAPPLE HAM DRESSING

1 cup pineapple chunks,
  partially drained
3 eggs
1 cup sugar

½ cup margarine, melted
1 cup milk
4 cups bread, cubed
1 thick slice of ham, cubed

Preheat oven to 400° F. Beat eggs well, mix in sugar, melted margarine, milk, pineapple and ham. Pour over bread chunks and blend. Bake in a greased 2-quart casserole for 45 minutes. Serves 6.

Donna Sievers (Staunton)

FARMERS' DELIGHT

2 pounds ground beef
1 16-ounce can whole kernel
corn, drained
1 16-ounce can cream style
corn

6 to 8 servings mashed
potatoes (I use instant)
Salt and pepper to taste

Brown hamburger. Salt and pepper to taste. Prepare mashed potatoes. Mix the corn together. Layer in a 2 to 2½ quart casserole as follows: ⅓ of mashed potatoes; ½ of hamburger; ½ of corn; ⅓ of potatoes; remaining hamburger; remaining corn; top with remaining potatoes. Pat potatoes with spoon to form small peaks. Heat in 350° F. oven for approximately 30 minutes or until potato peaks begin to brown and mixture is bubbly.

Diane L. Martin (Edwardsville)

SEVEN LAYER CASSEROLE

No precooking—just put in the layers and pop it into the oven. Start heating oven to moderate 350° F. Place the following ingredients in layers in a 2-quart dish with a tight fitting lid:

1 cup uncooked rice, washed
and drained
1 cup canned whole kernel
corn, drained
Sprinkle with salt and pepper
1 15-ounce can Hunts tomato
sauce
½ cup water
½ cup each finely chopped
onion and green pepper

¾ pound uncooked ground
beef
Sprinkle with salt and pepper
Pour second 15-ounce can
Hunts tomato sauce and
¼ cup water over top
Cover meat with:
4 strips of bacon, cut in half

Cover and bake for one hour. Uncover and bake about 30 minutes longer or until bacon is crisp. Makes 4 to 6 servings.

Mrs. George P. Eckert (Collinsville

HUNGARIAN GOULASH
OR BEEF STEW

4 tablespoons corn oil
2½ to 3 pounds beef stew
   meat (cut into 1½ inch
   cubes)
½ large onion, sliced
2 teaspoons beef bouillon
2 teaspoons salt

3 teaspoons paprika
½ teaspoon pepper
3 cups water
4 or 5 medium sized potatoes
   (cut into 12 pieces)
4 or 5 medium sized carrots
   (cut into 1½ inch lengths)

Brown meat in corn oil in a large skillet. Put into a large pot, deglaze skillet with some of water and add to meat. Add onion, bouillon, spices and water. Simmer for 1½ hours. Add vegetables (sprinkled with extra salt). Simmer another ½ hour. Thicken if desired. Serves 8 to 12.

Mary Jane Koeller (Godfrey)

MEATZA PIE

1 pound ground beef
½ cup bread or cracker
   crumbs
½ teaspoon garlic salt
⅔ cup evaporated milk
⅓ cup catsup

1 2-ounce can mushrooms,
   chopped
3 slices American cheese
2 teaspoons Parmesan cheese
¼ teaspoon oregano or
   poultry seasoning

Mix ground beef, garlic salt, and crumbs. Press in a 9-inch pie pan, raising rim about ½ inch. Spread catsup to rim. Arrange mushrooms on catsup. Criss-cross American cheese strips on top. Sprinkle with seasoning and Parmesan cheese. Bake at 400° F. for 20 minutes. Serves 4.

Verna Abert (New Douglas)

ONE MEAL CASSEROLE

1 pound ground beef
2 tablespoons oil
1 10-ounce can mushroom
   soup
1 10-ounce can cream of
   chicken soup
3 cups water

½ cup raw rice
2 onions, chopped
1 cup celery, chopped
4 tablespoons soy sauce
Pepper to taste
1 can chow mein noodles

Brown ground beef until crumbly, put into large baking dish. Add soups, water, rice, onions, celery and seasonings. Stir and bake at 350° F. for 1½ hours. Remove from oven and cover top with chow mein noodles and bake ½ hour more.

Mrs. Cletus Hediger (Highland)

ONION BEEF MACARONI CASSEROLE

1½ pounds hamburger
1 envelope onion soup mix
1 tablespoon flour
1 cup tomato sauce

2 cups water
1 cup macaroni
¼ cup grated cheese

Preheat oven at 400° F. Brown meat, pour off fat. Stir in soup mix, flour, tomato sauce and water. Simmer covered for 5 minutes. Cook macaroni in 1 quart salted water, drain. Add to meat mixture. Pour into 1½-quart casserole. Sprinkle with grated cheese. Bake for 15 minutes.

Ella Bentrup (Staunton)

QUICK PIGS IN A BLANKET

1 small head cabbage
½ cup chopped onion
1 pound ground beef
½ cup minute rice
½ teaspoon salt

¼ teaspoon pepper
1 10-ounce can tomato soup
1½ cups water
¼ cup grated Italian cheese

Chop cabbage into medium pieces. Spread in bottom of greased 13x9-inch baking dish. Brown meat and onions in skillet, breaking meat as it cooks. Stir in rice, salt and pepper. Spoon mixture over cabbage. In saucepan, heat tomato soup and water to boiling. Pour over all ingredients. Sprinkle with cheese. Cover tightly with foil and bake 1½ hours at 350° F. Serves 6.

Florence Dinwiddie (Roxana)

SLOPPY JOE CASSEROLE

1 pound ground beef
1 cup catsup
½ cup water
2 tablespoons instant minced
   onion
1 teaspoon instant beef
   bouillon or 1 beef bouillon
   cube

2 cups Bisquick baking mix
⅔ cup milk
Paprika

Heat oven to 400° F. Cook and stir ground beef in 10-inch skillet until brown; drain. Stir in catsup, water, onion, and bouillon. Heat to boiling; reduce heat. Simmer uncovered, stirring occasionally, 5 minutes. Mix baking mix and milk until soft dough forms; beat vigorously 20 strokes. Spread half of the dough in ungreased square pan, 8x8x2-inches. Top with beef mixture. Drop remaining dough by spoonfuls onto top; sprinkle with paprika. Bake until light brown, about 25 minutes. 8 servings.

Betty Heepke (Edwardsville)

SOUR CREAM NOODLE BAKE

1 8-ounce package medium
  noodles
1 pound ground beef
1 tablespoon butter
1 teaspoon salt
⅛ teaspoon pepper
¼ teaspoon garlic salt

1 cup tomato sauce
1 cup creamed cottage cheese
1 cup sour cream
½ cup green onions, chopped
1 cup sharp Cheddar cheese,
  shredded

Cook noodles in salted, boiling water. Rinse and drain. Brown meat in butter, then add salt, pepper, garlic salt and tomato sauce. Simmer 5 minutes. Combine cottage cheese, sour cream, chopped onions and noodles. Alternate layers of noodles mixture and meat mixture in 2-quart casserole, beginning with noodles and ending with meat. Top with shredded cheese. Bake in 350° F. preheated oven for 20 to 25 minutes or until cheese is melted and browned.

Mildred Dustmann (Dorsey)

SUNDAY EVENING STACK UPS

Mayonnaise or salad dressing
8 hamburger buns
1 beaten egg
¾ cup soft bread crumbs
1 pound ground beef
5 eggs

¼ cup milk
2 tablespoons butter
8 slices American cheese
8 lettuce leaves
½ teaspoon salt

Spread mayonnaise on cut surface of bun, set aside. In bowl, combine 1 egg, the crumbs, ½ teaspoon salt, beef and mix well. Shape meat into 8 patties. Broil 3 to 4 minutes on each side. Meanwhile beat together the remaining eggs, milk and ¼ teaspoon salt. In a skillet, scramble eggs in butter. Place cheese on top of burger and broil 1 minute. Place lettuce and burger on bottom half of bun. Spoon scrambled eggs on top and then cover with other half of bun.

Judy Ernst (Pocahontas)

SPRING VALLEY STEW

3 pounds hamburger
2 onions
1 10-ounce package frozen
  peas
Pinch of garlic salt
1 tablespoon Worcestershire
  sauce

1 15-ounce can red beans
1 15-ounce can chili hot beans
1 or 2 large potatoes
Salt and pepper to taste
1 tablespoon sugar

Brown chopped onion and hamburger. Slice potatoes thin. Place all ingredients in pot with hamburger mixture. Let boil well for a while then let simmer about 20 minutes. Our gang loved it. Makes 8 large servings.

Mae Grapperhaus (Troy)

TOMATOEY BEANS AND BURGER

1 pound ground beef
1 1½-ounce package Sloppy
  Joe Mix
1 cup water
1 6-ounce can tomato paste
2 16-ounce cans French style
  green beans, drained

1 4-ounce can mushrooms,
  drained
½ cup shredded Cheddar
  cheese

Brown hamburger. Drain. Add sloppy joe mix and water until thickened. Add tomato paste. Simmer 10 minutes. Stir in green beans and mushrooms. Put in 2-quart casserole. Top with cheese. Bake at 350° F. for 20 to 30 minutes. Yield: 5 large servings.

Diane L. Martin (Edwardsville)

WESTERN MAC

1 package macaroni and cheese dinner	2 cups whole kernel corn, drained
1 pound ground beef	1 6-ounce can tomato paste
½ cup sliced celery	½ cup water
¼ cup chopped green pepper	1 teaspoon salt
¼ cup chopped onion	Dash of pepper

Prepare dinner as directed. Brown meat, celery, green pepper, and onion; cook until tender. Stir in corn, tomato paste, water, salt and pepper. Add dinner; mix well. Pour into 2-quart casserole; bake at 350° F. for 15 to 20 minutes. Serves 6.

Cindy Hemann (New Douglas)

TATER TOT HOT DISH

1 pound ground beef	1 box tater tot frozen potatoes
1 onion, chopped	1 can cream of chicken soup
1 16-ounce can green beans or other vegetable of your choice	1 soup can milk

Brown ground beef and onion lightly. Place in baking dish. Add a layer of green beans or other vegetable. Place tater tots in a layer on top. Beat chicken soup with milk, using egg beater or fork. Pour over mixture in baking dish. Bake at 350° F. for 1 hour and 15 minutes or until tater tots are brown and crusty.

JoAnn Brase (Edwardsville)

ZUCCHINI-HAMBURGER CASSEROLE

1 pound zucchini, sliced	4 ounces sliced Velveeta cheese
1 pound ground beef, cooked	2½ cups canned tomatoes
1 to 1½ cups instant rice, cooked	
1 10-ounce can golden mushroom soup	

Place ½ of the zucchini in 2½-quart baking dish. Add by layers, cooked meat, instant rice, soup, rest of zucchini, cheese and tomatoes. Bake 1½ hours at 350° F.

Carol Roseberry (Alton)

SKILLET DINNER MEAT LOAF

2 pounds ground beef
2 slightly beaten eggs
1 cup cracker crumbs, about
   20 crackers
¼ cup chopped onion
½ teaspoon salt

¼ teaspoon pepper
6 medium baking potatoes,
   peeled and quartered
1 20-ounce package frozen
   green beans
1 stick butter

To prepare meat loaf, thoroughly combine ground beef, eggs, cracker crumbs, onion, salt and pepper. Shape into 2 rectangle loaf shapes. Preheat large size electric skillet to 325° F. Melt butter in skillet and reduce heat to 250° F. Place meat loaves in center of skillet. Place potatoes on one side of meat loaves and place frozen green beans on other end of skillet. Cover and cook for 35 to 45 minutes, or until potatoes are tender and meat is well cooked. Serves 6.

Judy Nagel (Alhambra)

BAKED ZUCCHINI AND GROUND BEEF

3 tablespoons oil
3 pounds zucchini, sliced
   ¼-inch
⅓ cup finely chopped onion
1 pound ground beef
1½ ounce envelope Italian
   spaghetti sauce

1¾ cups water
1 6-ounce can tomato paste
1 tablespoon oil
¼ cup Parmesan cheese
⅓ cup soft bread crumbs
1 8-ounce package Mozzarella
   cheese, sliced

Combine the first three ingredients and sauté until tender. Put into 2-quart casserole. In same skillet, brown ground beef. After ground beef is browned, add envelope of sauce, water, paste and 1 tablespoon oil. Heat to boiling; simmer 10 minutes. Pour over zucchini. Mix Parmesan cheese with bread crumbs; sprinkle over top and stir gently to mix. Top with Mozzarella cheese. Bake until cheese melts at 350° F.

Ruth Becker (Edwardsville)

ROAST AND VEGETABLES

1 3-pound beef roast
1 onion, sliced
Potatoes, peeled and chunked
Carrots, pared and cut
1 10-ounce can cream of
  mushroom soup

1 pint tomatoes
Salt and pepper to taste
1 #2 can green beans
1 #2 can corn

Place roast in an electric skillet, brown. Add water, onion, potatoes and carrots. Spoon cream of mushroom soup over meat and vegetables. Add tomatoes and salt and pepper to taste. Simmer until tender. Remove meat and vegetables and make gravy from liquid in skillet. Serve with one can green beans and one can corn.
Note: The next day these may all be combined to make beef stew.

Carol Roseberry (Alton)

ROUND STEAK AND POTATO CASSEROLE

1 pound round steak, cut into
  one-inch cubes
3 tablespoons shortening
3 small onions, sliced thin
1½ teaspoons salt
¼ teaspoon pepper
Dash of thyme

Dash of garlic powder
2 cups water
3 tablespoons flour
Thinly sliced potatoes
1 teaspoon salt
1 stick margarine
Paprika

Flour meat, brown in shortening and stir until tender. Pour into ungreased 9x13-inch baking dish. Sprinkle with flour. Add salt, pepper, thyme, garlic powder, onions and water. Bake in a 350° F. oven for 60 minutes. Increase temperature to 400° F. and arrange thinly sliced potatoes, sprinkled with salt, butter and paprika, over the top. Bake 30 minutes longer.

Mary K. Willaredt (Granite City)

SKILLET VEAL

6 boneless veal cutlets
(4 ounces each)
2 tablespoons shortening
1 teaspoon salt
1 16-ounce can tomatoes
1 1½-ounce package spaghetti
sauce mix with mushrooms
1⅓ cups Sherry

1 16-ounce can whole onions,
drained
1 6-ounce can sliced
mushrooms, drained
(reserve ¼ cup liquid)
1 16-ounce can peas and
carrots, drained

Pound meat until ¼-inch thick. Melt shortening in large skillet; brown meat. Season with salt. Stir in tomatoes, spaghetti sauce mix and sherry; heat to boiling. Reduce heat; cover and simmer 10 minutes, stirring occasionally. Add onions, mushrooms, reserved liquid and peas and carrots. Cover; simmer 10 minutes. Makes 6 servings, 305 calories each.

Louise Eckert (Collinsville)

SAUSAGE AND CABBAGE AU GRATIN

1 small head of cabbage
½ pound pork sausage, in
bulk
3 tablespoons sausage fat
3 tablespoons flour
1 cup milk

2 cups cabbage liquid
⅓ cup grated American
cheese
½ cup cracker crumbs
½ teaspoon salt

Chop cabbage coarsely and cook in boiling water with salt until tender. Season with salt and pepper to taste. Fry sausage and reserve 3 tablespoons drippings, discard remainder. Put drippings in saucepan; add flour and stir until blended. Gradually add milk and cabbage liquid and continue cooking and stirring for five minutes more. Grease a casserole, place a layer of cooked cabbage, then a layer of sausage. Pour white sauce over top and sprinkle with cheese and then with cracker crumbs. Repeat this procedure until all the mixture is in the casserole. Bake at 350° F. for 30 minutes or until crumbs are golden brown. Serves six.

Mrs. George P. Eckert (Collinsville)

EASY SAUSAGE MEAL

1 pound bulk pork sausage
12 slightly beaten eggs
¾ cup milk

6 medium cooked potatoes,
sliced
Salt and pepper to taste

Brown sausage well in skillet. Add milk to eggs and mix together. Add milk and egg mixture and sliced potatoes to sausage. Stir until eggs are well cooked. Serves 4 to 6.

Denise Nagel (Alhambra)

PORK CHOP AND POTATO DINNER

4 cups potatoes, thinly sliced
pared
2 tablespoons chopped onion
½ teaspoon salt

Dash pepper
4 pork chops
2 tablespoons oil

Preheat oven at 375° F. Place potatoes into a greased 2-quart baking dish. Sprinkle with onion, salt and pepper. Brown pork chops in oil on both sides and place on top of potatoes. Bake at 375° F. for 1¼ hours or until potatoes are tender.

Ella Bentrup (Staunton)

POTATO-SAUSAGE CASSEROLE

1 pound pork sausage
1 can cream of mushroom
soup
¾ cup milk
½ cup chopped onion

½ teaspoon salt
¼ teaspoon pepper
3 cups raw, sliced potatoes
½ pound grated cheese
Butter

Brown and drain sausage. Mix soup, milk, onion, salt and pepper together. In large casserole, layer potatoes, soup mixture and sausage. Repeat layers again and end with sausage. Dot with butter. Bake covered at 350° F. for 1¼ to 1½ hours. Sprinkle with grated cheese and melt in oven.

Mrs. Pam Heepke (Edwardsville)

SAUCY TWIST PORK DISH

4 ounces uncooked cork
screw shaped macaroni
½ cup finely chopped onion
⅓ cup chopped green pepper
1 tablespoon butter or
margarine
12 ounces pork, cut into
cubes (cooked)

1 can cream of mushroom
soup
½ cup catsup
⅓ cup shredded Cheddar
cheese

Heat oven to 400° F. Cook macaroni as directed on package. Drain. In a large skillet, cook and stir onion and green pepper in margarine. Stir in macaroni and remaining ingredients. Pour into ungreased 1½-quart casserole. Cover and bake 30 minutes. Serves 4 to 6 people.

Mary K. Willaredt (Granite City)

SAUSAGE PATTIES IN FRUIT SAUCE ON TOAST

(OR "PIGS IN THE ORCHARD")

1 pound pork sausage, bulk
1 16-ounce can fruit cocktail
1 tablespoon brown sugar
1 tablespoon lemon juice

½ teaspoon ginger
1½ teaspoons cornstarch
1 tablespoon cold water
Buttered toast slices

Shape pork sausage into eight finger-shaped patties, ½-inch thick. Brown patties in skillet and pour off drippings. Add fruit cocktail, brown sugar, lemon juice and ginger. Cover and simmer for 10 minutes. Remove patties from skillet. Pour in smooth paste made of the cornstarch and cold water; stir and simmer until thick. Patties may be put back into sauce at this point until you are ready to serve them. To serve, place two patties on each slice of buttered toast and top with fruit sauce. Serves four.

Delores Geiger (Alhambra)

MAIN DISH

MAIN DISH

MAIN DISH

MAIN DISH

VEGETABLES

Welcome
Lindendale Park
Helvetia Sharp Shooters
Home of Madison County Fair

Welcome
Lindendale Park
Helvetia Sharp Shooters
Home of Madison County Fair

Lindendale Park, Highland, is the home of the County Fair. Owned by the Sharp Shooters, it has also provided a home for the local high school football team, the summer stock car races, etc. The motif bears evidence of the Swiss heritage of the area.

ASPARAGUS CASSEROLE

4 tablespoons butter
3 tablespoons flour
1½ cups milk
¼ teaspoon salt
¼ teaspoon paprika
½ pound Cheese (grated or cut fine)
1 tablespoon pimento
2 eggs, hard boiled and chopped

2 tablespoons celery, cut fine
1 tablespoon onion, chopped fine
1 green pepper, chopped and fried in butter
1 can cream of mushroom soup
Dash garlic powder
2 or 3 cans asparagus, drained

Melt butter, add salt, paprika and flour. Gradually stir in milk until thick. Add cheese and stir until melted. Add pimento, eggs, celery, onion, green pepper and then add soup and garlic salt. Put in baking dish, layer of sauce and layer of asparagus until filled. Top with bread crumbs (buttered). Bake at 400° F. until browned on top.

VARIATION: Can be made with green beans or peas. All must be drained of juice.

Mildred Dustmann (Dorsey)

Add a few drops of lemon juice when cooking potatoes to make them whiter.

HOME BAKED BEANS

1 pound dried navy beans
6 cups water
½ pound salt pork, diced
1 cup chopped onion

¾ cup dark corn syrup
½ cup chili sauce
1 teaspoon dry mustard
¼ teaspoon pepper

Rinse beans, place in large saucepan and cover with water. Soak overnight. Cover; bring water to boil, simmer 1 hour or until beans are tender. Place beans in 3-quart bean pot or casserole. Stir in salt pork, onion, corn syrup, chili sauce, mustard and pepper. Cover and bake at 325° F. for 2 hours. Uncover and continue baking 30 minutes or until beans are browned and desired consistency. Makes 8 to 10 servings.

Marilyn Gass (Granite City)

SWEET-SOUR BEETS

1 1-pound can diced or sliced beets	2 teaspoons cornstarch
1 tablespoon minced onion	3 tablespoons vinegar
2 tablespoons butter	1 tablespoon horseradish
2 tablespoons brown sugar	½ teaspoon salt
	⅛ teaspoon pepper

Drain beets. Cook onion gently in butter 2 or 3 minutes. Stir in sugar mixed with cornstarch; add vinegar and horseradish; cook, stirring until smooth and clear. Add beets, then salt and pepper; heat thoroughly. Makes 4 servings.

Linda Gass (Granite City)

CREAMED GREEN BEANS

5 bacon strips	½ cup Parmesan cheese, grated
1 medium onion	
1 #3-can green beans	Onion Rings, French fried
½ cup evaporated milk	(optional, canned)
1 11-ounce can cream of mushroom soup	

Dice and brown onion with 5 strips of bacon. Drain and mix with beans and evaporated milk. Place in casserole dish and pour soup over top and dot with butter. Sprinkle cheese over all. Bake covered in 350° F. oven for 25 minutes. Add onion rings last 5 minutes and bake uncovered.

Donna Price (Granite City)

BARBECUED GREEN BEANS

2 16-ounce cans green beans	½ cup catsup
1 large onion, diced	¼ cup vinegar
3 slices bacon, cut up	½ cup sugar

Brown bacon and onions. Add catsup, vinegar and sugar. Simmer until slightly thick. Drain beans and put in casserole. Pour sauce over beans, stir. Bake at 325° F. until bubbly, about ½ hour.

Mrs. Edward Barth (Brighton)

GREEN BEAN CASSEROLE

½ cup chopped onion
4 tablespoons butter
4 tablespoons flour
1 cup cream
1 cup milk
1 cup chicken broth

½ teaspoon salt
⅛ teaspoon pepper
1½ cups grated Swiss cheese
2 cups green beans, cooked
½ cup cracker crumbs

In saucepan, sauté onions in butter. Mix in flour. Add cream, milk, broth, salt and pepper. Cook over low heat, stirring until mixture thickens. Stir in cheese. When melted, add green beans. Pour mixture into casserole dish and sprinkle top with cracker crumbs. Bake in 350° F. oven for 30 minutes.

Velma Ernst (Alhambra)

BROCCOLI BAKE

½ cup chopped onion
½ cup chopped celery
1 cup rice, cooked
1 package chopped frozen
broccoli

1 can cream of mushroom
soup
1 can cream of chicken soup
1 8-ounce jar Cheez Whiz

Mix all ingredients together. Bake in buttered casserole at 375° F. for 30 minutes. Serves 8.

Marilyn Gass (Granite City)

BROCCOLI CASSEROLE

3 8-ounce packages frozen
chopped broccoli
2 10½-ounce cans cream of
mushroom soup
½ cup milk
½ pound mild Cheddar
cheese (cut into cubes)

1 8-ounce can sliced water
chestnuts, drained
1 can French fried onion
rings

Cook broccoli to a fast boil, drain well. Combine with other ingredients, except onion rings. Place broccoli mix in 9x13-inch baking dish and top with onion rings. Bake at 325° F. for 30 minutes.

Ruth Keller (Edwardsville)

BROCCOLI CASSEROLE

2 8-ounce packages frozen
broccoli
1 cup real mayonnaise
1 8-ounce package shredded
Cheddar cheese
½ cup diced onion

1 10-ounce can cream of
mushroom soup
Salt and pepper to taste
1 can French fried onion
rings

Cook broccoli as directed on package and drain. Mix cheese, diced onion, soup, salt and pepper. Pour over broccoli in casserole dish. Top with French fried onion rings. Bake at 350° F. for 30 minutes.

Charlene Bandy (Moro)

BROCCOLI CASSEROLE

1 cup or less chopped onions
1 stick margarine
1 cup minute rice
1 8-ounce jar Cheese Whiz or
8 ounces Velveeta cheese

1 can cream of celery soup
1 large bunch broccoli,
cooked until tender, and
well drained

Sauté onions in margarine. Mix all ingredients together and bake in 9x13-inch pan at 350° F. for 30 minutes.

Irma Henkhaus (Alhambra)

BROCCOLI CORN BAKE

1 16-ounce can creamed corn
1 10-ounce package frozen
chopped broccoli (cooked
and drained)
1 egg, beaten
½ cup cracker crumbs
1 tablespoon onion, chopped

2 tablespoons margarine,
melted
½ teaspoon salt
Dash pepper
½ cup cracker crumbs
1 tablespoon margarine,
melted

Combine corn, broccoli, egg, ½ cup cracker crumbs, onion, 2 table-spoons margarine, salt, pepper. Turn into 1-quart casserole. Combine ½ cup cracker crumbs and remaining tablespoon of margarine. Sprinkle over vegetable mixture. Bake uncovered in 350° F. oven for 35 to 40 minutes.

Janice Bradley (Marine)

CHEESE BROCCOLI

2 small packages frozen
   broccoli
2 cups cooked Minute Rice
1 stick butter

1 large onion, diced
1 can cream of mushroom
   soup
1 4-ounce jar Cheez Whiz

Sauté onion in butter. Mix all ingredients. Bake at 350° F. for 45 minutes in a 2-quart greased baking dish.

Donna Koenig (Edwardsville)

BROCCOLI SUPREME

2 10-ounce packages frozen
   broccoli cuts, cooked with
   salt and pepper to taste
1 8-ounce package
   Philadelphia cream cheese

½ stick butter
3 tablespoons corn flake
   crumbs

Cook broccoli in ½ to ¾ cup salted water until tender. Drain if more than ½ cup liquid remains, add the butter and cheese. Stir until melted and blended together. Put into 1½-quart casserole, sprinkle top with crumbs. Bake, uncovered, in a 325° F. oven about 30 minutes, until heated through and bubbly.
NOTE: Spinach is good prepared this way.

Mary Jane Koeller (Godfrey)

BROCCOLI AND RICE CASSEROLE

1 10-ounce package frozen
   broccoli, chopped
½ cup rice, uncooked
¼ cup onion, chopped
1 can cream of mushroom
   soup, undiluted

½ cup celery, chopped
½ stick butter or margarine
3 slices bread, toasted

Cook broccoli and rice separately according to package directions. Combine first five ingredients and put in a buttered casserole dish. Set aside. Melt margarine in small saucepan and crumble toasted bread into margarine in pan. Place bread crumbs on top of casserole and bake in 350° F. oven for 45 minutes. Yield 4 servings.

VARIATION: Use grated cheese instead of bread and omit the butter.

Helen Ernst (New Douglas)

SCALLOPED CABBAGE

1 medium head (2½ pounds)
  cabbage
¼ pound coarse cracker
  crumbs
¼ pound butter
¼ teaspoon cayenne pepper

½ teaspoon salt
1 cup half and half cream
¾ cup milk
½ cup liquor from boiled
  cabbage

Wash and cut cabbage in small pieces. Boil cabbage in salted water, to which cayenne pepper has been added, for 10 minutes. Drain cabbage; save ½ cup of liquor. Layer half of cabbage in buttered 2-quart baking dish. Sprinkle with half of cracker crumbs; repeat, ending with crackers. Dot with butter, sprinkle with salt. Mix cream, milk, and cabbage liquor and pour over all. Bake at 400° F. for 30 minutes or until lightly browned. Yield 6 servings.

Kay Losch (East Alton)

CORN PUDDING

2 eggs, slightly beaten
1 small box Jiffy corn muffin
  mix
1 18-ounce can cream style
  corn

1 18-ounce can whole kernel
  corn
1 cup sour cream
½ cup margarine, melted
4 ounces Swiss cheese

Combine the beaten eggs, muffin mix, corns, sour cream and margarine. Put into ungreased casserole dish. Bake at 350° F. for 35 minutes. Place the Swiss cheese on top and bake 10 minutes more.

Ruth Becker (Edwardsville)

SCALLOPED CORN AND OYSTERS

1 1-pound can cream style
  corn
½ pint oysters
1 egg, beaten

¼ cup milk
1 tablespoon butter
3 cups cracker crumbs
Salt and pepper to taste

Mix corn, egg, milk and butter. Alternate layers of corn and oysters in baking dish with cracker crumbs in between. Make top layer crumbs. Bake at 350° F. for 30 minutes.

Marilyn Gass (Granite City)

CHEESE SCALLOPED CORN

2 tablespoons melted butter
⅔ cup cracker crumbs
2 1-pound cans whole kernel or cream style corn
1 cup shredded Cheddar cheese

¼ cup milk
¼ cup chopped onion
2 tablespoons chopped green pepper

Toss butter and cracker crumbs. Spread half on bottom of greased casserole. Combine corn, cheese, milk, onion and green pepper and spread over crumb mixture. Sprinkle remaining crumbs on top. Bake at 350° F. for 30 to 40 minutes.

Ruth Nungesser (Highland)

CARROTS ELEGANTE

1 stick margarine
2 teaspoons salt
2 teaspoons sugar

2 pounds coarsely grated carrots
½ cup orange juice

Place first four ingredients in a heavy fry-pan. Cover. Cook over medium heat about 10 minutes. Stir several times during the cooking. Stir in orange juice and cook 5 minutes longer or until crisply tender. Garnish with fresh orange and parsley.

Cornelia Parrill (Edwardsville)

CARROTS PLUS

1 pound carrots, pared and thinly sliced
¼ cup butter or margarine
2 medium onions, cut in thin strips

2 medium apples, pared and thinly sliced
1 teaspoon lemon juice
¼ teaspoon salt
⅛ teaspoon white pepper

Steam carrots. Meanwhile, in a 10-inch skillet, melt butter; add onion and cook over moderate heat, covered, until transparent, 10 to 15 minutes. Add apple slices and continue cooking, covered, until just tender, about 5 minutes. Drain carrots and add to skillet, stir in lemon juice, salt and pepper and heat through. Makes 6 servings.

Mrs. Lawrence Wall (New Douglas)

CANDIED CARROTS

1 1-pound package carrots
½ teaspoon salt
1 cup water
½ cup brown sugar, firmly
  packed

4 tablespoons butter or
  margarine
1 tablespoon lemon juice

Pare carrots, cut diagonally in thin slices. Combine with salt and water and cook until tender, drain thoroughly. Add brown sugar, butter and lemon juice. Heat slowly until butter melts. Allow to set about 20 minutes so carrots are richly glazed.

Louise Eckert (Collinsville)

CARROT CASSEROLE

2 pounds carrots, sliced
½ pound Velveeta cheese

2 sticks butter or margarine
24-26 saltine crackers

Preheat oven to 350° F. Boil carrots 10 minutes. Melt 1 stick of butter and ½ pound cheese. Pour over carrots and put into a 2-quart casserole dish. Roll crackers into crumbs. Stir crackers into the remaining stick of butter which has been melted. Pour over carrots. Bake 30 minutes.

Vera Mae Henschen (Alhambra)
Norma Meyer (Edwardsville)

DILL BUTTERED CARROTS

¼ cup butter
3 cups carrot strips
1 teaspoon instant chicken
  flavor bouillon

½ teaspoon dill weed
¼ teaspoon salt

In a heavy 2-quart saucepan, melt butter over medium heat. Add remaining ingredients. Cover; cook over medium heat for 12 to 15 minutes or until carrots are tender. Serve immediately. Makes 4 ½ cup servings.

Carleen Paul (Worden)

EGGPLANT

1 eggplant, peeled and sliced   ¼ cup milk
thin (¼ to ⅜ inches thick)   Cracker crumbs
1 egg

Spread slices and salt according to taste. Mix egg and milk together and dip eggplant slices into this and then into cracker crumbs. Fry on well greased griddle and serve *immediately*. For variation, can use corn meal or flour, but burns easily.
Note: Zucchini may be used instead of eggplant.

Florence Rapp (Edwardsville)

SCALLOPED EGGPLANT

1 medium sized eggplant   1 tablespoon butter
½ cup water   ½ cup half and half cream
1 teaspoon salt   3 tablespoons butter
1 small onion, finely chopped   ¾ cup soda cracker crumbs

Pare and dice eggplant. Simmer in ½ cup water and salt until tender. Drain. Sauté onion in 1 tablespoon butter. Add to drained eggplant. Add cream. Melt 3 tablespoons butter and add cracker crumbs. Alternate layers of eggplant and cracker crumbs in 1-quart greased casserole, ending with crumbs. Bake in 375° F. oven for 30 minutes.

Ruth Brave (Granite City)

SCALLOPED CELERY

3 cups celery, sliced   ½ can cream of celery soup
1 cup chopped green peppers   Salt and pepper to taste
Onion, chopped, to taste   Bread crumbs

Cook celery, green peppers and onion in small amount of water until tender. Drain. Add soup and seasoning. Place in greased 1-quart casserole. Top with cracker crumbs. Bake at 350° F. until heated through.

Olga Blom (Alhambra)

EGGPLANT PARMIGIANA

1 medium eggplant
¼ cup all-purpose flour
½ teaspoon salt
1 beaten egg
½ cup grated Parmesan
  cheese

1 recipe tomato sauce
1 6-ounce package sliced
  Mozzarella cheese

Peel eggplant and cut into ½-inch slices. Combine flour and salt. Dip eggplant into beaten egg, then in flour mixture. Brown in hot oil in large skillet. Drain well on paper towel. Place 1 layer of eggplant in a 10x6x2-inch baking dish, cutting to fit. Sprinkle with ½ of the Parmesan, then ½ each of the tomato sauce and Mozzarella cheese. Repeat layers and top with remaining Mozzarella cheese. Bake uncovered in 400° F. oven for 20 minutes. Makes 6 servings.

TOMATO SAUCE FOR EGGPLANT PARMIGIANA:

⅓ cup chopped onion
¼ cup celery, chopped fine
½ clove garlic, minced
1 teaspoon parsley flakes
2 tablespoons cooking oil
1 16-ounce can Italian
  tomatoes

⅓ cup tomato paste
½ teaspoon salt
½ teaspoon dried oregano
¼ teaspoon pepper

In saucepan, cook the onion, celery, garlic, and parsley flakes in the cooking oil until tender. Add tomatoes, tomato paste, salt, oregano and pepper. Simmer gently uncovered 45 to 50 minutes.

Lorene Genczo (New Douglas)

FRIED OKRA

Enough okra for a meal,
  ⅓ pound per person
Shortening—oil or Crisco

Salt, flour
1 egg, slightly beaten

Wash and slice tender okra. Add the egg and stir to cover okra. Add enough flour to coat okra well. Salt and pepper to taste. Melt shortening in heavy iron skillet, about ½ cup. Put okra in skillet to fry. Fry slowly at first and then on high until crisp.

Reita Sparrowk (Bethalto)

SCALLOPED DELUXE HASHED BROWNS

1 2-pound package frozen
   hashed brown potatoes
1 can cream of potato soup
1 can cream of celery soup
Chopped onion and green
   pepper to taste

1 8-ounce carton sour cream
Salt to taste
Pepper to taste
Parsley flakes and paprika

Put into a bowl; let stand 30 minutes. Mix. Put into lightly greased 9x13-inch casserole dish. Sprinkle with parsley flakes and paprika. Bake uncovered at 300° F. for 1½ to 2 hours.

Ruth Becker (Edwardsville)

CHEESE POTATOES

6-8 medium potatoes, cooked
1 8-ounce package
   Philadelphia cream cheese
1 egg

⅓ cup finely chopped onion
1 teaspoon salt
Pepper
Dash of nutmeg (optional)

Using mixer, beat cooked potatoes. Add remaining ingredients and mix. Pour into greased casserole and bake in 350° F. oven for 45 minutes.

VARIATION: Make individual patties, coat both sides with crushed corn flakes and bake on greased cookie sheet until they puff. Bake in 400° F. oven for 20 to 30 minutes.

Ruth Brave (Granite City)

MASHED POTATOES

8 or 9 potatoes or 16 serving
   instant potato package
1 large carton sour cream
1 8-ounce package
   Philadelphia cream cheese

Garlic to taste
Salt to taste
Pepper to taste

Cook potatoes, and mash. Add Philadelphia cream cheese and sour cream. Place in 9x13-inch baking dish, dot with butter, and sprinkle with paprika. Bake at 350° F. for 30 minutes.

Ruth Keller (Edwardsville)

HASH BROWN POTATOES
IN CHEESE SAUCE

8 or 9 potatoes (more if small)
¼-½ pound grated Cheddar
  cheese

2 cups half and half milk
⅓ cup butter
Salt

Cook potatoes about 48 hours ahead. When cold, peel and grate. Place in 9x13-inch pan and sprinkle with cheese and salt. Melt butter in milk and pour over potatoes. Bake one hour at 350° F.

Vera Mae Henschen

VOLCANO POTATO BAKE

5 or 6 medium potatoes,
  scrubbed
1¼ cups evaporated milk
2 egg yolks, beaten
2 tablespoons melted
  margarine

½ cup grated American
  cheese
Dash of salt and pepper

Boil unpeeled potatoes in salted water until tender. Drain, remove skins and mash. Add 1 cup milk to give desired consistency; beat until fluffy. Season with salt and pepper. Heap potatoes in greased pie plate; make crater in top, the size of a custard cup. Combine egg yolks, margarine, ¼ cup milk, cheese and a dash of salt and pepper. Pour into crater. Bake in 450° F. oven for 15 minutes or until topping browns, cracks and runs down sides of "volcano."

Name Unknown

POTATOES IN FOIL

6 potatoes
Small onion
Water

3 slices bacon
Butter
Salt and pepper

Cut aluminum foil in 12x12-inch pieces and spread flat. Place 1 sliced potato in foil. Cover slices with ½ slice bacon, (more bacon if desired), thin slice of onion, just a dab of butter, teaspoon of water, salt and pepper. Seal foil and place in 300° F. oven for 30 minutes. Check for doneness.

Olga Blom (Alhambra)

EASY BAKED RICE

1 cup raw rice (not minute rice)
1 can beef broth or consomme
1 can onion soup

1 4-ounce can mushrooms
1 stick margarine minus 1 tablespoon, cut into small pieces

Preheat oven to 350° F. Bake for 1 hour. Put all ingredients together in casserole and bake. Serves 6 to 8.

Charlyne Kruckeberg (Edwardsville)

JEWEL RICE & PEAS

2 tablespoons butter or margarine
½ cup chopped onion
1 cup uncooked long grain rice
1 chicken bouillon cube
2 cups water

1 teaspoon salt
⅛ teaspoon pepper
½ teaspoon dried leaf thyme
1 10-ounce package frozen peas thawed and drained
1½ cups orange sections

In large skillet, melt butter, add onion and cook until tender, about 5 minutes. Add rice and cook until golden. Stir in chicken bouillon cube, water, salt, pepper and thyme. Bring to boil, cover and simmer 15 minutes. Add peas and cook 5 minutes, until rice is tender and liquid absorbed. Add orange sections, heat. Makes 6 servings.

Ruth Keller (Edwardsville)

SOUTHERN DINNER RICE

1 stick margarine
1 medium onion, chopped
¼ cup slivered almonds

1 4-ounce can mushrooms
1 cup rice, uncooked
2 cans beef consomme

Sauté the chopped onion in melted oleo until clear. Add almonds and mushrooms and heat through. Add the uncooked rice and two cans of consomme. Bake in casserole for about 45 minutes at 350° F. Serves four.

Charline Rehberger Tucker (Highland)

VARIATION: 1 can onion soup may be used in place of 1 can beef consomme and 1 chopped onion.

Mrs. Hilda Brakhane (Edwardsville)

SAUERKRAUT & APPLESAUCE

1 #2 can sauerkraut
1 #2 can applesauce
1 medium onion, chopped

6 Mayrose brown and serve
sausages

Combine all ingredients in casserole. Bake 35 to 40 minutes at 350° F.

Lois Beckmann (Granite City)

FETTUCINE AND SPINACH

1 (10-ounce) package frozen
   chopped spinach
1 clove garlic, chopped
½ teaspoon basil leaves
½ teaspoon salt
¼ cup vegetable oil
1 teaspoon chicken flavored
   bouillon

½ cup water
1 cup cottage cheese
1 (8-ounce) package fettucine
   or linguini noodles, cooked
   and drained
¼ cup grated cheese

Cook spinach, garlic, basil leaves and salt in vegetable oil for 5 minutes. Dissolve bouillon in water. Add bouillon, spinach mixture and cottage cheese to cooked noodles. Add grated cheese. Toss until mixed. Serve in heated dish. Makes 4 to 6 servings.

Virginia Schuette (Staunton)

SPINACH CASSEROLE

6 eggs
4 10-ounce packages frozen
   spinach, cooked and
   drained
8 tablespoons flour
1 stick butter, cut up

Salt and pepper to taste
2 pounds cottage cheese
½ pound American cheese,
   cut in small pieces
½ pound Brick cheese, cut in
   small pieces

Beat eggs in large bowl. Mix spinach, flour, butter, salt and pepper into eggs. Fold cheeses into egg mixture. Place in casserole. Bake uncovered at 350° F. for one hour. Let cool and set for 10 to 15 minutes before cutting.

Joan Willaredt (Edwardsville)

BAKED SPINACH

2 10-ounce boxes frozen
   spinach
10 small soda crackers
½ stick butter, cut up

2 eggs
Salt and pepper to taste
White sauce
1 hard-boiled egg

Cook spinach in ½ cup water for 5 minutes. Crush 10 crackers and mix with butter, beaten eggs, salt and pepper and spinach. Bake in greased casserole at 350° F. for 35 minutes. Unmold and cover with white sauce. Decorate with sliced, hard-boiled egg.

Louise M. Kipp (Edwardsville)

QUICK CREAMY SPINACH

2 1-pound cans spinach,
   drained
1 10-ounce can cream of
   chicken soup

2 tablespoons Worcestershire
   sauce
2 tablespoons butter

Drain spinach well and place in saucepan with soup, Worcestershire sauce and butter. Mix well and heat on stove top.

Linda Gass (Granite City)

SWEET POTATO & CRANBERRY BAKE

½ cup flour
½ cup brown sugar
½ cup quick oats
1 teaspoon cinnamon
⅓ cup margarine

2 cans yams
2 cups cranberries
1½ cups miniature
   marshmallows

Preheat oven to 350°. Cut together first five ingredients until mixture resembles coarse crumbs. Toss 1 cup crumb mixture with two cans yams. Add cranberries, place in 1½-quart casserole. Top with remaining crumbs. Bake for 35 minutes. Sprinkle with marshmallows. Broil until lightly browned. Makes 6 servings.

Donna Sievers (Staunton)

SPICED SWEET POTATOES

2 pounds sweet potatoes
½ teaspoon nutmeg
½ teaspoon cinnamon
¼ teaspoon salt

¼ cup packed brown sugar
2 tablespoons butter
¼ cup heavy cream or Milnot
3 eggs, separated

Preheat oven to 400° F. Grease 1½-quart baking dish. Cook sweet potatoes until tender 20 to 30 minutes. Drain, peel and mash. Add spices, salt, sugar, butter and cream; mix well. Stir in egg yolks thoroughly. Beat egg whites until stiff peaks form; fold into potato mixture. Pour into baking dish. Bake for 35 minutes at 400° F. Makes 6 servings.

Dorothy Biesk (Wood River)

SOMETHING SPECIAL SWEET POTATOES

2 15-ounce cans sweet
  potatoes
1 20-ounce can crushed
  pineapple, undrained
½ cup pitted prunes
  (presoaked), cut in quarters

1 tablespoon grated orange
  rind
¼ cup slivered almonds
1 tablespoon butter

Combine sweet potatoes, pineapple, prunes and orange rind. Turn into a 1-quart casserole and sprinkle with almonds, dot with butter and bake at 350° F. for 40 to 45 minutes. Makes 6 to 8 servings.

Mrs. George P. Eckert (Collinsville)

SWEET POTATOES

1 large can sweet potatoes
½ cup white sugar
½ cup brown sugar
½ stick butter

½ cup frozen orange juice
  concentrate
2 tablespoons cornstarch

Arrange sweet potatoes in baking dish. Cook remaining ingredients in saucepan until thickened. Pour over sweet potatoes. Bake 45 minutes at 375° F.

Dorothy Marti (Pocahontas)

SPAGHETTI SQUASH

Scrub—leave whole, prick skin with a fork in several places. Place in pan with water, cook 30 to 45 minutes, according to size. Let cool to handle. Cut in half, scoop seeds out. Then take fork and scrape "spaghetti" out.

May be seasoned with spaghetti sauce, butter, beef or chicken broth. You can also make a cheese sauce like macaroni and cheese.

Kay Losch (East Alton)

SCALLOPED TOMATO CASSEROLE

1 cup finely chopped onion
1 29-ounce can tomatos,
    drained, cut in pieces
⅓ cup cheese cracker crumbs
1 tablespoon parsley flakes
1½ teaspoons sugar

1 teaspoon seasoned salt
1 cup sour cream
3 slices crisp toast, cubed
2 tablespoons butter, melted
Parsley flakes

Preheat oven to 325° F. Mix the first six ingredients in a greased 1¼-quart shallow baking dish. Spoon on sour cream. Coat the bread cubes with melted butter and spread on top. Sprinkle with parsley flakes. Bake for 20 minutes. Serves 6.

Donna Sievers (Staunton)

TOMATO AND CORN SCALLOP

1 1-pound can whole kernel
    corn
2 eggs
⅔ cup evaporated milk
¼ cup melted butter
¼ teaspoon salt
⅛ teaspoon pepper

⅛ teaspoon nutmeg
1 1-pound can cream style
    corn
2 1-pound cans stewed
    tomatoes
2 cups coarse cracker crumbs

Drain whole kernel corn; reserve ¼ cup liquid. Beat eggs slightly. Add reserved corn liquid, milk, butter, salt, pepper and nutmeg. Blend well. Stir in whole kernel corn, cream style corn, tomatoes and cracker crumbs. Turn into a greased 3-quart baking dish. Bake at 325° F. for 1 hour 10 minutes or until golden brown and set around edges. Makes 8 to 10 servings.

Marina Brugger (East Alton)

ONION STUFFED ACORN SQUASH

2 medium acorn squash
1 10-ounce package frozen
  tiny onions
1 cup shredded sharp cheese

1 cup soft bread crumbs
2 tablespoons snipped parsley
2 tablespoons melted
  shortening

Preheat oven to 350° F. Cut squash in half lengthwise and remove seeds. Place cut side down in shallow baking pan and bake for 35 to 40 minutes. Meanwhile, cook onions according to package directions, stir in cheese until melted. Turn squash cut side up, sprinkle with a little salt and spoon in onion mixture. Combine melted shortening, bread crumbs and parsley and sprinkle on top of onions. Bake 20 minutes more.

Suzanne Blattner (Madison)

AUTUMN BUTTERNUT

1 Butternut squash, 2½ to
  3 pounds
¼ teaspoon salt
Pinch of white pepper
1 tablespoon brown sugar

1½ quarts red Jonathan
  apples, cored, unpeeled and
  sliced
1½ tablespoons shortening
¼ cup granulated sugar

NUTTY TOPPING:

4 cups corn flakes, coarsely
  crushed
½ cup chopped pecans

2 tablespoons melted butter
½ cup brown sugar

STEP 1—Cut squash in half lengthwise. Scrape out seeds, steam 30 minutes or bake upside down on foil in a moderate oven until tender. Scrape out pulp and mash or beat in mixer until smooth. Set aside.

STEP 2—Core and slice apples, heat shortening in skillet, add apples, sprinkle with sugars. Cover and simmer on low heat until apples are barely tender. Spread in a 9-inch round or 8-inch square casserole (1½ quarts).

STEP 3—Prepare nutty topping by mixing together corn flakes, pecans, butter and brown sugar.

STEP 4—Assemble by spooning the squash over the apples evenly. Bake in moderate oven 325° to 350° F. until lightly browned, about 12 to 15 minutes. Serve piping hot. Yield: 8 generous servings.

Mrs. Edward Barth (Brighton)

VEGETABLE CASSEROLE

1 10-ounce box frozen
chopped broccoli
1 10-ounce box frozen
cauliflower
1 10-ounce box frozen French
green beans

1 12-ounce jar small onions
2 10¾-ounce cans cream of
mushroom soup
1 cup grated Cheddar cheese
¼ cup butter

Cook vegetables 4 to 5 minutes or until crisp. In baking dish, place alternate layers of vegetables, onions, butter, soup and cheese. Cover and bake 30 minutes at 350° F. Uncover and bake 15 minutes more.

Florence Dinwiddie (Roxana)

VEGETABLE CASSEROLE

10 carrots, peeled and sliced
1 large head cauliflower
2 cups grated Cheddar cheese
3 tablespoons butter

1 cup bread crumbs
2 10¾-ounce cans cream of
chicken soup

Cook carrots about 10 minutes. Cook cauliflower 5 minutes and break into flowerets. Layer carrots and flowerets and cheese into 3-quart casserole. Melt butter in small skillet, add bread crumbs and coat. Pour soup over vegetables and cheese and sprinkle bread crumbs on top. Bake at 350° F. for 45 to 50 minutes.

Lois Beckmann (Granite City)

COMPANY VEGETABLE CASSEROLE

1 10-ounce package frozen
peas
1 10-ounce package frozen
chopped broccoli

1 can mushroom soup
1 small jar Cheez Whiz
Bread crumbs

Cook peas and broccoli separately and drain well. Melt mushroom soup and small jar of Cheez Whiz together. Mix peas, broccoli and sauce together. Put into a casserole oven dish. Top with bread crumbs and heat for 25 to 30 minutes at 350° F. Serves 10 to 12.

Melba Helmkamp (East Alton)

BAKED VEGETABLE CASSEROLE

1 16-ounce can mixed
  vegetables, drained
1 package frozen chopped
  broccoli, thawed
1 can cream of chicken soup
2 tablespoons milk

½ teaspoon lemon juice
½ cup Miracle Whip salad
  dressing
Velveeta cheese
Catherine Clark's sage and
  onion stuffing mix

Put a layer of vegetables and then a layer of broccoli in casserole dish and repeat this procedure. Pour sauce made from chicken soup, milk, lemon juice and salad dressing over top of vegetables. Top with Velveeta cheese slices. Cover all with stuffing mix. Bake 45 minutes in 350° F. oven with the casserole covered. Remove cover and bake 5 to 10 minutes longer. Large recipe but yummy.

Mrs. George P. Eckert (Collinsville)

Add a pinch of baking powder when mashing potatoes to make them extra fluffy.

HOT MIXED VEGETABLE CASSEROLE

1 10-ounce package frozen
  baby lima beans
1 10-ounce package French
  green beans

1 10-ounce package frozen
  peas

Cook each one and drain.

SAUCE:

1 cup salad dressing
2 eggs, boiled, chopped
3 tablespoons lemon juice
2 tablespoons onion, minced
1 teaspoon mustard
1 teaspoon Worcestershire
  sauce

2 tablespoons butter
2 tablespoons sugar
Dash of garlic salt
Dash of tabasco sauce

Heat through and pour over hot vegetables.

Mrs. Louis A. Schmidt (Edwardsville)

ZUCCHINI AND MUSHROOMS

1 medium or 2 small zucchini,
   diced or sliced thick
¼ stick margarine

½ cup water
1 teaspoon bouillon, chicken
   or beef

Stir fry until barely tender.

1 small can mushrooms
1 tablespoon soy sauce

1 tablespoon cornstarch
Salt to taste

Add to above and cook only long enough to thicken.

Evelyn Neubauer
Florence Rapp (Edwardsville)

ZUCCHINI-TOMATO CASSEROLE

1 medium zucchini, sliced thin
2 large tomatoes, peeled and
   chopped
1 medium onion, sliced thin
   and separated
½ cup Cheddar cheese, grated

3 slices bacon, cooked and
   crumbled
Butter
Salt and pepper
Buttered bread crumbs or
   croutons

In buttered casserole, layer tomatoes, onion and zucchini. Dot with butter and scatter cheese and crisp crumbled bacon over each layer. Salt and pepper lightly. Cover with bread crumbs (buttered). Bake covered in 400° F. oven about an hour, uncovered for the last 20 minutes. Yields 3 to 4 servings.

Lorene Genczo (New Douglas)

ZUCCHINI GRAVY WITH DUMPLINGS

1 onion, chopped fine
1 stick margarine
Caraway seeds to taste
4 tablespoons flour

3 large zucchini squash
1 can (13-ounce) Milnot
4 to 6 tablespoons vinegar
Salt to taste

Peel and grate zucchini. Salt and let set ½ hour. Then squeeze liquid out thoroughly. In large pot, saute onion in butter, add caraway seeds and flour. Add grated squash, stir, add Milnot slowly while stirring. Add vinegar and salt. Let cook while making drop dumplings. Freezes well.

DROP DUMPLINGS:

4 cups flour
2 eggs
Pinch baking powder
2 tablespoons butter

1 tablespoon cream of wheat
Salt to taste
Milk, enough for thick paste

Drop teaspoonfuls of dough into boiling water, boil until dumplings rise to top. Spoon dumplings out of water into glass bowl. Serve dumplings with zucchini gravy on top and with pork chops, fried and sprinkled with caraway seed; or pork roast and sweet sour green beans.

Brenda Norwood Dusek (Collinsville)

VEGETABLES

VEGETABLES

VEGETABLES

VEGETABLES

BEEF, PORK, POULTRY AND SEAFOODS

BEEF, PORK, POULTRY AND SEAFOODS

The County Court House found in downtown, Edwardsville, has been the seat of government since 1833.

BEEF STEW

2 pounds boneless beef
1 large can tomatoes (#2) or 1
  quart homecanned tomatoes
  plus liquid
1 cup celery, cut into bite size
  pieces
1 cup onions, diced
1 cup carrots, cut into bite
  size pieces

2 cups potatoes, cut into bite
  size pieces
2 tablespoons sugar
2 tablespoons tapioca
1 tablespoon Lawry season
  salt
Salt and pepper to taste

Stir all ingredients together. Bake at 300° F. for four hours or until done. Have in covered dish or pan. You may wise to stir occasionally.

Doris Gvillo (Edwardsville)

BRISQUET

1 4 or 5-pound brisquet
1 onion, sliced
½ cup chili sauce

2 tablespoons brown sugar
1 clove garlic, minced
1 can beer

Place brisquet in roaster, put sliced onion on top. Mix in bowl the chili sauce, brown sugar, garlic and beer. Pour sauce on top of meat and put in oven with lid on roaster. Bake at 350° F. for three hours. Thicken gravy a little if you like.

Virginia Herrmann (Edwardsville)

ELEGANT BEEF

1 pound round steak, cut into
  strips 1-inch x ¼-inch
1 small onion
1 4-ounce can mushrooms
  with juice
1 10-ounce can golden
  mushroom soup

¼ cup vinegar
1 teaspoon garlic salt
2 cups rice (prepared as
  directed on package)

Brown steak, cut onion into slices and brown. Add mushrooms, soup, vinegar and salt. Simmer about 1 hour. Serve over rice or noodles. Serves 5.

Mrs. Charlene Bandy (Moro)

CHICKEN FRIED STEAK

1 or 2 eggs, slightly beaten
1 tablespoon milk
2 pounds round steak
1 cup bread or cracker
   crumbs

3 to 4 tablespoons fat
Salt to taste
Pepper to taste

Add eggs to milk; mix. Cut steak into serving pieces. Dip steak into egg mixture; dip into crumbs. Brown steak on both sides in hot fat. Season. Cover; steam over low heat for 1 hour or until meat is tender.

GRAVY:

Heat 2 tablespoons fat. Stir in 2 tablespoons flour until brown and bubbly. Stir in 1 cup milk until thickened. Season to taste. 6 to 8 servings.

Reita Sparrowk (Bethalto)

JERKY

3 pounds lean, boneless meat
½ cup soy sauce
2 tablespoons Worcestershire
   sauce
½ teaspoon garlic powder

½ teaspoon black pepper
1 teaspoon onion powder
2 teaspoons Hickory Smoke
   Flavor salt

Cut meat in thin strips and toss with other ingredients. Marinate overnight. Lay meat on cooling racks and place over cookie sheets (sprayed with Pam). Bake at 150° F. for 7 hours.

Abby Daugherty (Granite City)

JOHN'S FAVORITE BEEF

2½-3 pound piece of lean beef
   brisket
¼ cup soy sauce

¼ cup lemon juice
¼ cup brown sugar
Garlic powder to taste

Marinate beef in soy sauce, lemon juice, brown sugar and garlic for 1 hour at room temperature or overnight (covered) in refrigerator. Roast in marinade at 300° F. until desired doneness. Slice thinly and serve with juices. Leftovers are delicious reheated and served on onion rolls or French bread.

Carolyn Losch (East Alton)

CHUCK WAGON PEPPER STEAK

1 3-pound round-bone arm
chuck or boneless round
roast, 2 inches thick
2 teaspoons unseasoned meat
tenderizer
2 tablespoons instant minced
onion
2 teaspoons thyme

1 teaspoon marjoram
1 bay leaf, crushed
1 cup vinegar
½ cup olive oil
3 tablespoons lemon juice
2 tablespoons coarsely
crushed peppercorns

Sprinkle meat evenly on both sides with meat tenderizer; pierce deeply all over with a fork. Place in a shallow baking pan. Mix instant onion, thyme, majoram, bay leaf, vinegar, olive oil and lemon juice in a small bowl; pour over and around meat. Let stand at room temperature 1 to 2 hours, turning meat every 30 minutes to marinate well. When ready to grill, remove meat from liquid; sprinkle both sides with peppercorns and pound into meat. Place on charcoal grill and cook about 35 minutes on each side. 6 servings.

Reita Sparrowk (Bethalto)

PEPPER BEEF

6 tablespoons margarine
1 clove garlic
2 green peppers, cut in strips
2 cups sliced onions
1 pound round steak, cut in
¼-inch strips

Flour
½ cup wine
10 ounce package noodles,
prepared as directed on
package

In large skillet, melt 3 tablespoons margarine over medium heat. Sauté garlic clove until golden brown. Discard. Add peppers and onions, sauté lightly. Remove from pan and drain. Dredge beef strips lightly in flour, shaking off excess. Melt remaining margarine in skillet, brown beef thoroughly. Add wine and simmer 10 minutes. Return peppers and onions to skillet. Simmer 5 minutes, or until heated through. Serve over noodles.

Anna Holman (Granite City)

PEPPER STEAK WITH RICE

3 cups hot cooked rice
1 pound round steak
1 tablespoon paprika
2 tablespoons butter
1½ cups beef broth
2 cloves crushed garlic

1 cup sliced onions
2 green peppers, sliced
2 tablespoons cornstarch
¼ cup soy sauce
¼ cup water
2 fresh tomatoes

While rice is cooking, pound steak to ¼-inch thickness and slice in ¼-inch strips. Sprinkle meat with paprika and allow to stand. Brown meat in butter in skillet. Add garlic and broth. Cover and simmer for 30 minutes. Stir in onions and green peppers. Cover and cook 5 minutes more. Blend cornstarch, water and soy sauce and stir into meat mixture. Cook, stirring until clear and thickened (2 minutes). Add tomatoes and stir gently. Serve over bed of rice. 6 servings.

Delores Geiger (Alhambra)

PEPPER STEAK WITH RICE

2 tablespoons oil
1-2 pounds round steak, cut
   into 1-inch strips
Salt and pepper
½ cup chopped onion
2 green peppers, cut into
   strips

1½ cups water
2 bouillon cubes
2 tablespoons cornstarch
¼ cup soy sauce
¼ cup water
1 cup rice, cooked according
   to directions on box

Heat oil in 10-inch skillet. Season meat with salt and pepper. Brown meat in hot oil. Push meat to the side of the pan and lightly sauté onions and green peppers. Put 2 bouillon cubes in 1½ cups water and bring to boil. Add beef broth to the meat and simmer for 1 hour. In measuring cup put ¼ cup soy sauce, ¼ cup water and 2 tablespoons cornstarch. Mix and add to skillet. Serve over cooked rice.

Sue Urban (Highland)

The average homemaker walks over 3000 miles a year.

MUSHROOM STEAK

1 large round steak, cut into serving size pieces
Oil
1 cup sliced mushrooms

1 medium onion, diced
2 cups water
Flour
Salt and pepper to taste

In a large heavy skillet, put enough oil to brown meat. When meat has been browned on both sides, add mushrooms and onion on top of meat. With skillet covered, cook on low heat until tender. When meat is tender, remove from skillet and add two cups water, flour to thicken and salt and pepper to taste. This makes a good rich mushroom sauce for steak or gravy. Preparation time: about one hour.

VARIATION: Brown steak fast on both sides, then add on top of the meat one quart tomatoes, one onion sliced and one cup fresh mushrooms or canned mushrooms. Cover and put on lowest heat for about one hour. Add salt and pepper to taste and flour to thicken.

Marie Mindrup (Alhambra)

SHISH-KA-BOBS

1½ pounds beef, cut in 1-inch cubes
1½ pounds pork or veal, cut in 1-inch cubes
6 small potatoes, cooked half done

1 medium onion, cut into 6 wedges
1 medium green pepper, cut into 6 wedges

Marinate meat cubes overnight in a mixture of:

1 cup vegetable oil
1 teaspoon garlic salt
¼ cup brown sugar
2 tablespoons Worcestershire sauce or 2 tablespoons soy sauce

Salt and pepper

Put one cube of beef and one of pork between each vegetable on a skewer. Grill over medium low fire, brush with marinade and grill until desired doneness.

Helen Miller (Granite City)

OVEN SWISS STEAK

1½ pounds round steak
¼ cup flour
1 teaspoon salt
1 16-ounce can stewed
  tomatoes
½ cup chopped celery

½ cup chopped carrot
2 tablespoons chopped onion
½ teaspoon Worcestershire
  sauce
¼ cup shredded American
  cheese

Pound flour and salt into meat. Brown meat in a small amount of fat. Place meat in a shallow baking dish. Blend remaining flour with drippings in skillet. Add remaining ingredients except cheese. Cook until it boils. Pour over meat. Cover and bake at 350° F. for 2 hours. Top with cheese and return to oven for a few minutes, until cheese melts.

Carol Russell (Bethalto)

SWISS STEAK

3¼ pounds round steak cut
  ½ inch thick
Adolph's unseasoned
  tenderizer
Salt and pepper
1 tablespoon shortening or
  margarine
⅓ cup onion, chopped fine
⅓ cup carrots, chopped fine
⅓ cup celery, chopped fine

1 can cream of mushroom
  soup
1½ cans beef stock or water
3 tablespoons Heinz chili
  sauce
1 cup flour
1½ teaspoons salt
¼ teaspoon pepper
2 teaspoons paprika

Trim fat from meat and cut in serving pieces. Sprinkle with Adolph's tenderizer, salt and pepper. If there is time, let stand a couple of hours before pounding in flour. I think it gets more tender. Using flour as needed, cover the steak and pound in with edge of saucer until well coated on both sides. Brown a few pieces at a time in hot fat and place in roasting pan or casserole. In same skillet on medium heat, sauté the carrots, celery and onion using 1 tablespoon fat or margarine. Sauté vegetables for about three minutes. Mix the flour, salt, pepper and paprika together and add one tablespoon of this mixture to the vegetable mixture and stir until brown. Mix together the soup, beef stock or water and chili sauce until smooth. Then add gradually to the above mixture, stirring constantly until smooth. Cook for a few minutes, then pour over meat in roasting pan. Bake in 450° F. oven for 10 minutes. Then bake in 350° F. oven for one hour or until tender.

Martha Blom (Alhambra)

BAKED ROUNDSTEAK

1 pound round steak,
tenderized
1 10-ounce can cream of
mushroom soup

1 package onion soup mix
3 tablespoons A-1 sauce
Salt
Pepper

Preheat oven to 250° F. Place tenderized steak in baking dish or pan. Salt and pepper to taste. Sprinkle with A-1 sauce. Add soups, cover well. Bake for 2½ hours.

Suzanne Blattner (Madison)

BEEF SALAMI

2 pounds lean ground beef
¼ teaspoon pepper
¼ teaspoon onion salt
½ teaspoon garlic powder
½ teaspoon salt

1 tablespoon mustard seed
2 tablespoons Morton tender
quick salt
¾ cup water
1 tablespoon liquid smoke

Mix all ingredients together in a large bowl. Shape in roll. Wrap in heavy duty foil. Punch holes all over with fork. Refrigerate 24 hours, then bake at 350° F. for 1 hour on rack still in foil. After baking and cooling, add another layer of foil and refrigerate again for 24 hours. Makes 2 pounds and can be frozen. You can use ground turkey but then bake at 325° F. for 1¼ hours. 3½ ounces equals 1 serving.

Beverly Meyer (Edwardsville)

BOUILLON BURGER

1 pound ground beef
1 tablespoon beef bouillon
granules
¼ cup boiling water

1 cup soft bread crumbs
½ cup chopped onion
¼ teaspoon pepper

Dissolve bouillon in water, mix the ground beef, bread crumbs, onion, pepper and dissolved bouillon. Form into 4 patties and broil.

Mary Jane Koeller (Godfrey)

CHEDDARBURGER SKILLET

1 pound ground beef
1 medium onion, chopped
1 can cream of mushroom
  soup

1 can Cheddar cheese soup
¼ cup water

In skillet, brown beef and cook onion until tender. Stir to separate meat. Pour off fat. Stir in soups and water. Heat, stir occasionally. Cook about another ten minutes.

Lorene Genczo (New Douglas)

CHEESE BURGER LOAVES

2 cups corn flakes cereal
1 egg
1 8-ounce can stewed
  tomatoes or tomato juice
1 teaspoon salt

⅛ teaspoon pepper
1 pound ground beef
3 slices American cheese, cut
  in half diagonally

Crush corn flakes to make 1 cup crumbs. Place in mixing bowl, add egg, tomatoes or juice, salt and pepper. Mix well. Add ground beef. Mix. Shape into six loaves. Place in single shallow baking pan. Bake in 350° F. oven for 30 to 45 minutes. Remove from oven, add cheese to each loaf. Return to oven. Bake 10 minutes longer or until cheese melts.

VARIATION: Potatoes and carrots may be added to the loaves of meat and baked, omitting the cheese or it may be added at the finish.

Rose Schrage (Edwardsville)

TASTY BARBECUED HAMBURGER

1 pound ground beef
½ medium onion
3 tablespoons butter
1 cup ketchup
⅛ cup vinegar
2 tablespoons brown sugar

1 teaspoon mustard
1 tablespoon Worcestershire
  sauce
⅛ teaspoon salt
½ tablespoon Liquid Smoke

Brown ground beef, drain and set aside. Sauté onions in butter. Add all remaining ingredients and hamburger to onions. Simmer ten minutes. Serves four. Serve on warm buns.

Cindy Hemann (New Douglas)

GLORIFIED HAMBURGER

1¼ pounds ground chuck or
   hamburger
1 beaten egg
1 medium onion, chopped
8 small cracker squares,
   crumbled

Milk, if mixture is dry
1 can mushroom steak sauce
1 can water

Mix first five ingredients together and form into patties. Brown in skillet. Remove from pan and drain grease. Put mushroom steak sauce and water in pan and simmer. Return hamburger patties to sauce in pan and cover tightly. Simmer until hot.

Bernice Willaredt (Granite City)

HAMBURGER SKILLET

1 pound ground beef
1 16-ounce can cut green
   beans, undrained
Dash pepper
1 10½-ounce can pizza sauce
   or tomato sauce

2 teaspoons instant minced
   onion
1 cup package biscuit mix
⅓ cup milk

In skillet, brown beef, spoon off fat. Season with pepper. Stir in beans, pizza sauce and onion. Heat until boiling. Combine biscuit mix and milk; beat vigorously until stiff but sticky. Drop by rounded tablespoons on top of boiling meat mixture. Cover and simmer about 12 minutes. *Do not lift cover during cooking.* Yields 4 or 5 servings.

Mary Lou Sutton (Alton)

MEAT LOAF

1 pound ground beef
½ pound ground pork
1½ teaspoons salt
¼ cup catsup
¾ cup milk

1 cup corn flakes
1 egg
1 cup celery, cut fine
½ cup onion, cut fine

Combine all ingredients. Mix well. Bake at 325° F. for 1 to 1¼ hours. Serves 6.

Georgia Engelke (Granite City)

HAMBURGER PORCUPINES

2 pounds ground beef
½ cup chopped onion
2 teaspoons salt
⅛ teaspoon pepper
1 egg

1 cup uncooked regular rice
3 cups tomato juice
¼ cup oil
1 teaspoon instant beef broth

Mix ground beef with first five ingredients and ¼ cup tomato juice, shape into one-inch balls. Brown half at a time in oil in large skillet. Pour off excess oil and combine remaining tomato juice and beef broth in same skillet. Return meatballs to skillet and bring to a boil. Lower heat, cover and simmer one hour. Serves eight.

Lois Beckmann (Granite City)

SALISBURY STEAK

1½ pounds hamburger
¼ teaspoon celery salt
¼ teaspoon garlic powder
Salt and pepper to taste

¼ cup Western or Catalina
dressing, or season as
desired

Mix, shape into patties. Cook in baking dish until half done.

Mix together:

1 envelope brown gravy mix
1 cup water

1 small onion thinly sliced

Pour the above mixture over patties. Cover and cook six to eight minutes or until meat reaches desired doneness.

Linda Brase (Edwardsville)

MEATLOAF

⅔ cup ketchup
⅔ cup evaporated milk
1 cup oatmeal

2 eggs
1 package onion soup mix
3 pounds hamburger

Mix all the above ingredients together and put into a pan of your choice or shape into a loaf. Bake uncovered at 350° F. for 1½ hours.

Carleen Paul (Worden)
County Committee Secretary

MEAT LOAF AND DRESSING

1 pound beef, ground	2 cups coarse soft bread,
1 teaspoon salt	broken up
⅛ teaspoon pepper	2 tablespoons minced onion
1 egg, beaten	2 tablespoons butter, melted
¼ cup ketchup	½ teaspoon salt
½ teaspoon Worcestershire	⅓ cup celery
sauce	2 tablespoons hot water

Mix the first 6 ingredients together. Grease a 1½-quart casserole, put ½ hamburger mixture in bottom of the casserole. Put in all the bread crumbs which have been mixed with the onion, butter, celery and hot water. Then add the remaining hamburger mixture on top. Bake in 350° F. oven, put casserole in shallow pan of water and bake about 2 hours. This is real good, easy casserole dish.

Ruth M. Rogier (Highland)

MEAT BALLS AND SAUCE

1½ pounds ground beef	¼ teaspoon pepper
¼ cup cracker crumbs	½ cup milk
1 clove garlic	1 onion
1½ teaspoons salt	¼ cup oil

Chop onion and garlic and mix the remaining ingredients well. Form into balls and brown evenly in oil. Remove to plate. While oil is still hot start sauce.

SAUCE:

¼ cup flour	¼ teaspoon salt
1 cup sour cream	⅓ cup sherry
1 can consommé	1½ cups ripe olives, diced
3 tablespoons catsup	
1 teaspoon Worcestershire	
sauce	

Sauté flour in hot oil until golden. Add remaining ingredients except olives. After sauce has thickened and been well mixed add meat balls and simmer gently for about 1 hour. Just before serving add olives.

Suzanne Blattner (Madison)

MEAT LOAF

4 pounds ground beef
1 can tomato soup
2 beaten eggs
1 cup fine dry bread crumbs
1 large chopped onion

2 tablespoons Worcestershire
  sauce
2 teaspoons salt
½ teaspoon pepper

Heat oven to 350° F. Combine all ingredients thoroughly. Shape into 2 loaves. Bake for 1 hour. One loaf may be frozen before baking for future use. Increase baking time to about 1½ or 1¾ hours for frozen loaf.

Betty Heepke (Edwardsville)

MOTHER'S MEAT LOAF

1 cup sliced mushrooms or
  one small can
½ cup chopped onions
2 tablespoons butter or
  margarine
½ cup sour cream
2 eggs

⅔ cup milk
1½ pounds ground beef
¾ cup bread crumbs
2 teaspoons salt
1 teaspoon Worcestershire
  sauce

Sauté the mushrooms and onions in butter or margarine. Remove from heat, stir in sour cream. Set mixture aside. Combine remaining ingredients. Shape half of mixture into oval in a shallow baking pan. Form a well in the middle for the filling. Spoon the sour cream mixture into the well of indentation. Shape the rest of meat mixture over filling, using fingers, pinch meat together around filling so you have a seam (seal). Bake in 350° F. oven for one hour. Let stand ten minutes before slicing.

Olga Blom (Alhambra)

HAM BAKE

1 cup brown sugar
½ teaspoon pumpkin pie
  spice

1 20-ounce can crushed or
  sliced pineapple
Maraschino cherries

Add brown sugar and spice to drained pineapple juice. Let stand for ½ hour to dissolve sugar and spice. Put this on ham and bake in the last two hours required to complete baking ham. Baste every twenty minutes. The crushed or sliced pineapple is placed on the ham in the last two hours of baking also. Maraschino cherries may be added in center of sliced pineapple.

M. L. Maedge (Highland)

HAM WITH CHERRY SAUCE

1 10-ounce jar apple jelly
1 tablespoon prepared
  mustard
⅓ cup pineapple juice

1 pound 17-ounce can cherry
  pie filling
5-6 pound ham

Place ham fat up in 325° F. oven for about 1½ hours. Take out of oven and score fat in diamonds. In saucepan, combine first four ingredients. Heat to boil and stir, simmer 2 to 3 minutes. Pour ⅓ over ham and return to oven. Spoon remaining glaze at two 10-minute intervals. In same pan heat cherry filling and add glaze from baking ham to cherry sauce. Bring to boil again. Spoon over ham on a platter. Use remainder for use at the table.

Lois Beckmann (Granite City)

HONEYED PORK CHOPS

4 pork chops 1-inch thick
¾ cup strained honey
½ cup vinegar
½ teaspoon ginger

¼ cup soy sauce
1 clove garlic
½ teaspoon salt

Place pork chops in 8x8-inch baking dish. Mix remaining ingredients and pour over chops. Marinate overnight or all day. Bake uncovered in marinade in 325° F. oven for 1 hour. Take out of marinade to serve.

Kay Losch (East Alton)

HAM GLAZE

1 ham
1 20-ounce can sliced
  pineapple
½ cup brown sugar

2 teaspoons dry mustard
2 tablespoons Argo
  cornstarch

Place ham in oven at 325° F. While ham is heating, make glaze. Drain pineapple juice into saucepan. Add brown sugar and dry mustard. Stir and bring to a boil. Slowly add a thickener made from cornstarch and small amount of water. Slowly pour into boiling pineapple sugar mixture, stirring constantly. Mixture should be the consistency of a very thick syrup. Arrange pineapple slices on top of ham. About 1½ hours before ham is done, pour glaze over the ham and return to oven, uncovered.

Dottie Suhre (Alhambra)

GINGER PORK LOIN ROAST

5 pound pork loin roast
½ cup pineapple juice

1 tablespoon ginger
2 tablespoons light molasses

Place pork roast in shallow roasting pan; fat side up. Insert meat thermometer into loin part of roast. Combine remaining ingredients to make a glaze. Roast at 325° F. for 2½ to 2¾ hours or until thermometer reads 170° F. Baste with glaze every half hour. Serves eight to ten people.

Florence Highlander (Hamel)

PORK CHOPS SUPREME

4 lean pork chops, one inch
  thick
4 lemon slices or ¼ teaspoon
  lemon juice per chop

Salt
4 thin onion slices
Brown sugar
4 tablespoons ketchup

Heat oven to 350° F. Place chops in baking pan. Salt well. Top each chop with a lemon slice or juice, and a thin onion slice; sprinkle generously with brown sugar. Pour 1 tablespoon ketchup over each chop. Cover and bake one hour. Uncover and bake 30 minutes longer, basting occasionally.

Ruth Becker (Edwardsville)

214

BARBECUE

¼ cup ketchup
1 24-ounce bottle Maull's
  barbecue sauce
1 button garlic, chopped
2 onions, diced
2 tablespoons vinegar
2 tablespoons sugar, more
  if desired

2 tablespoons salad mustard
Salt to taste
¼ teaspoon chili powder,
  more if desired
2 pounds pork
2 pounds beef

To make sauce, mix the above ingredients, except meat, in a heavy saucepan and bring to a boil. In another heavy pan, cook pork and beef in a small amount of water, cover tightly. Simmer until tender. Cut up meat, then add to sauce and simmer for 3 hours. Use broth from cooked meat for making noodle soup.

Esther Schuette (Staunton)

BBQ PORK CHOPS

½ cup brown sugar
½ cup soy sauce

6-8 pork chops, one inch thick

Marinate one inch thick pork chops in mixture at least 4 hours. (Overnight is best). Barbecue 45-60 minutes, basting often. One chop will satisfy the heartiest.

Ronnie Sommers (Godfrey)

BAR-B-QUE PORK

6 pork steaks
¾ cup Open Pit hickory
  smoke barbecue sauce

1 cup Maull's barbecue sauce
2 tablespoons brown sugar
2 tablespoons lemon juice

Score fat around edge of steak, place them in a large size Pyrex utility dish. Mix the four ingredients together and pour over the steak and cover with foil for 1 hour, remove the foil and continue baking for ½ hour longer. Bake in 300° F. oven.

Mary Jane Koeller (Godfrey)

215

BAKED CENTER-CUT PORK CHOPS

6 center-cut pork chops,
  one-inch thick
Salt
Pepper

2 large red apples
1 tablespoon lemon juice
2 tablespoons brown sugar,
  firmly packed

Season pork chops with salt and pepper. Arrange chops, about two inches apart, in a large shallow baking dish. Bake in oven at 350° F. for 1¼ hours. Core apples, but do not pare. Cut into ½-inch slices. Place apple slices on each chop. Brush apple with lemon juice and sprinkle with brown sugar. Cover loosely with aluminum foil. Bake 15 minutes or until chops are tender. Makes six servings.

Pam Heepke (Edwardsville)

PORK CHOPS AND SWEET POTATOES

6 pork chops (¾-inch thick)
Salt to taste
Pepper to taste
2 tablespoons shortening
2 or 3 fresh sweet potatoes,
  peeled
½ cup firmly packed brown
  sugar

1 orange, peeled and sliced
  into 6 cartwheels
¼ teaspoon ground cloves
  (if desired)
⅔ cup freshly squeezed
  orange juice

Season pork chops with salt and pepper. Brown both sides in hot shortening. Cut peeled sweet potatoes into ½-inch slices and place over bottom of baking pan or casserole. Sprinkle with brown sugar. Add layer of browned pork chops and top each with orange cartwheel. Pour mixture of ground cloves and orange juice over all. Tightly cover and bake at 350° F. for 45 minutes. Remove cover and bake 15 minutes longer—basting with juice. Allow 1 to 2 pork chops per serving.

Wilma Willaredt (Collinsville)

Be careful when you talk in the country, because the corn has ears, the potatoes have eyes and the beanstalk.

216

ROLY-POLY PORK LOAVES

Bake 1—Freeze 1 for future.

3 pounds ground pork
1 8-ounce can tomato sauce
1 egg
¼ cup finely chopped green
  pepper

2 teaspoons salt
2 teaspoons chili powder
⅛ teaspoon pepper
corn bread stuffing*
2 tablespoons catsup

Combine pork, tomato sauce, egg, green pepper and seasonings. Pat out ½ of mixture on waxed paper into a 10x8 inch rectangle. Place ½ of stuffing in layer over meat, pressing lightly, Roll up from short end (jelly roll fashion) to form a loaf. Seal ends; place seam side down on rack in roasting pan. Bake in moderate oven at 350° F. for 1 hour and 15 minutes. Spread with catsup and bake 5 to 10 minutes longer. Prepare second loaf; freeze, wrap and store at 0° F. or below for 2 to 3 weeks. To cook frozen loaf, bake as directed, increasing original time to 1½ to 1¾ hours. Yield 2 loaves, 6 to 8 servings each.

CORN BREAD STUFFING:

1 8½-ounce package Corn
  Muffin mix
¼ cup finely chopped onion
½ cup finely chopped celery

1 tablespoon butter or
  margarine
1 teaspoon sage
¼ cup water

Make corn bread according to package directions; cool and crumble. Brown onion and celery in butter. Stir in corn bread, sage and water.

Diane L. Martin (Edwardsville)

CHICKEN SALAD

1 chicken, cooked, boned and
  ground
¼ teaspoon salt
⅛ teaspoon pepper
1 teaspoon sugar

1 teaspoon mustard
1 teaspoon salad dressing
1 teaspoon vinegar or lemon
  juice

Mix the ground chicken and remaining ingredients together. You can freeze only the ground chicken. When you need meat for sandwiches, thaw and add the above mixture and you have a quick chicken salad.

Verna Kasubke (New Douglas)

CHICKEN SALAD

2 chickens, cooked, boned and diced
¾ cup diced celery
1 cup seedless white grapes, halved
1 cup mandarin oranges
½ cup mayonnaise
½ cup sour cream
2 tablespoons finely chopped parsley

2 tablespoons finely chopped onion
1 tablespoon lemon juice
½ teaspoon salt
½ teaspoon pepper
½ teaspoon Herb Italian spices
¼ cup toasted slivered almonds

Mix all ingredients together, toss lightly. Chill before serving. Serve with lettuce, rolls, olives, etc.

Gracie Koeller (Godfrey)

HOT CHICKEN SALAD

2 cups cut-up cooked chicken
2 cups thinly sliced celery
1 cup toasted bread cubes
1 cup mayonnaise

½ cup toasted sliced almonds
2 tablespoons lemon juice
2 teaspoons grated onion
½ teaspoon salt

TOPPING:

½ cup grated Cheddar cheese   1 cup bread cubes

Combine first eight ingredients and pile loosely in a casserole and sprinkle with the topping mixture. Bake in 450° F. oven 10 to 15 minutes.

Mary K. Willaredt (Granite City)

CHICKEN CASSEROLE

1 frying chicken, cut in pieces
1 cup uncooked rice
1 10-ounce can cream of celery soup

1 10-ounce can cream of mushroom soup
1 package of onion soup mix

Preheat oven to 250° F. Put rice, celery soup and mushroom soup in pan, lay chicken on top and sprinkle onion soup mix over top. Cover with lid or foil, and bake for three hours.

Suzanne Blattner (Madison)

CHICKEN SALAD

6 cups diced, cooked chicken
4 hard boiled eggs (coarsely
  chopped)
2 cups thinly sliced celery
¼ cup finely diced red
  bermuda onion
1 cup slivered pitted ripe
  olives

2 teaspoons salt
¼ teaspoon pepper
½ cup mayonnaise or salad
  dressing
6 tablespoons lemon juice

Place chicken, eggs, celery, onions, olives, salt and pepper in a bowl.
Blend mayonnaise and lemon juice together, add chicken mixture and
gently toss together. Chill about 1 hour. Serve over shredded lettuce
and garnish with sliced tomatoes. Serves 10 to 12.

Ruth Keller (Edwardsville)

BAKED CHICKEN SALAD

2 cups diced, cooked chicken
1 can cream of chicken soup
½ cup mayonnaise
1 cup diced celery
1 cup cooked rice (Minute)

1 teaspoon grated onion
1 teaspoon lemon juice
½ teaspoon salt
3 hard boiled eggs (diced)

TOPPING:

½ cup slivered almonds

1 cup buttered corn flakes

Mix all ingredients together and place in greased 2-quart casserole
dish and top with topping mix. Bake at 350° F. for 25 minutes until
bubbly.

Ruth Keller (Edwardsville)

OVEN BAKED CHICKEN

1 chicken, cut up and skinned
1 egg, beaten with 2
  tablespoons water

Instant potato flakes

Dip chicken in egg mixture and then in instant potatoes. Season with
salt and pepper. Place on pan that has been sprayed with Pam. Bake
at 400° F. for 1 hour. Turn after ¾ of an hour.

Beverly Meyer (Edwardsville)

HOT CHICKEN SALAD

1 3-pound chicken
2 cups cooked rice
1 cup diced celery
¾ cup mayonnaise
½ cup slivered almonds or
pecans
1 10½-ounce can condensed
cream of chicken soup
3 hard cooked eggs—mashed

2-ounce jar pimientos,
chopped
2 tablespoons chopped green
pepper
2 tablespoons chopped onion
1 tablespoon lemon juice
¼ teaspoon salt
½ cup dry bread crumbs

Simmer chicken in water until tender. Cool in broth. Skin and bone chicken. Cut into ¾-inch cubes. Mix with the remaining ingredients (except crumbs). Pour into buttered 8x12-inch baking dish. Sprinkle with crumbs. Bake at 350° F. for 45 minutes or until golden brown. Makes six generous servings. It's good the second day, either cold or warm.

Edna Suessen (Edwardsville)

CHICKEN 'N DUMPLINGS

1 stewing hen
2 teaspoons salt
Water to cover chicken
2 cups sifted flour

1 cup hot broth
1 beaten egg
2 chicken bouillon cubes

Prepare stewing hen for cooking by cutting into serving size pieces. Place in large pot and cover with water and add salt. Simmer until tender. When tender, remove meat from broth (debone if you prefer). Put meat in pan and keep warm while making dumplings.

DUMPLINGS:

Sift flour into a large bowl, make a well in the center of the flour. Pour into it, the hot broth, mixing with fork as you pour. Then stir in beaten egg. As soon as dough becomes difficult to stir with fork, work with fingers until it is smooth and medium stiff, adding flour as needed. Knead the dough for a few seconds on floured board. Divide dough into four or five parts. Roll as thin as possible and cut rounds into strips 1½ or 2 inches wide. Break these into 2 inch long pieces and drop into *boiling* broth. (They may be cut into squares instead of breaking them.) Cook 10 to 15 minutes. (One cup of hot broth and 1 egg will make 8 to 10 servings.)

Wilma Schoen (New Douglas)

BARBECUED BAKED CHICKEN

1 large chicken, cut up
4 tablespoons brown sugar
½ teaspoon paprika
2 teaspoons salt
1 teaspoon mustard
¼ teaspoon chili powder
1 tablespoon Worcestershire
  sauce

1½ cups water
¼ cup vinegar
2 cups tomato juice
¼ cup catsup
¼ teaspoon curry powder
¼ teaspoon celery salt
⅛ teaspoon turmeric

Brown chicken pieces and put in baking dish. Meanwhile, mix all other ingredients and pour over chicken that has been browned. Cover with aluminum foil. Bake 1 hour and 10 minutes at 350° F. Remove chicken pieces and thicken sauce with cornstarch. Serve chicken with baked potatoes, buttered peas and salad. Yield: 8 servings.

Mrs. Edward Barth (Brighton)

CHICKEN DELIGHT

2 cups cooked-boned and
  skinned chicken, cut up
Salt to taste
Pepper to taste
Poultry seasoning to taste
¼ cup chopped onion
¼ cup chopped green pepper
¼ cup chopped celery
2-3 tablespoons margarine or
  oil

1 10½-ounce can chicken
  noodle soup
1 10¾-ounce can cream of
  mushroom soup
1 6-ounce can Pet or Milnot
  evaporated milk
1 2-ounce can Chow Mein
  noodles
8 slices of bread, chunked
2 sticks margarine

Sauté chopped onions, green peppers and celery in 2 or 3 tablespoons of margarine. Add next four ingredients and add chicken salt and pepper and mix well and pour into a well greased casserole. Top with 8 or more slices of bread (chunked) and mixed with 2 sticks of melted margarine. Bake 30 to 35 minutes in 350° F. oven.

VARIATION: 1 12½-ounce can tuna or 2 cups diced ham may be used instead of chicken. 1 can cream of celery soup may be substituted for ¼ cup celery.

Irma Henkhaus (Alhambra)

CHICKEN BROCCOLI CASSEROLE

1 package Betty Crocker
  Noodles Romanoff
2 cups diced chicken
1 10-ounce package chopped
  frozen broccoli
1 4-ounce can mushrooms,
  sliced

1 can cream of mushroom
  soup
4 ounces shredded Cheddar
  cheese
1 3-ounce can fried onion
  rings

Prepare noodles according to package directions except use ½ cup milk instead of ⅓ cup. Mix with chicken, broccoli (cooked and drained), mushrooms, soup and put into casserole. Cover with cheese and onion rings. Bake 25 minutes in a 350° F. oven.

Wilma Becker (Moro)

CHICKEN AND BROCCOLI BUFFET BAKE

2 10-ounce packages frozen
  broccoli, cooked and
  drained
3 cups cooked and cut-up
  chicken
1 4-ounce can drained
  mushrooms

½ cup flour
1½ cups water
1 cup milk
2 chicken bouillon cubes
1 cup mayonnaise
2⅔ cups crushed corn flakes
2 tablespoons margarine

Arrange broccoli in baking dish. Place chicken over broccoli. Place mushrooms on top of chicken. Set aside. Make sauce of water, flour, milk and bouillon; stir while cooking. After cooking sauce, add mayonnaise. Pour over the first mixture. Melt margarine, stir in corn flakes. Mix and add as topping. Bake 30 minutes in 350°F. oven. This dish freezes well.

Mary K. Willaredt (Granite City)

CHICKEN AND STUFFING CASSEROLE

4 to 6 boned and skinned
  half chicken breasts
Swiss cheese slices
⅓ cup cooking sherry

1 can cream of chicken soup
2 cups stuffing mix
1 stick melted butter

Place breasts in casserole. Top with cheese slices. Combine soup and sherry. Pour over chicken, Top with stuffing. Pour melted butter over all. Bake at 350° for 45 minutes.

Reita Sparrowk (Bethalto)

CHICKEN CASSEROLE

4 cups cooked chicken
1 can cream of chicken soup
  or cream of celery soup

1 cup Velveeta cheese
2 cups cooked noodles
1 4-ounce bag of potato chips

SAUCE:

8 tablespoons flour
8 tablespoons butter

2 cups broth (chicken)

In baking dish, place in layers as follows: Layer chips, chicken, soup, noodles, cheese (diced). Cover with sauce, then layer of crumbled potato chips. Bake one hour in 325° F. oven in a 9x13-inch baking dish.

Carleen Paul (Worden)

CHICKEN AND DRESSING CASSEROLE

1 heavy fryer, cooked and
  boned
1 package prepared dressing
  mix

1 can mushroom soup
1 small jar pimento, chopped
1 egg

Cut cooked chicken into large pieces. Prepare dressing mix according to package directions, using broth from chicken and 1 well beaten egg. Make layers of dressing, then chicken, soup and pimento until all are used. Bake at 350° F. for 45 minutes or until soup bubbles through the mixture.

Norma Albrecht (Worden)

CHICKEN AND DRESSING CASSEROLE

1 3-pound chicken, boiled and
  deboned
1 can cream of mushroom
  soup or 1½ cups milk
1 can cream of chicken soup

1 can chicken noodle soup
4 tablespoons melted
  margarine
2 eggs
10 slices bread

Tear bread into small pieces. Mix all ingredients together. Pour into 9x13-inch greased baking dish. Bake at 375° F. for 30 to 35 minutes. Thicken chicken broth to make gravy and pour over top when served. Serve with a green salad. Yield: 12 servings.

Mrs. Edward Barth (Brighton)

CHICKEN DELITE CASSEROLE

1½ cups diced cooked
  chicken
1½ cups chicken broth
1 8-ounce package shell
  macaroni, cooked and
  drained

1 cup cubed process cheese
½ cup chopped ripe olives
1 4-ounce can mushrooms,
  drained
1 4-ounce can pimiento,
  chopped

Combine chicken and broth with macaroni. Add cheese and stir over low heat until cheese melts. Add olives, pimiento, mushrooms. Turn into buttered 2-quart casserole. Bake at 350° F. for 20 to 30 minutes. Serves 6 to 8.

Alice Stille (Alhambra)

CHICKEN LOAF

1 4-pound chicken
2 cups ground bread crumbs
1 cup cooked rice
1 tablespoon salt
1 teaspoon pepper or paprika

½ cup pimentos
4 eggs, well beaten
¼ cup chicken fat
1½ pints broth
1 4-ounce can mushrooms

Cook chicken until tender. Pick meat from bones, cut into small pieces. Grind gizzard and skin. Add all other ingredients and stir together well. Bake in 9x1-inch pan in 325° F. oven for one hour. Serve with sauce and add one can mushrooms. Cut in squares and serve.

SAUCE: Milk gravy and mushrooms.

Louise M. Kipp (Edwardsville)

HUNTINGTON CHICKEN

1 4-pound chicken
2 cups shell macaroni
½ pound cheese, diced
4 cups chicken broth

8 tablespoons flour
2 tablespoons butter
1½ cups dry bread crumbs

Cook chicken, bone and dice. Cook macaroni in salted water and drain. Add flour to broth and cook until thickened. Add cheese, macaroni and chicken. Pour into greased 8x12-inch pan. Heat crumbs in butter and spread over top. Bake at 325° F. 30 minutes. Cut in squares and serve hot. Serves 12.

Martha Blom (Alhambra)

OVEN BARBECUED CHICKEN

1 cut-up frying chicken
⅓ cup chopped onion
1 small clove garlic, minced
2 tablespoons salad oil
1 can (10¾-ounce) tomato
   soup

2 tablespoons brown sugar
1 tablespoon vinegar
1 tablespoon Worcestershire
   sauce
½ teaspoon prepared mustard
Dash of hot pepper sauce

Preheat oven at 375° F. In a 2-quart saucepan cook onion and garlic in oil until tender. Add remaining ingredients (except chicken). Simmer 15 minutes. Place chicken, skin down in a 9x13x2-inch pan. Spread half the sauce on chicken. Bake for 30 minutes, then turn chicken and spread the remaining sauce. Bake 30 more minutes or until done. Remove chicken, spoon off fat. Thin sauce if desired with water, then serve with chicken.

Ella Bentrup (Staunton)

CHICKEN WITH RICE

1 envelope dehydrated onion
   soup mix
¾ cup rice (½ white, ½ wild)
2½ pounds chicken parts
   (thighs, legs and breasts)

1 10½-ounce can cream of
   chicken soup
½ soup can of milk
½ soup can of water

Sprinkle dry soup in the bottom of an ungreased 9x13-inch ovenproof glass baking dish. Wash rice and place in a layer on top of soup. Salt chicken lightly and place in a single layer on top of rice. Mix chicken soup with milk and water. Pour over chicken and bake uncovered, 325° F. for 2 hours. Watch carefully toward the end and add water, if needed. If chicken is getting too brown, cover pan with foil. Makes 6-8 servings. NOTE: All breasts may be used instead of chicken parts. This is a good dinner for parties. Very little work with just a salad, rolls and dessert to complete the meal.

Ruth Keller (Edwardsville)

OVEN FRIED CHICKEN PARMESAN

½ cup grated Parmesan
  cheese
¼ cup flour
1 teaspoon paprika
½ teaspoon salt
Dash pepper

2½ to 3 pound broiler-fryer,
  cut up
1 egg, slightly beaten
1 tablespoon milk
¼ cup melted margarine

Combine cheese, flour and seasoning. Dip chicken in combined egg and milk, coat with cheese mixture. Place in baking dish, pour margarine over chicken and bake at 350° F. one hour or until tender. Makes 3 to 4 servings.

Ruth Keller (Edwardsville)

TURKEY HASH

¼ cup chopped green pepper
¼ cup chopped celery
¼ cup chopped onion
3 tablespoons margarine
2 cups cooked turkey, cut up
3 cups turkey gravy (or plain
  gravy made with water)

1 teaspoon Poultry seasoning
2 tablespoons grated Cheddar
  cheese (sharp, medium or
  mild to suit taste)
2 hard cooked eggs, chopped
Chow Mein noodles, optional

Sauté peppers, celery and chopped onions in margarine. Add cut up, cooked turkey, gravy and poultry seasoning. Heat, then simmer to get fullest flavor. Cheese and eggs can be added in last minute of heating or can be saved as garnish.

OPTIONAL: Some cheese can be added during cooking and more for garnish. If additional salt is needed, use seasoned salt for added flavor. Serve over Chow Mein noodles.

Irma Henkhaus (Alhambra)

BARBECUED RABBIT

1 teaspoon salt
⅛ teaspoon pepper
½ cup catsup
½ cup water
1 tablespoon vinegar

1 tablespoon brown sugar
2 tablespoons Worcestershire
   sauce
½ teaspoon salt
1 medium onion

Brown rabbit in lard. Pour off drippings. Season with one teaspoon salt and pepper. Mix together remaining ingredients and add to rabbit. Cover tightly and bake in oven until nice and tender. Bake in 350° F. oven.

Lorene Genczo (New Douglas)

FISH FILLETS

2 pounds frozen cod or
  halibut fillets
1 cup chicken broth
¼ cup lemon juice
1 bay leaf, crumbled
1 clove garlic, minced
1 tablespoon grated onion
½ teaspoon salt

¼ teaspoon thyme
4-6 onion slices
4-6 tomato slices
¼ cup cornflake crumbs
2 tablespoons grated
  Parmesan cheese
3 tablespoons butter

Cut frozen fish into 4-6 portions. Put in shallow buttered casserole. Mix above ingredients and pour over fish. Let stand until fish thaws, spooning sauce over fish occasionally. When ready to bake, top each fish with onion and tomato slices. Sprinkle over top, a mixture of crumbs and cheese; dot with butter. Bake at 350° F. for 25-30 minutes or until fish flakes easily and topping is golden brown. Serve with sauce from pan.

Edna Suessen (Edwardsville)

POACHED FISH

2 1-pound blocks frozen cod,
  haddock or perch
1 tablespoon butter or
  margarine
½ cup canned tomatoes or
  1 fresh tomato, sliced

1 teaspoon salt
1 onion, sliced
1 green pepper, sliced in
  strips

Melt butter in heavy skillet. Place frozen fish blocks in skillet; sprinkle with salt. Layer tomatoes, onions and peppers over fish blocks. Cover tightly. Simmer until fish flakes easily with fork, about 25 minutes. Lift out of skillet onto platter, leaving any juice in skillet. Cut into 6 servings.

Kay Losch (East Alton)

SCALLOPED OYSTERS

1 pint oysters
2 cups coarse cracker crumbs
⅛ teaspoon pepper
½ teaspoon salt
1 cup milk

½ cup melted butter or
  margarine
¼ teaspoon Worcestershire
  sauce

Drain oysters. Combine cracker crumbs, salt, pepper and melted butter. Butter a 1½-quart casserole, then sprinkle ⅓ of cracker mixture in, followed by a layer of oysters; repeat layers, ending with cracker mixture. Add Worcestershire sauce to milk and pour over the top. Bake at 375° F for 30 minutes. Yield: 6 servings.

Kay Losch (East Alton)

SEAFOOD SHELLS

1 can crabmeat
1 can shrimp
1 cup celery, cut fine
1 medium onion, grated
1 medium green pepper, cut
  fine

½ teaspoon salt
¼ teaspoon pepper
1 cup mayonnaise
1 can mushrooms
1 cup buttered crumbs

Mix together and put in sea shells, or individual casseroles; put crumbs on top. Bake in oven at 350° F. for 30 minutes. Serves six.

Virginia Herrmann (Edwardsville)

SHRIMP TOWERS

4 hamburger buns, split and
  toasted
2 tomato slices
32 shrimp, cleaned and
  cooked

Bacos product
8 slices process Cheddar
  cheese

Spread cut sides of buns with butter. Top each bun half with remaining ingredients in order listed. Set oven control at broil and/or 550° F. Place sandwiches on rack in broiler pan. Broil 5 or 6 inches from heat for 2 to 3 minutes or until cheese is melted and bubbly. Makes 8 open faced sandwiches.

Louise Eckert (Collinsville)

SEVEN SEAS CASSEROLE

1 can cream of mushroom or
   celery soup
1¼ cups water or milk
¼ teaspoon salt
Dash pepper
1⅓ cups minute rice,
   uncooked

1 can tuna, drained
1 box frozen peas or 1 can
   peas
Cheese slices

Mix soup, water or milk, salt and pepper in saucepan. Bring to boil. Put ½ the soup mixture in a 2-quart casserole, layer with rice, tuna and peas. Pour on rest of soup mixture and top with your favorite cheese slices. Cover and bake for 20 minutes in a 375° F. oven.

Cheryll Sievers (Staunton)

SIMPLE TUNA HOT DISH

½ cup uncooked rice
1 12-ounce can tuna
1 10¾-ounce can cream of
   mushroom soup

1 cup milk
Velveeta cheese to taste

Combine all ingredients and place in a 2½-quart casserole dish. Bake for 1 hour at 350° F. Yields five servings.

Carol Roseberry (Alton)

TUNA CASSEROLE

½ cup chopped celery
1½ cups chopped onion
1 cup tuna fish

1 cup mushroom soup
1 cup cashew nuts
1 cup chow mein noodles

Mix celery, onions, tuna, soup and nuts together and put into a baking dish. Sprinkle with chow mein noodles. Bake for 25 minutes (or less) at 350° F.

VARIATION: 1 can of chicken, or 1 can of turkey may be substituted for tuna.

Jackie Thomas (Carlinville)

TUNA BOATS

1 12-ounce can tuna
2 tablespoons chopped
  pickles or relish
2 tablespoons chopped onion

3 hard boiled eggs
½ cup mayonnaise
¼ cup American cheese, diced

Combine all ingredients and place on a weiner bun; wrap in foil and bake in 350° F. oven for 15 minutes or until warm through.

Janice Bradley (Marine)

TUNA BURGERS

1 7-ounce can tuna
1 cup chopped celery
½ cup diced process yellow
  cheese (Velveeta)

1 small onion, minced
¼ cup mayonnaise
Salt and pepper to taste

Split and butter 6 hamburger buns. Fill buns with tuna mixture and replace tops. Heat in foil on baking sheet at 350° F. for 15 minutes.

Gracie Koeller (Godfrey)

BEEF, PORK, POULTRY AND SEAFOODS

BEEF, PORK, POULTRY AND SEAFOODS

BEEF, PORK, POULTRY AND SEAFOODS

HOW MEN COOK

Southern Illinois University-Edwardsville campus is nestled on
a 2,600 acre campus. Madison County residents secured this
branch from Carbondale in the late 1950's.

UNCLE BUD'S ONION-BEEF CHEESE BALL

2 8-ounce packages cream
  cheese
2 6-ounce packages chipped,
  dried beef or smoked beef

2 bunches green onions
½ teaspoon garlic salt
2 teaspoons Worcestershire
  sauce

Cream garlic salt and Worcestershire sauce into cream cheese. Chop onion, keep white and green tops separate. Chop beef. Add white of onion and beef to cream cheese mixture. Form into a ball and roll in green tops. Serve with Wheat Thins or other crackers of your choice.

Gene Losch (East Alton)

SALAMI

2 pounds ground beef
2 tablespoons Morton tender
  quick salt
½ teaspoon mustard seed
½ teaspoon garlic powder

1 teaspoon marjoram
¼ teaspoon sage
1 teaspoon black pepper
1 cup water

Mix all ingredients well. Wrap in foil and twist each end. Put in refrigerator for 3 days. Punch holes in foil, cover with water. Cook on top of stove for one hour and 10 minutes.

Leslie J. Cooper (Dorsey)

CHICKEN PARMESAN

½ cup butter
1 broiler-fryer (about 2½ to
  3 pounds), cut up
¾ cup grated Parmesan
  cheese
⅓ cup cracker crumbs

1 teaspoon parsley flakes,
  finely crushed
1 teaspoon onion powder
½ teaspoon salt
⅛ teaspoon white pepper
Paprika

Place butter in a 2-quart bowl. Microwave on HIGH for 1 to 2 minutes or until melted. Rinse chicken pieces and pat dry. Dip in melted butter. Combine remaining ingredients except paprika. Roll each chicken piece in the combined mixture. Arrange skin side up with the thickest meaty pieces to the edges of a 12x8 inch dish. Sprinkle with paprika. Microwave uncovered on HIGH for 18 to 20 minutes until meat is tender. Let stand covered for 5 minutes before serving. Makes 4 servings.

Frank R. Thomas (Carlinville)

MAKE AHEAD SALAD

½ head lettuce, chopped
1 small head cauliflower
½ pound bacon, fried crisp

1 small onion, chopped
⅓ cup Parmesan cheese
½ cup mayonnaise

In a large bowl, layer ingredients in order given. Cover and let sit in refrigerator 3 hours to overnight. Toss before serving.

Don Mancell

TONI'S ITALIAN SALAD DRESSING

2 cups red wine vinegar
2 tablespoons oregano
2 tablespoons salt
1 tablespoon ground black
  pepper

3 tablespoons dehydrated
  garlic
6 cups olive oil
7 cups Arcola oil

Put all ingredients in a gallon jar and shake well to mix. Keep chilled in refrigerator until used. Use over tossed lettuce salad, sprinkled with celery seed. Garnish salad with black olives, sliced egg, pepperacini and tomato. Serve with bread sticks.

Fred Losch (East Alton)

HAMBURGER SOUP

1 pound ground beef
1 can vegetable soup

1 tablespoon Worcestershire
  sauce

Mix all ingredients together and cook about 1 hour, until meat seems thoroughly cooked. Makes generous serving for 2.

Chet Sommers (Godfrey)

FRANK'S CHILI

1 pound ground beef
2 medium onions
2 tablespoons fat
2 teaspoons salt

⅛ teaspoon pepper
2 tablespoons chili powder
1 #2-can tomatoes
1 #2-can red kidney beans

Cook onions and beef in fat until brown. Add seasonings and tomatoes. Simmer for one hour. Add kidney beans and simmer five minutes. Serves 6.

Frank R. Thomas (Carlinville)

CHILI

1½ pounds ground chuck
2 31-ounce cans Brooks chili
  beans
1 quart tomatoes
1 6-ounce can tomato paste

1 large onion
2 tablespoons margarine
2 tablespoons chili powder
1 can beer
1 teaspoon salt

Cook onion until transparent in margarine. Add ground chuck and cook until brown. Stir in tomatoes, tomato paste, chili powder, beer and salt and cook 15 minutes. Then add chili beans and cook 45 minutes more.

Harold Price (Granite City)

BEER BATTER FISH

Fish fillets (enough for meal)
Salt
Pepper

Pancake mix, Hungry Jack—
  extra light
1 12-ounce can beer

Use enough pancake mix with the can of beer to make a batter that doesn't coat the fish too heavy but still does not run off the fish when dipped into it. Salt and pepper each fish to taste. Dip into batter and then into hot oil that has reached temperature of 375° F. Fry until brown on one side then turn over and brown other side. Remove to platter and eat.

Harold Price (Granite City)

HUSHPUPPIES

1½ cups cornmeal
¾ cup flour
2 teaspoons baking powder
1 tablespoon sugar
1 teaspoon salt
½ teaspoon pepper

¼ teaspoon onion powder
1 small onion, chopped
6 onion tops, chopped
1 egg
¾ cup milk

Use deep fryer for this recipe, heat oil to 350° F. Mix egg and milk together and set aside. Sift all dry ingredients together and mix. Add all onions and continue mixing. Add egg and milk mixture and blend well. Shape into oblong balls about 1½ to 2 inches long and ½ to 1 inch thick. Fry in hot oil until they float and are a light golden brown.

Bob Schrumpf (Highland)

BARBECUED BEANS

1 pound ground beef
½ cup chopped onion
½ teaspoon salt
¼ teaspoon pepper
1 1-pound-12-ounce can pork
and beans

½ cup catsup
1 tablespoon Worcestershire
sauce
1 tablespoon vinegar
2 tablespoons brown sugar

Brown beef and onions. Drain off fat. Add remaining ingredients and mix well. Pour into a 1½ quart casserole. Bake at 350° F. for 40 minutes. Serves 6. NOTE: I use hickory flavored catsup and Country Style pork and beans for improved flavor.

Frank R. Thomas (Carlinville)

ITALIAN DELUXE MOSCOTOLLI

1 1-pound box moscotolli
2 pounds hamburger
3 medium onions
1 large stalk celery
2 cloves garlic
1 grated carrot
1 tablespoon Worcestershire
sauce
3-5 tablespoons Italian
seasoning

4-5 tablespoons sugar
1 16-ounce can tomatoes
1 4-ounce can mushrooms
1 6-ounce can tomato paste
1 15-ounce can tomato sauce
6-7 tablespoons cooking oil
Salt and pepper to taste
8-10 slices American cheese
1 3-ounce can Parmesan
cheese

Preheat oven to 350° F. Brown hamburger in separate skillet and drain off excess grease. Cut up fine, onions, garlic, celery and carrot. Add 3-4 tablespoons of cooking oil and sauté slowly. Add ½ cup of water if needed. Add hamburger, tomato sauce, tomato paste, diced whole tomatoes, mushrooms, sugar, Worcestershire sauce, Italian seasoning and salt and pepper to taste. Simmer 1 hour. Add 6-8 ounces of water if needed. Cook moscotolli per package instructions. (Approximately 12 minutes. *DON'T* over cook.) Oil a 12x14 inch casserole with cooking oil, then add moscotolli, sauce, Parmesan cheese and cut up American cheese. Bake in moderate oven for 30 minutes at 350° F. Uncover and cook for an additional 10 minutes. Serve with salad and Italian bread. NOTE: This recipe won a $50.00 prize in a contest that this young man entered.

Victor H. Daiber (Marine)

TONI'S SPAGHETTI SAUCE

5 pounds beef neck bones
1 #10 can tomato paste
1 #10 can tomato puree
½ cup olive oil
1 large onion
4 tablespoons sugar
1 tablespoon cracked pepper
2 tablespoons salt

2 teaspoons dried garlic
2 tablespoons dried sweet
  basil
2 tablespoons Parmesan
  cheese
1 large bay leaf
½ cup red wine

Bake beef neckbones until brown at 375° F. Mix all ingredients together in a pan that holds at least 3 gallons. Bring to boil, then simmer 3 to 4 hours. Strain. Meat can be picked off and used in spaghetti sauce. Yield 6 quarts. This sauce may be divided in small amounts and frozen. Serve over cooked spaghetti or any other cooked pasta.

Fred Losch (East Alton)

TONI'S BEEF MEAT BALLS

10 pounds ground chuck
4 cups bread crumbs
2 tablespoons salt
2 tablespoons black pepper

2 tablespoons dried parsley
4 eggs
2 teaspoons dehydrated garlic
2 cups water

Mix all ingredients together well. Make into meatballs about the size of a walnut. Bake in 350° F. oven for 35 minutes. Drain drippings off and heat meatballs in Toni's spaghetti sauce to be served over pasta. Makes about 120 meatballs. Serves 30 to 40 people.

Fred Losch (East Alton)

TONI'S PORK MEAT BALLS

10 pounds pork butt, ground
4 cups bread crumbs
2 tablespoons black pepper
1 tablespoon fennel
1 tablespoon mustard seed

½ teaspoon nutmeg
1 teaspoon poultry seasoning
Pinch red pepper
2 cups water

Mix all ingredients together well. Make into meatballs about the size of a walnut. Bake in oven at 350° F. for 45 minutes. Drain drippings off and heat meatballs in Toni's spaghetti sauce to serve over pasta. Should serve 30 to 40 people. Makes about 120 meatballs.

Fred Losch (East Alton)

COTTAGE CHEESE BREAD

1 package dry yeast
½ cup lukewarm water
1 cup small curd cottage
 cheese
¼ cup shortening
2 tablespoons sugar

1 teaspoon salt
1 tablespoon dill
1 tablespoon onion, minced
¼ teaspoon baking soda
1 egg, beaten
2½ cups flour (approximately)

Dissolve yeast in water. Combine cottage cheese, shortening, sugar, salt, dill, onion, and soda. Beat well. Add yeast, egg and enough flour to make a stiff dough. Cover, let rise until double. Punch down and let rest for 15 minutes. Shape into a loaf and place in a 9x5x3 inch loaf pan. Let rise until double again. Bake for 50 minutes at 350° F.

Frank R. Thomas (Carlinville)

MY DAD'S BREAD PUDDING

3 cups soft bread crumbs
2 cups scalded milk
¼ cup butter
½ cup sugar
2 eggs, slightly beaten

¼ teaspoon salt
1 teaspoon cinnamon or
 nutmeg
½ cup seedless raisins

Put bread crumbs in 1½ quart baking dish. Blend in remaining ingredients. Put the baking dish in a pan of hot water 1 inch deep. Bake at 350° F. for 40 to 45 minutes or until knife comes out clean when inserted in middle. Makes 6-8 servings. Serve warm.

Melvin Paul (Worden)

CHERRY DESSERT

2 cups flour
1 teaspoon salt
2 tablespoons sugar
1 cup shortening

1 egg, separated
⅔ cup milk
2 cans cherry pie filling

Mix together flour, salt, sugar, shortening, egg yolk and milk. Roll out half of dough and put in jelly roll pan. Cover with cherry pie filling. Dot with butter and cover with other half of dough. If dough comes apart just pinch together. Brush with slightly beaten egg white. Bake 375° F. for 35 minutes. After removing from oven put on glaze of powdered sugar and milk.

Rodney Keck (St. Jacob)

CHEESE CAKE SQUARES

⅓ cup butter
⅓ cup brown sugar
1 cup flour
½ cup chopped nuts
8 ounces cream cheese

¼ cup sugar
1 egg
1 tablespoon lemon juice
2 tablespoons milk
½ teaspoon vanilla

Cream together butter and brown sugar, add flour and nuts. Blend together and set aside one cup for topping. Press remainder into 8 inch square baking pan. Bake 350° F. for 12 minutes. Beat cream cheese, sugar, egg, lemon juice, milk, vanilla and spread over crust. Sprinkle with cup of reserved crumbs. Bake at 350° F. for 25 minutes. Cool and cut in squares.

Ralph Keck (St. Jacob)

CHILDRENS

Built in 1854, the Godfrey Memorial Chapel speaks of the New England background of the builder. Photographs of the church are preserved in the Library of Congress.

AUNT HELEN'S CHEESE BALL

2 8-ounce packages cream
  cheese, softened
2 tablespoons grated
  Parmesan cheese

¾ tablespoon Blue cheese
¼ cup milk
½ tablespoon garlic salt
½ cup pecan pieces

Mix all the above ingredients, except nuts, with electric mixer until well blended. Shape into a ball. Chill overnight and pat the pecan pieces around the cheese ball. Serve with crackers of your choice.

Constance Paul (Worden)

SNACK PARTY SANDWICH

3 pounds Velveeta cheese
2 pounds pork sausage
2 pounds ground beef

2 teaspoons oregano
Party rye bread
Mozzarella cheese

Mix together Velveeta cheese, sausage, ground beef and oregano and fry. Spread mixture on party rye bread and top with mozzarella cheese. Put in oven long enough to melt cheese. Serve as snacks or can be frozen for further use.

Brian Keck (St. Jacob)

SAUSAGE-BEAN SOUP

¼ pound bacon, chopped
½ pound Italian sausage,
  chopped
2 onions, chopped
1 pound can tomatoes,
  chopped
½ cup rice
½ cup dried beans, soaked or
  1 pound can Pinto beans

½ cup celery, chopped
1 cup carrots diced
6 cups meat stock
¼ head cabbage, shredded
1½ teaspoons salt
¼ teaspoon pepper

Fry bacon and sausage together until lightly browned. Add onion, tomatoes, rice, soaked beans, celery, carrots and stock. Simmer until beans are tender. Skim off fat frequently. Add shredded cabbage, seasonings and simmer until soup is thick and vegetables are soft. Serves 6.

Linda Gass (Granite City)

BUTTER DIPS

¼ cup butter
1¼ cups flour
⅔ cup milk

2 teaspoons sugar
2 teaspoons baking powder
1 teaspoon salt

Melt butter in baking pan in oven. Mix flour, milk, sugar, baking powder and salt to a soft dough in bowl with a fork. Gently smooth the dough into a ball on a covered pastry board. Knead ten times. Roll the dough into an eight inch square. Cut the square in half, then cut each half crosswise into nine strips. (Dip the knife in flour to keep the dough from sticking.) Dip each strip into the melted butter, turning to coat completely. Arrange the strips close together in two rows in the pan. Bake 15-20 minutes or until golden brown. If using self-rising flour, omit the baking powder and the salt.

Constance Paul (Worden)

HOT DOG CHEESIES

2 cups boiling water
8 frankfurters
8 slices bread
Soft butter

Prepared mustard
8 slices American cheese
¼ cup butter

Drop frankfurters into boiling water and lower heat; cover and simmer 5 to 8 minutes. Spread one side of bread with butter and prepared mustard. Place on baking sheet. Top each slice with American cheese and a frankfurter. Fold over to make a triangle shape. Fasten with wooden picks. Melt butter in small pan over low heat. Brush each triangle with the butter. Set oven at broil. Broil sandwiches with tops 4 to 5 inches from heat for about 2 minutes or until golden brown. Makes 8 servings.

Louise Eckert (Collinsville)

AUNT DOROTHY'S ONION DIP

1 16-ounce carton sour cream
1 package onion soup mix

¼-½ cup milk

Mix the sour cream and onion soup mix together until well blended. Add enough milk to make the dip creamy and easy to dip chip into. Use as a dip or use it with baked potatoes.

Scott Paul (Worden)

CHEESE DREAMS

3 English muffins, cut in half
Soft butter

6 slices bacon, cut in half

Set oven at broil and/or 550° F. Place muffin halves, which have been spread with soft butter, and bacon slices on rack in broiler pan. Broil with tops of muffins 3 inches from heat until bacon is light brown, about 2 minutes. Remove muffins and turn bacon over. Broil bacon 1 minute longer.

Top each muffin with:

1 thick tomato slice
2 pieces bacon

2 thin slices process
American Cheese

Return muffins to broiler. Broil about 1 minute or until cheese is melted. Serve at once. Makes 6 servings.

Louise Eckert (Collinsville)

CORN FRITTERS

1⅓ cups flour
1½ teaspoon baking powder
¾ teaspoon salt
1 tablespoon sugar

⅔ cup milk
1 egg
1 small can drained corn or
fresh sweet corn

Mix together and spoon onto griddle or waffle iron. May use pancake and waffle mix if you are in hurry.

Darla Sievers (Staunton)

NOODLE CASSEROLE

1 pound ground beef
1 small onion, chopped
1 tablespoon shortening
1 10-ounce can celery or
mushroom soup
2 eggs

¼ cup milk
¼ cup grated cheese
(Velveeta)
1 10-ounce package egg
noodles

Fry ground beef, onion and shortening. In bowl, mix soup, eggs, milk, cheese and cooked noodles. Add ground beef mixture. Place in greased baking dish. Lay some Velveeta cheese on top. Bake at 350° F. for 30 minutes.

Michael Keck (St. Jacob)

TOMATO-MEAT SAUCE
(Spaghetti Sauce)

1 small onion	1 cup finely cut-up canned or
1 tablespoon fat or oil	cooked beef or pork
1 cup canned or cooked	1 teaspoon Worcestershire
tomatoes	sauce

Chop onion and cook in fat or oil in a skillet until tender and lightly browned. Stir in remaining ingredients. Cook over low heat about 30 minutes to blend flavors. Add a little water during cooking, if needed. Makes two servings about ½ cup each. Serve over hot cooked spaghetti or macaroni or rice.

Linda Bauer (Granite City)

PIZZA WITH A HAMBURGER CRUST

Heat oven to 425° F.
Mix with spoon in a large bowl:

1 pound ground beef	1 teaspoon salt
½ cup dry bread crumbs	½ teaspoon oregano

Stir in:

½ cup tomato sauce*

Spread meat mixture in ungreased 10-inch pizza pan or on the bottom and side of 10-inch tube pan.

Pour on top:

½ cup tomato sauce*

Spread on tomato sauce:

1 8-ounce can kidney beans, drained

Cut into strips:

3 slices Cheddar or Mozzarella cheese

Arrange cheese strips in criss-cross design on beans. Bake uncovered 20 minutes. Makes 4 servings.
*You will need 1 8-ounce can tomato sauce.

Louise Eckert (Collinsville)

250

MINI PIZZA

English muffins, hamburger
   buns or thick sliced bread

Pizza Quick or Pizza Magic
Mozzarella cheese

Spread pizza sauce on one of the kinds of bread. Sprinkle cheese on top. Bake at 350° F. for 10 to 12 minutes or until cheese is melted. (My grandma's stove lights automatically. If yours doesn't, have someone do it for you. I love making this as an after school snack.)

Camille Merkle (Alhambra)

CARAMEL NUT ROLLS

¼ cup butter, melted
¾ cup brown sugar
⅓ cup water
½ cup chopped nuts

2 cans refrigerator
   biscuits (20)
½ teaspoon cinnamon

Combine butter, brown sugar and water in Pyrex pie pan or round Pyrex cake pan. Stir on low heat until blended. Sprinkle in nuts, and cinnamon. Arrange biscuits overlapping. Bake at 400° F. until golden brown. Remove and let set 5 minutes, then place plate over pan and turn upside down. Serve warm.

Dana Sievers (Staunton)

FUNNEL CAKES

2 eggs, beaten
1½ cups milk
2 cups all-purpose flour,
   sifted

1 teaspoon baking powder
½ teaspoon salt
2 cups cooking oil

Combine eggs and milk. Sift together flour, baking powder and salt. Add egg mixture; beat smooth with rotary beater. (Test mixture through funnel. If too thick, add milk; if too thin, add flour.) In skillet, heat cooking oil to 360° F. Cover funnel opening with finger; and pour in ½ cup batter. Remove finger and release batter into hot oil in a spiral shape. Fry until golden brown, about 3 minutes. Using spatula and tongs, turn cake carefully. Cook 1 minute more. Drain on paper towel; sprinkle with sifted confectioners' sugar. Serve hot. Makes 4 cakes.

Darla Sievers (Staunton)

CHERRY CHEESE CAKE

CRUST:

3 cups graham cracker   ½ cup butter, melted
  crumbs

Mix graham cracker crumbs and melted butter together. Put all crumbs on the bottom of a 9x13x2 inch pan, except 4 tablespoons, which you sprinkle on the top of the cheese cake when it is done.

FILLING:

1½ cups powdered sugar
2 8-ounce packages cream
  cheese, softened
2 packages Dream Whip,
  made according to
  directions on the package

1 21-ounce can cherry pie
  filling
4-6 tablespoons lemon juice
  (optional)

Mix powdered sugar and softened cream cheese with a mixer on low speed until blended. Slowly blend in the whipped Dream Whip. Mix in the lemon juice. Pour mixture into a pan and let set in the refrigerator until firm. Spread the cherry pie filling on the top and the cracker crumbs.

Scott Paul (Worden)

CHEESE COOKIES

1 8-ounce package cream
  cheese, softened
2 sticks butter

2 cups flour
Jam, your favorite kind

Blend the cream cheese, butter, flour and chill this mixture in the refrigerator for at least 4 to 5 hours. Roll out the mixture and cut into 2 inch squares. Put a teaspoon of jam in the center of each cookie. Fold corners into the center and press all the edges together tightly. Bake in the oven at 350° F. for 15 to 18 minutes.

Constance Paul (Worden)

CHOCOLATE ICE CREAM

1 can Eagle Brand
  Condensed Milk
⅓ cup Hershey's Chocolate
  Syrup

2 cups Cool Whip

Mix milk and chocolate syrup together in a large bowl. Then add Cool Whip and mix together. Put into a foil lined loaf pan and freeze.

Linda Bauer (Granite City)

CHURCH WINDOW COOKIES

1 12-ounce package chocolate
  chips
1 10-ounce package colored
  miniature marshmallows

Flaked coconut (optional)
1-2 cups chopped pecans
½ cup margarine

Melt chocolate and margarine. Cool. Stir in nuts and marshmallows. Sprinkle coconut on large pieces of waxed paper. Spoon stiff batter in a log form and press into a roll. Makes two log forms; wrap and refrigerate. When thoroughly cooled, slice.

Dana Brase (Worden)

GRAHAM CRACKER BROWNIES

3 eggs
1 cup brown sugar
1 cup granulated sugar

1 cup chopped nuts
28 crushed graham crackers

Beat eggs, add sugar, beat well. Add crushed graham crackers and nuts. Pour into greased and floured oblong pan. Bake at 350° F. for 20 minutes. Cut into squares while warm.

Karen Mueller (East Alton)

EGG NOG

¾ cup milk
1 egg beaten
2 teaspoons sugar

½ teaspoon vanilla
⅛ teaspoon nutmeg
Pinch of salt

Blend all ingredients in blender. Makes 1 cup.

Dana Brase (Worden)

PEANUT BUTTER BALLS

1 pound creamy peanut
  butter
2½ cups Rice Krispies
1 stick butter or margarine

1 pound powdered sugar
1 pound chocolate chips
¼ pound paraffin

Mix the first 4 ingredients together by hand and shape into round balls. Melt in top of double boiler, the chocolate chips and paraffin. Dip balls into chocolate and put on wax paper to cool.

Scott Paul (Worden)

PEANUT BUTTER KISSES

2 cups dry milk
1 cup peanut butter

½ cup honey
¼ cup coconut, shredded

In a 2 quart bowl, mix dry milk, peanut butter and honey. Roll dough into balls. Roll the balls in coconut. Makes 24 kisses.

Constance Paul (Worden)

EASY PUDDING MILK SHAKE

4 cups cold milk
1 3½-ounce package Jello
  instant pudding, any flavor

4 scoops ice cream, any flavor

Pour 2 cups milk in bowl or 2 quart shaker. Add pudding mix. Beat slowly with beater until blended, about 2 minutes or shake vigorously until blended about 30 seconds. Add remaining milk and ice cream. Beat or shake until thoroughly mixed. Serve at once. Makes 6 servings.

Kevin Meyer (Staunton)

FROZEN PUDDING TREATS

1 package instant pudding,
  any flavor

2 cups cold milk

Combine pudding mix and milk in bowl. Beat slowly until well blended about 2 minutes. Pour into six, 5-ounce paper cups. Insert wooden stick down into pudding. Press a square of foil or waxed paper down onto pudding to cover, piercing center of foil with handle. Freeze until firm, at least 5 hours. Press firmly on bottom to release pop. Yield: 6 pops.

Kevin Meyer (Staunton)

DOUBLE DECKER PEACH SURPRISE

1 package pie crust sticks
2 tablespoons water
1 tablespoon granulated
  sugar
½ teaspoon cinnamon

1 29-ounce can sliced peaches
½ cup chilled whipping cream
2 tablespoons powdered
  nutmeg

Heat oven to 475° F. Take out 1 pie crust stick. (Save remaining for another time.) Prepare pastry for one-crust pie as directed on package except do not roll out. Divide the pastry into 8 equal parts. Shape each into a ball. Pat each ball into a 3½ inch circle on ungreased cookie sheet. Prick each pastry circle with a fork at ½ inch intervals, making holes big enough so they won't close up when you bake the circles. Mix 1 tablespoon granulated sugar and ½ teaspoon cinnamon in custard cup or small dish. Sprinkle the pastry circles with the sugar-cinnamon mixture. Bake in 475° F. oven for 7 minutes or until light brown. Lift circles to rack with pancake turner. You can make these ahead to save time. Beat the whipping cream and powdered sugar in a chilled bowl. Place 1 baked circle on each of 4 dessert plates. Spoon some whipped cream mixture and some peaches onto each. Cover with remaining circles and top with the rest of the whipped cream and peaches. Sprinkle with nutmeg.

VARIATIONS: You can use cherry, peach, apple or your favorite pie filling in place of the peaches. You may also use pudding in place of the fruit.

Scott M. Paul (Worden)

FROZEN POPS

1 package 3 ounce Jell-O
  gelatin, any flavor
1 envelope Kool-Aid Instant
  soft drink mix, any flavor

1 cup sugar
2 cups boiling water
2 cups cold water

Dissolve Jell-O gelatin, instant soft drink mix, and sugar in boiling water. Add cold water. Pour into ice cube trays, small paper cups, or frozen pop molds. Insert wooden sticks diagonally in each ice cube section for handles. If desired, pops may be partially frozen before handles are inserted. Freeze until firm about 2 to 3 hours. Makes about 20 to 24 pops.

Dawn Brase (Edwardsville)

POPCORN BALLS

2 cups uncooked popcorn
2 cups white Karo Syrup
1 cup sugar

1 tablespoon vinegar
½ stick butter
Pinch of baking soda

Pop 2 cups uncooked popcorn. Mix together the syrup, sugar, vinegar, and butter in saucepan. Bring to a boil; (soft ball stage). After it reaches the soft ball stage, add a pinch of baking soda. Pour over popcorn and stir to cover all popcorn. Use cold wet hands to form balls.

Dawn Brase (Edwardsville)

PUDDING-WICHES

1½ cups cold milk
½ cup creamy peanut
butter

1 3-ounce package instant
pudding mix
24 graham crackers

Add milk gradually to peanut butter, in a deep, narrow-bottom bowl, blending until smooth. Add pudding mix. Beat slowly with hand beater or at lowest speed of electric mixer until well blended, about 2 minutes. Let stand 5 minutes. Spread filling ½ inch thick on 12 of the graham crackers. Top with remaining crackers. Freeze until firm, about 3 hours. Makes 12 Pudding-wiches.

Karen Mueller (East Alton)

ROASTED PUMPKIN SEEDS

2 cups pumpkin seeds,
unwashed
1½ tablespoons melted butter
or oil

1¼ teaspoons salt

Don't throw away your pumpkin seeds. Separate seeds from pumpkin fiber, but do not wash. Mix seeds, butter and salt and mix thoroughly. Spread seeds in single layer over bottom of shallow pan and bake at 250° F. until crisp and brown.

Dana Sievers (Staunton)

RICH CHOCOLATE SHAKE

5 spoonsful vanilla ice cream   ½ cup milk
2 tablespoons chocolate syrup

Place about 5 big spoonsful of vanilla ice cream in a shaker or jar. Add chocolate syrup to ice cream in jar. Mix a bit with spoon. Add the milk. Cover shaker or jar tightly with lid; shake hard. Pour in glass. This makes 1 milk shake. (For a vanilla shake, omit the chocolate syrup.)

Dawn Brase (Edwardsville)

FAST AND FABULOUS FRUIT

1 20-ounce can crushed   1 cup Cool Whip
   pineapple and juice
1 4-ounce package instant
   vanilla pudding

Reserve small amount of drained fruit for garnish, if desired. Combine pudding mix and rest of fruit and juice in bowl. Blend in Cool Whip. Garnish with reserved fruit. Yield: 6 servings.

Kimberly Meyer (Staunton)

YELLOW CAKE

1½ cups sugar   2 cups flour
½ cup butter   1 cup milk
2 teaspoons baking powder   1 teaspoon vanilla
¼ teaspoon salt   2 eggs

Mix all ingredients well. Pour into 9x13x2 inch greased and floured pan. Bake at 350°F for 30 to 35 minutes.

Dana Brase (Worden)

PLAY MODELING CLAY

2 cups flour   Few drops of oil
1 cup salt   Food coloring
¾ to 1 cup water

Mix together and separate into several balls, then add a different food color to each.

Debra Sievers (Staunton)

CHILLDRENS

LEISURE COOKING

Nestled on the Pleasant Ridge Road, Collinsville Township, is this quaint Lutheran Church. Glistening as new fallen snow is an E.V. Lutheran Church bearing this inscribed information "St. Johannes Kirche VAC 1859." The German heritage is given away by this inscription.

CHOCOLATE CANDY CLUSTERS

1 6-ounce package milk
  chocolate morsels
1 12-ounce package
  butterscotch chips

1 8-ounce package Spanish
  peanuts

Put butterscotch and chocolate chips in big Pyrex bowl for 7 minutes on Low or 60% in microwave. Then add peanuts and drop by teaspoon on wax paper and let cool. Then you have chocolate covered peanuts like you buy in the store, delicious.

VARIATION: You can add coconut, raisins, cashews, Rice Krispies, or split it up and use half nuts and other half raisins.

Kathy Erspamer (Edwardsville)

QUICK MICROWAVE FUDGE

1 pound powdered sugar
½ cup cocoa
¼ cup milk

¼ pound butter or margarine
1 tablespoon vanilla
½ cup chopped nuts, walnuts

In a large mixing bowl, combine and blend sugar and cocoa. Add milk and margarine. (Do not stir.) Cook with Hi-power 2 minutes. Remove from oven and stir just to combine ingredients. Add vanilla and nuts. Stir until blended. Pour into greased 8x8 inch pan. Refrigerate 1 hour. Cut into serving pieces.

Deborah I. Becker (Moro)

MICROWAVE PEANUT BRITTLE

½ cup light corn syrup
1 cup sugar
1 cup peanuts
1 teaspoon butter or
  margarine

1 teaspoon vanilla
1 teaspoon baking soda

Combine corn syrup and sugar in 1½ quart round microwave glass baking dish. Stir well. Microwave on High four minutes. Stir in nuts. Microwave again on High three to five minutes, until light brown. Stir in butter and vanilla, blending well. Microwave on High one to two minutes. Add soda and stir gently, just until light and foamy. Quickly pour onto lightly greased baking sheet. Cool, and break into small pieces and store in air-tight container.

Lorene Genczo (New Douglas)

BAKED APPLES

4 medium apples   Butter or margarine
¼ cup sugar

Core and slice thin circles of peel from top of each apple. Arrange apples in 9x2 inch round dish. Spoon 1 tablespoon sugar into each apple cavity and place small piece of butter on each apple. Cover with plastic wrap. Cook in Microwave oven, covered, on full power for 3 to 4 minutes or until apples are tender. Let stand few minutes before serving.

VARIATION: Apples may be filled with mincemeat, whole cranberry sauce or raisins and nuts.

Donna Price (Granite City)

SPICED PEACHES

2 large cans peach halves   1 teaspoon whole cloves
2 tablespoons cider vinegar   4 cinnamon sticks
1 teaspoon whole allspice

Drain peaches, reserving syrup. In large bowl, combine syrup and spices. Microwave 4 to 6 minutes on High, or until mixture boils. Reduce setting to Medium and microwave 4 minutes. Remove cloves, add peaches and microwave 5 minutes on Medium, basting peaches several times. Serve hot or cold.

Linda Brase (Edwardsville)

BAKED CUSTARD

1⅔ cups milk, scalded   ¼ teaspoon salt
3 eggs   ½ teaspoon vanilla
4 tablespoons sugar   Dash nutmeg

To scald milk, heat in heat resistant glass or plastic measuring cup for 3 to 4 minutes on Full power, or until bubbles appear around edges of cup. Beat eggs slightly, add sugar, salt, vanilla and slowly add milk. Divide custard among 5 glass custard cups. Place custard dishes in a circle on outer edge of turntable. Heat, uncovered on Roast temperature for 5 to 5½ minutes or until custard just begins to boil. Center will become firm during standing time. Chill.

Donna Price (Granite City)

BROWNIES

2 squares unsweetened
  chocolate
⅓ cup butter
1 cup sugar
2 eggs

1 teaspoon vanilla
⅔ cup flour
½ teaspoon salt
½ cup nuts

Melt butter in microwave. Add sugar, eggs, vanilla to the melted butter and beat for 2 minutes. Mix in flour, salt and nuts until well blended. Pour in 8 inch round pan. Microwave 4 minutes Full power. Rotate every minute or so. Ice with Chocolate Frosting of your choice.

Donna Price (Granite City)

UNBELIEVABLE LEMON PIE

1 14 ounce can sweetened
  condensed milk
1 cup water
½ cup reconstituted lemon
  juice
½ cup Bisquick

3 eggs
¼ cup butter
1½ teaspoons vanilla
1 cup flaked coconut or
Cherry pie filling

Combine condensed milk, water, lemon juice, Bisquick, eggs, butter and vanilla in blender and blend for 3 minutes on low. Pour into greased 10-inch pie plate and let stand for 5 minutes. Flaked coconut may be sprinkled over top. Bake in microwave oven on Roast for 20-22 minutes, or until filling is set and knife comes out clean when inserted in middle. Should be turned every 5 minutes. For conventional oven bake at 350° F. for 35 to 40 minutes. Instead of coconut before baking, a can of cherry pie filling may be spread over top of pie after it has cooled. Tastes like cheese cake.

Barbara Brase (Edwardsville)

PORK CHOPS WITH BAR B-Q SAUCE

3 or 4 pork chops

Bar B-Q sauce

Arrange chops in pie plate with bones toward the center of the plate. Coat with sauce. Cover with Saran Wrap. Cook at High for 10 minutes.

Donna Price (Granite City)

BARBECUED COUNTRY-STYLE RIBS

2½ to 3 pounds country-style ribs
½ cup bottled barbecue sauce

¼ cup bottled Italian salad dressing
1 teaspoon dried parsley flakes

Place ribs in 3 quart, 13x9 inch, glass baking dish, cover with wax paper. Microwave for 25 minutes on Roast (medium, 70% power). Drain. Combine remaining ingredients and brush over ribs. Recover and continue cooking for 30 to 35 minutes on Roast, or until meat is fork tender (about 170 degrees). Let stand, covered 5 minutes. 4 to 6 servings.

Betty Heepke (Edwardsville)

MEAT LOAF

1½ pounds ground beef
¼ cup catsup
1 small onion, diced
1 egg
1½ teaspoons salt
¼ teaspoon pepper

3 or 4 slices of bread, broken into pieces
¼ cup red or green diced bell peppers may be added for additional color and flavor

Mix the above ingredients together well. Shape into four individual loaves. Place loaves in two quart glass utility dish or ten inch glass pie pan in a ring. Cook in microwave oven for seven minutes on High (cover with paper towel to prevent splattering). Drain off juice and turn each loaf and bake an additional seven minutes or until done.

Barbara Brase (Edwardsville)

BROCCOLI EGG BAKE

3 eggs, hard boiled, sliced
2 10-ounce packages frozen broccoli, cooked
1 cup Cheddar cheese, (4-ounces, shredded, processed)

⅓ cup milk
1 10¾-ounce can cream of mushroom soup
½ cup cornflake crumbs
2 tablespoons butter or margarine, melted

Arrange egg slices on top of broccoli in 10x6x1½ inch baking dish; sprinkle with cheese. Blend milk and soup; pour over all. Cook covered at Medium High for 10 minutes until hot. Combine crumbs and butter; sprinkle on top.

Donna Price (Granite City)

NIPPY MEATBALLS IN MUSHROOM SAUCE

1 onion, chopped fine
2 tablespoons oil
2 pounds lean ground beef
1 pound lean ground pork
4 eggs
1 cup seasoned bread crumbs
1 12-ounce can beer
1 tablespoon dill

1 teaspoon pepper
1 4-ounce can mushrooms,
  drained and cut up
1 10½-ounce can condensed
  cream of mushroom soup
2 tablespoons lemon juice
chopped parsley
1 teaspoon salt

Lightly brown onion in oil. Mix meats with onion, eggs, bread crumbs, beer, dill, salt and pepper. Shape into meatballs. Brown in ungreased skillet. Blend mushrooms with undiluted soup and lemon juice. Layer meatballs in crock pot, moistening thoroughly with sauce and cover. Cook 4 hours on low. Skim off fat. Adjust seasonings. Remove to warmed serving bowl and sprinkle with parsley. Makes 9½ dozen meatballs. Allow 6-8 per serving.

Betsy Knezevich (Godfrey)

SWISS STEAK

2 pounds round steak, ½ inch
  thick
¼ cup flour
1 teaspoon salt
⅛ teaspoon pepper
3 tablespoons shortening
1 onion, sliced
½ cup chopped celery

1 28-ounce can tomatoes,
  mashed
½ green pepper, chopped
1 button garlic, sliced
¼ cup water
½ teaspoon salt
¼ pound Mozzarella cheese,
  thinly sliced (optional)

Pound meat with meat mallet to tenderize. Dredge meat in mixture of flour, salt and pepper. On cooktop, heat shortening in skillet, brown meat on both sides. Place in four quart casserole. Cook onions until transparent. Add remaining ingredients, including flour mixture. Stir well, then pour over steak, be sure the meat is covered with liquid. Cover and cook on Low for 45 minutes or until meat is tender. Turn casserole one quarter turn every 15 minutes. Top with cheese slices, return to oven and cook on Low five minutes more or until cheese melts. Makes 4 to 6 servings.

Kay Losch (East Alton)

TUNA AND CHEESE ROLL

1 8-ounce can refrigerator
  biscuits, rolled and
  flattened
½ 11-ounce can condensed
  Cheddar cheese soup

2 6½-ounce cans tuna fish,
  drained
1 cup milk
1 cup chopped onion
1 tablespoon chopped parsley

Arrange biscuits in two rows in a 1½ quart baking dish. Mix soup, tuna fish and milk; spoon mixture over biscuits. Make roll. Cook eight minutes on High or until biscuits are no longer doughy. Spoon sauce over biscuits once during last half of cooking time. Serve with chopped onion and parsley.

Karen Mueller (East Alton)

TUNA CHOW MEIN

2 tablespoons butter
½ cup finely chopped onion
1 cup finely chopped celery
2 tablespoons finely chopped
  green pepper

1 can mushroom soup
1 3-ounce can chow mein
  noodles, reserve ⅓ cup
1 6½-ounce can tuna, drained
Salt and pepper to taste

Combine butter, onion, celery and green pepper. Microwave four minutes on High, or until onion is transparent. Add soup, noodles, salt and pepper. Mix well, cover. Cook 5 minutes on High. Let stand 3 minutes, covered. Top with reserved noodles.

Linda Brase (Edwardsville)

FILLET OF FISH

Turbot fillets
Waxed paper
Olive oil
Pinch of salt

Pinch of rosemary
Pinch of marjoram
Pinch of turmeric

Lay fillet on piece of waxed paper large enough to enclose a 6-7 ounce fillet, and coat both sides with olive oil. Add a pinch each of salt, rosemary, marjoram, and turmeric to the top of each fillet. Fold wax paper around fillet to make a pouch and secure with a toothpick. Cook in microwave 1½ to 2 minutes on High or until fish flakes, and is hot throughout. Pouches may be rearranged halfway through cooking in order to cook all evenly.

Barbara Brase (Edwardsville)

ONE DISH SPAGHETTI

1 tablespoon butter
1 large onion, sliced
1 clove garlic, pressed
1 pound ground beef
1 teaspoon parsley flakes
½ teaspoon salt

¼ teaspoon pepper
½ teaspoon oregano
2 8-ounce cans tomato sauce
1½ cups water
¼ pound uncooked spaghetti

Combine butter, onion and garlic in 2 quart casserole. Microwave 2 to 3 minutes on High or until onion is transparent. Crumble ground beef into casserole, microwave 4 to 5 minutes on High or until pink color is gone. Add parsley, salt, pepper and oregano and tomato sauce and water. Cover. Microwave 4 minutes on High. Break spaghetti in half and mix into sauce. Cover. Microwave 10 to 12 minutes on High or until spaghetti is tender, stirring twice. Let stand 5 to 10 minutes, covered.

Linda Brase (Edwardsville)

CHEESE AND EGG SCRAMBLE

6 eggs
¼ cup milk
¼ teaspoon salt
Dash of pepper
2 tablespoons margarine or
   butter

1 3-ounce package cream
   cheese, cubed
Chopped chives, optional

Mix eggs, milk, salt and pepper. Melt butter in a 2 quart casserole on High for 30 seconds. Pour in egg mixture. Cook on Low for six minutes, stirring occasionally the last three minutes of cooking. Add cream cheese cubes. Cook on Low for 45 to 60 seconds. Sprinkle with chives. Makes four servings.

Kay Losch (East Alton)

TOMATO SOUP

1 quart tomato juice
3 cups milk

1 tablespoon sugar
1 teaspoon baking soda

Heat tomato juice and milk in separate glass bowls to same temperature. Add baking soda to tomato juice and stir well. Then combine milk and tomato juice. Add sugar. Serve while hot with crackers.

Kay Losch (East Alton)

CHEESY BROCCOLI-ONION CASSEROLE

2 10-ounce packages frozen,
  chopped broccoli
1 10¾-ounce can condensed
  cream of mushroom soup
1 16-ounce can whole onions,
  drained

½ teaspoon seasoned salt
4 ounces processed cheese
  spread, sliced
2 tablespoons butter or
  margarine
⅓ cup dry bread crumbs

Microwave broccoli in covered 1½ quart glass casserole for 10 to 12 minutes or until thawed. Drain. Stir in soup, onions and salt; arrange evenly in dish. Top with cheese slices. Microwave butter in glass dish ½ minute or until melted. Stir in crumbs; sprinkle over cheese. Microwave, uncovered, 10 to 12 minutes or until heated through, rotating dish once or twice. Serves 6 to 8 people.

Jacqueline Thomas (Carlinville)

ESCALLOPED CORN

1 #2 can cream style corn
1 #2 can whole kernel corn,
  drained
1 cup cracker crumbs

1 5¾ ounce can evaporated
  milk
1 egg, slightly beaten
2 tablespoons butter

Combine corns, crumbs and milk in 1 quart casserole. Mix well. Stir in egg. Dot with butter. Cover. Microwave 7 minutes, 30 seconds on '8' or until set. Let stand 3 to 5 minutes covered. Garnish with paprika, if desired.

Linda Brase (Edwardsville)

SCALLOPED POTATOES

5-6 medium potatoes
1 10-ounce can cream of
  mushroom soup

½ soup can milk
Butter
Paprika

Peel and slice potatoes. Arrange half of potatoes in a 2 quart casserole. Pour half of the soup on potatoes. Add rest of potatoes. Fill half empty can with milk and stir to blend remaining soup and milk, then pour over top of potatoes. Dot with butter and sprinkle with paprika. Bake in Microwave oven 10 minutes on High. Turn dish and continue cooking with lid on for 10 minutes more or until tender.

Barbara Brase (Edwardsville)

OVEN PANCAKE

2 tablespoons margarine   ¼ teaspoon salt
¾ cup flour   2 eggs, beaten
1½ teaspoons sugar   1¼ cups milk
½ teaspoon baking powder

Melt margarine in 9-inch Pyrex cake pan for 30 seconds in microwave. Sift together flour, sugar, baking powder and salt. Slowly add beaten eggs and milk. Pour batter into hot margarine in pan. Bake 3 minutes on High; turn pan, bake 2 minutes more. Serve immediately with syrup or fruit sauce or fresh fruit.

You may bake this in regular oven 425° F. until golden brown and puffy. The texture between the product from the two ovens will be entirely different. However, the microwave gives a real tasty quickie.

Cornelia Parrill (Edwardsville)

SCATTER MIX

6 tablespoons butter   2 cups Wheat Chex
4 teaspoons Worcestershire   2 cups Rice Chex
   sauce   2 cups pretzels, thin sticks
1 teaspoon seasoned salt   1½ cups mixed nuts (12
2 cups Corn Chex   ounces) or peanuts

In 13x9x2 inch dish, place butter, Worcestershire sauce and salt, microwave at High for 1 minute or until butter is melted. Stir well. Add cereals, pretzels and nuts. Mix thoroughly to coat. Microwave at High 3 to 6 minutes. Stir after 3 minutes. Continue to bake until evenly toasted. Makes about 2½ quarts.

Donna Price (Granite City)

CROCK POT APPLE BUTTER

8 cups thick apple pulp   4 cups sugar
½ cup vinegar   2 teaspoons cinnamon

Core and slice apples but do not peel. Add only enough water to cover and cook apples till soft. Press through fine sieve and measure. Combine all ingredients. Cook until mixture remains in a smooth mass when a little is cooled. Stir occasionally in crock pot. Cook about 12 hours on low. Pour into sterilized jars to within ½ inch from the top. Process in boiling water bath 10 minutes.

Reita Sparrowk (Bethalto)

FESTIVE FILLED ONIONS

4 medium onions
1 10-ounce package frozen
  chopped spinach
¼ cup milk
2 tablespoons all-purpose
  flour
½ teaspoon salt
2 tablespoons butter or
  margarine

½ cup shredded Cheddar
  cheese
1 tablespoon butter or
  margarine
3 tablespoons dry bread
  crumbs

Peel onions and halve each crosswise. Place cut-side-down in an 8-inch round glass baking dish. Cover with waxed paper. Microwave 7 to 9 minutes or until onions are tender-crisp. Remove centers from onions and set aside for use in other dishes. Separate onion halves into about two shells each, leaving 2 to 3 layers of onion in each. Place shells, cut-side-up in baking dish. Set aside.

Microwave spinach in covered glass bowl 5 to 6 minutes or until thawed. Drain well. Combine milk, flour and salt; stir into hot spinach mixture. Add butter. Microwave, uncovered, 2 to 2½ minutes or until thickened. Stir in cheese. Microwave 1 tablespoon butter in small glass dish about ½ minute or until melted. Stir in bread crumbs. Spoon spinach mixture into onion shells; top with buttered crumbs. Cover and set aside until ready for final heating. Microwave, covered with waxed paper, 3 to 4 minutes or until heated through. Serves 8 to 10.

Jacqueline Thomas (Carlinville)

CHOLENT
(Meat & Lima Bean Stew)

1 cup dried lima beans	2 onions, sliced
2 pounds boneless chuck	1 clove garlic, minced
5 tablespoons oil	1 cup Pearl barley
1 teaspoon salt	2 cups tomato juice
½ teaspoon pepper	1 bay leaf
½ teaspoon paprika	Chopped parsley
½ teaspoon ground ginger	

Soak lima beans overnight in water to cover by 2 inches. Next day, brown meat in 2 tablespoons oil. Sprinkle all over with ⅔ teaspoon salt, ¼ teaspoon pepper, paprika, ginger; remove from pan. Add 3 tablespoons oil to skillet and brown onions and garlic; sprinkling them with a little salt and pepper. Drain limas and mix with barley. In crock pot, layer half the onions, the meat, remaining onions, beans and barley. Rinse skillet with tomato juice and 2 cups water, then pour over contents of crock pot. Bury bay leaf and cover. Cook 12 hours on low or until beans are tender. Adjust seasonings. Turn into warmed serving dish and dust with parsley. Makes 8 servings.

Betsy Knezevich (Godfrey)

SLOW COOKER STUFFING

½ cup butter	½ teaspoon salt
1 cup chopped onion	⅛ teaspoon pepper
1 cup chopped celery	12 cups toasted bread cubes*
1 8-ounce can mushrooms,	2 eggs, well beaten
sliced and drained	1½ cups chicken broth or
¼ cup chopped parsley	bouillion
1½-2 teaspoons poultry	
seasoning	

Melt butter in skillet; add onion and celery and sauté until tender. Stir in mushrooms and parsley. Combine seasonings and sprinkle over bread cubes. Add eggs, bouillion (or broth), and onion mixture and toss thoroughly until combined. Spoon lightly into slow cooker. Cover and set on high for 1 hour. Reduce heat to low and cook 1 to 2 hours longer. Makes 7 to 8 cups.
NOTE: *Cube 22 bread slices and toast for 15 minutes in a 300° F. oven to get 12 cups of toasted bread cubes.

Janice Bradley (Marine)

HEARTY BEEF STEW

2 pounds stew beef, cut in 1 inch cubes
5 carrots, cut in 1 inch slices
1 large onion, cut in chunks
3 stalks celery, sliced
1 large size can tomatoes
½ cup quick-cooking tapioca
1 whole clove (or ½ teaspoon ground clove)
2 bay leaves
Salt and pepper to taste

Trim all fat from meat. Put all ingredients in Crock Pot. Mix thoroughly, cover and cook on low 12 hours. (High for 5 to 6 hours)

Mrs. Louis A. Schmidt (Edwardsville)

SPINACH CASSEROLE

2 10-ounce packages frozen spinach
2 cups cottage cheese (small curd)
1½ cups American cheese
3 eggs
¼ cup flour
1 teaspoon salt

Break spinach chunks apart. Cut American cheese into small cubes. Beat eggs slightly. Mix spinach, cottage cheese, American cheese, eggs, flour and salt together. Pour into greased crock-pot and cover and cook on low for 4½ hours.

Kathryn Cook (Marine)

LEISURE COOKING

LEISURE COOKING

EATING SLIM

Religious programs and services are conducted at SIU-E in the building provided by business and organizations of the area. Buckminster Fuller engineered the structure with the geodetic design indicated.

FREE CABBAGE SOUP

2 cups tomato juice
4 cups coarsely chopped
cabbage
1 4-ounce can mushrooms,
drained
2 tablespoons vinegar
1 teaspoon chili powder

2 teaspoons artificial
sweetener or 1 package
Sweet and Low
2 cups water
2 ribs celery, diced
2 chicken bouillon cubes
2 tablespoons onion flakes

Put all above ingredients in pot and bring to boil. Reduce heat and simmer until cabbage is done.

Bernice Willaredt (Granite City)

CABBAGE DELIGHT

1 small head of cabbage
(less may be used)
1 small minced onion
1 can tomato soup

1 pound ground beef
⅓ cup uncooked rice
1 soup can of water

Chop cabbage in small pieces and place in the bottom of a 2 quart baking dish which has been sprayed with Pam. Brown meat and onion. Drain fat. Stir uncooked rice into browned meat. Top cabbage with this mixture and then cover casserole with tomato soup and water. Bake at 350° F. for at least 1 hour. Check during cooking time to be sure it doesn't get too dry. An additional small can of tomato sauce may be added if necessary. Covering casserole also helps from drying out.

Betty Heepke (Edwardsville)

SPICY TOMATO DRESSING
(Low Calorie—15 per tablespoon)

1 8-ounce can tomato sauce
½ small onion, cut up fine or
1 tablespoon dry flakes
½ cup cider vinegar
2 tablespoons sugar

2 tablespoons salad oil
2 teaspoons Worcestershire
sauce
½ teaspoon oregano leaves
½ teaspoon salt

Blend, cover and refrigerate. It is best made several days before using. Very good on tossed salad or plain lettuce.

Cornelia Parrill (Edwardsville)

PICKLED CAULIFLOWER

1 head cauliflower   Liquid from a jar of dill
pickles (32-ounce)

Pour liquid into a sauce pan. Add cauliflower which has been broken into floweretts. Cook about 15 minutes, stirring to make sure all floweretts get their turn in hot liquid. Cook until tender-crisp (not mushy). Store in refrigerator. Good for snacks.

Donna Price (Granite City)

RED JELLO SALAD

2 packages strawberry
  D-ZERTA gelatin
2 cups boiling water
1 8-ounce can crushed
  pineapple in juice

1 cup low fat cottage cheese
1 package whipped D-ZERTA
  whipped topping

Dissolve gelatin in boiling water. Set in refrigerator until it starts to jell. Then add pineapple in juice, and cottage cheese. Mix well and fold in whipped topping. Chill in refrigerator. I use this as a diabetic salad. Add a few pecans and it is very good. Makes a large bowl.

Marie Mindrup (Alhambra)

DIETER'S BEEF

3 pounds chuck (trim off fat)
1 can beer
¾ cup catsup
2 onions chopped
1 celery rib with leaves, press
  2 whole cloves in celery rib

1 teaspoon paprika
½ teaspoon white pepper (you
  can use black pepper, too)
1 bay leaf

Simmer all ingredients with meat on low heat until tender, about 3 hours. Skim off any fat after removing beef. Simmer liquids half hour to sort of thicken. Put meat back in for 10 more minutes. Serves seven to eight persons, depending on the waste of fat and gristle discarded.

VARIATION: Good served over Kasha too. Also good over rice or noodles.

Mildred Urban (Highland)

DIETER'S BEEF RAVIOLI

Prepare roast according to recipe for Dieter's Beef. This recipe of beef roast can be cooled. Then beef stripped of all gristle, fat and bones. Put beef into food chopper and grind with celery leaves and parsley leaves. Some people add an egg, too. Season meat to make filling for ravioli with salt and pepper only.

DOUGH FOR RAVIOLI:

1¾ cups flour
½ teaspoon salt

2 beaten eggs
⅓ cup water

Mix all ingredients together to make dough. Knead 15 to 20 times. Cover dough with bowl and let stand ten to fifteen minutes. Divide dough in half. Roll out and cut into squares. Put spoonfull of meat mixture on dough, seal edges. Have boiling water with teaspoon of salt ready. Drop ravioli in boiling water for 8 minutes. Serve with your favorite tomato sauce.

Mildred Urban (Highland)

ZUCCHINI-HAMBURGER CASSEROLE
(Lasagne-type casserole)

1 pound hamburger
1 medium onion, chopped
1 medium zucchini, diced
1 8-ounce can tomato sauce
1 teaspoon oregano

Garlic powder to taste
Salt and pepper to taste
1 tablespoon diet margarine
2 slices Mozzarella cheese

Brown hamburger, add onion, salt and pepper. Drain. Sauté diced zucchini in 1 tablespoon diet margarine. Add tomato sauce, oregano, garlic powder and drained hamburger. Put in 2 quart casserole and top with 2 slices Mozzarella cheese. Bake at 350° F. oven for 35 minutes. Makes 4 servings.

Diane L. Martin (Edwardsville)

DIET JELLO

1 12-ounce diet soda
1 package unflavored gelatin

½ cup water
1 tablespoon lemon juice

Boil soda. Mix water and gelatin with lemon juice. Add sweetener to taste. Add soda. Chill until firm.

Carleen Paul (Worden)

HALIBUT WITH VEGETABLES

2 pounds Halibut fillets
1 teaspoon salt
¼ teaspoon pepper
¼ teaspoon paprika
2 carrots

3 stalks celery
6 green onions
1 teaspoon salt
1 tablespoon lemon juice

Heat oven to 350° F. Place fish in ungreased dish or pan, 13x9x2 inches. Season with 1 teaspoon salt, the pepper and paprika. Cut carrots, celery and onions (with tops) into 1-inch lengths. Place in blender; add enough water to cover. Chop, watching carefully. Drain thoroughly. (Or carrots can be shredded and celery and onions chopped finely by hand.) Spread vegetables on fish; season with 1 teaspoon salt. Sprinkle with lemon juice. Cover and bake 30 minutes or until fish flakes easily with fork. Makes 6 servings. 180 calories each.

Louise Eckert (Collinsville)

GINGER GLAZED CARROTS

1 tablespoon margarine
1 tablespoon brown sugar
½ teaspoon salt
¼ teaspoon ground ginger
¼ teaspoon ground cinnamon

5 medium carrots, sliced into
   coins or cut into uniform
   strips
1 tablespoon water

Combine all ingredients in saucepan along with one tablespoon water. Cover and simmer for 20 to 30 minutes or until carrots are just tender, stirring occasionally. Yield 4 servings. 70 calories per serving.

VARIATION: Microwave: Combine all ingredients in microwave proof dish and cook for 5 minutes, stirring once.

Mr. George P. Eckert (Collinsville)

LOW CAL HOT CHOCOLATE

1 8-quart size box Carnation
   non fat dry milk powder
1 1-pound box Nestle's Quick

1 8-ounce jar Coffee Mate
1 cup powdered sugar

Mix all together. Use ⅓ cup of dry mix for each cup of hot chocolate. Simply add hot water and stir.

Helen Brase (Worden)

PINEAPPLE CHEESE CAKE

2 envelopes unflavored
   gelatin
1 cup boiling water
1 teaspoon vanilla
2 teaspoons lemon juice
1 pound lowfat cottage
   cheese

1 large can crushed pineapple
   (1-pound, 4-ounce can
   packed in its own juice)
1 8-ounce container Cool
   Whip
½ cup graham cracker
   crumbs

Put into blender, the gelatin, boiling water, vanilla, lemon juice and cottage cheese, and blend until smooth. Stir in pineapple (including juice). Fold in Cool Whip. Pour into baking dish 9x13 inches. Sprinkle lightly with graham cracker crumbs. Refrigerate. 1 Serving (¹⁄₁₀ of cheese cake) = 100 calories.

Vera Mae Henschen (Alhambra)

FRUIT PUNCH

½ cup unsweetened pineapple
   juice
½ cup fresh orange juice
¼ cup fresh lemon juice
1½ cups water

Artificial sweetener
   equivalent to ½ cup sugar
1 12-ounce can sugar free
   lemon-lime soda

Mix all ingredients, serve over ice. Yield: 4 1-cup servings, 1 fruit exchange each serving. Nutrient value per serving: Calories, 35: carbohydrates, 10 grams; protein, 0; fat, 0.

Kay Losch (East Alton)

NO SUGAR HOT COCOA

1½ tablespoons cocoa
2 cups skim milk
Dash salt
Vanilla to taste

Artificial sweetener
   equivalent to 1 tablespoon
   sugar

Mix cocoa with ½ cup milk. Stir in remaining milk. Cook over low heat, stirring until mixture comes to low boil. Remove from heat. Add salt, vanilla and artificial sweetener. Yield: 2 (1-cup) servings, one milk exchange each. Nutrient value per serving: Calories, 105; carbohydrates, 15 grams; protein, 9 grams; fat, 1 gram.

Kay Losch (East Alton)

EATING SLIM

284

COOKIES
AND COOKIE BARS

Diamond Mineral Springs still provides a restaurant for those desiring food and a visit to the eastern part of the county. The health spa facet of this operation disappeared several years earlier.

CHOCOLATE FUDGE BROWNIES

6 squares chocolate or ¾ cup
  cocoa
2 sticks plus 2 tablespoons
  margarine
5 eggs
2¼ cups sugar

1 teaspoon salt
2 teaspoons vanilla
1¾ cups flour, sifted
¾ cup walnuts or pecans,
  chopped

Melt chocolate and margarine over low heat and remove. Meanwhile, beat 5 eggs and add sugar, salt and beat again. Add chocolate mixture and vanilla. Beat well and add flour, beat again. Add chopped nuts, if desired. Bake in greased 14x10x2 or 9x14x2 inch pan in 350° F. oven for about 25 to 30 minutes. Test with toothpick.

ICING:

½ cup cocoa
6 tablespoons margarine
1 teaspoon vanilla

¼ cup milk or cream
¾ box powdered sugar

In a saucepan, over low heat, melt margarine and cocoa. Remove from heat and add vanilla and milk. Stir well and add powdered sugar. Beat by hand. It will be stiff. Beat until smooth and add milk a little at a time until desired spreading consistency. Pour over *hot* brownies as soon as done and let set awhile. Cool and cut in squares.

Madelyn Grotefendt (Marine)

CHOC-CHIP BAR COOKIES

1 stick margarine
1 cup crushed graham
  crackers
1 6-ounce package chocolate
  chips

1 cup coconut
1 cup nuts
1 can Eagle Brand milk

Melt margarine in 8½x13 inch pan in oven. Add the remaining ingredients one at a time, as listed, spreading over the entire pan. Bake at 325° to 350° F., watch heat, do not have too high. When brown, not too brown, remove from oven and cool on cake rack. Can be cut when slightly warm. Easy as 1-2-3.

Ruth M. Rogier (Highland)

FUDGE FROSTED BROWNIES

½ cup butter or shortening
1 cup sugar
2 eggs
2 1-ounce squares
  unsweetened chocolate,
  melted

1 teaspoon vanilla
½ cup enriched flour
½ cup chopped nuts

Cream butter and sugar, add eggs and beat thoroughly. Blend in melted unsweetened chocolate and vanilla. Stir in flour and chopped nuts. Pour into greased 8-inch square pan and bake at 325° F. for 35 minutes.

FROSTING:

1 cup sifted powdered sugar
1 tablespoon cocoa

2 tablespoons cream
1 tablespoon butter

Combine powdered sugar, cocoa, cream and butter and cook till mixture boils around side of pan. Remove from heat; beat until frosting is of spreading consistency.

Wilma Willaredt (Collinsville)

PEANUT BUTTER BAR COOKIES

½ cup margarine
¾ cup sugar
2 eggs
1 teaspoon vanilla
¾ cup flour
½ cup chopped pecans
2 tablespoons unsweetened
  cocoa

¼ teaspoon baking powder
¼ teaspoon salt
2 cups tiny marshmallows
1 6-ounce package semisweet
  chocolate chips
1 cup peanut butter
1½ cups Rice Krispies

Cream margarine and sugar. Beat in eggs and vanilla. Stir together flour, nuts, cocoa, baking powder and ¼ teaspoon salt. Stir into egg mixture. Spread in bottom of greased 13x9x2 inch pan. Bake in 350° F. oven for 15 to 20 minutes, until bars test done. Sprinkle marshmallows evenly on top. Bake 3 minutes. Cool. In small saucepan combine chocolate chips and peanut butter. Cook and stir over low heat until chocolate is melted. Stir in cereal. Spread mixture on top cooled bars. Chill. Cut into bars. Refrigerate.

Lorene Genczo (New Douglas)

DATE BARS

1 cup sifted flour
½ cup butter or margarine
1 cup sugar
2 eggs

1 teaspoon baking powder
½ teaspoon salt
1 teaspoon vanilla
1½ cups chopped dates

Preheat oven at 375° F. Sift flour, baking powder and salt. Cream butter, blend in sugar and add 1 egg at a time. Beat until light and fluffy. Add vanilla and dry ingredients, blend well. Fold in chopped dates. Spread in a 7x11 inch greased pan. Bake for 30 minutes. Sprinkle with powdered sugar and cut in squares.

Mrs. Ella Bentrup (Staunton)

DATE NUT BARS

1 cup sifted all purpose flour
½ teaspoon baking powder
½ teaspoon salt
½ cup butter or margarine
1 cup sugar

2 eggs
1 teaspoon vanilla
11 ounces finely cut dates
1 cup coarsely chopped nuts

Sift together flour, baking powder, salt. Cream butter, gradually blend in sugar. Add eggs, one at a time, and beat until light and fluffy. Add vanilla. Gradually blend in dry ingredients, beating well after each addition. Fold in dates and nuts. Spread evenly in a greased, 8 inch square pan. Bake in 375° F. for 30 minutes until firm when touched. When cool, sprinkle with confectioners sugar and cut into bars.

Mrs. William Kaufman (Alhambra)

YUM YUM SQUARES

1 stick butter, melted
1 cup graham cracker crumbs
1 cup semi-sweet chocolate
   chips
1 cup butterscotch chips

1 cup chopped pecans, coarse
1 cup angel flake coconut
1 cup Bordens sweetened
   condensed milk

Grease a 9x13 inch pan. Put in melted butter. Spread crumbs over butter, then spread chocolate chips over crumbs. Put pecans over this and then the coconut. Dribble milk over the top evenly. Bake in 350° F. oven for 30 minutes. Cut into squares when cool, not cold.

Gracie Koeller (Godfrey)

SAUCEPAN BROWNIES

⅓ cup shortening
2 squares unsweetened
   chocolate
½ teaspoon vanilla
1 cup sugar

2 eggs
¾ cup sifted flour
¼ teaspoon salt
½ cup chopped nuts

Melt shortening and chocolate in saucepan over low heat. Beat, into above, the vanilla and sugar. Add eggs one at a time. Stir, into above, flour and salt. Add nuts. Turn into a well greased 8x8 inch square pan. Bake in 350° F. oven for 25 to 30 minutes. Cool, cut into serving pieces. May ice with melted chocolate chips or sprinkle with powdered sugar. (Optional)

Norma Lesko (Granite City)

CARAMEL SQUARES

1 14-ounce package light
   caramels
⅓ cup evaporated milk
1 package German Chocolate
   cake mix

¾ cup margarine, melted
⅓ cup evaporated milk
1 cup chopped nuts
1 6-ounce package chocolate
   chips

Preheat oven to 350° F. Melt caramels and ⅓ cup evaporated milk. Set aside. Combine cake mix, margarine and ⅓ cup evaporated milk. Press ½ of the above mixture in 9x13 inch pan. Bake 6 minutes. Pour chips and nuts over this baked dough. Spread melted caramel mixture on nuts and chips. Crumble (or spoon it on and spread) rest of cake mixture on top. Return to oven and bake 15-20 minutes. Cool well and cut when firm.

Ginger Schuette (Staunton)

GRAHAM CRACKER ROLL

1 pound graham crackers,
   crushed
1 8-ounce can crushed
   pineapple
¾ pound dates, chopped

⅔ pint single cream, whipped
1 cup ground pecans
5-6 ounces miniature
   marshmallows
8 graham crackers, crushed

Mix first six ingredients by hand. Form into a roll. Roll in crumbs from 8 graham crackers. Refrigerate overnight. Cut into 1 inch slices and serve with whipped cream.

Shirley Beck (Pocohontas)

OATMEAL DATE SQUARES

1¾ cups raw cooking oatmeal
1½ cups flour
1 cup light brown sugar

1 teaspoon soda
½ teaspoon salt
¾ cup butter

Mix dry ingredients and work in butter thoroughly. Pack half of mixture in bottom of greased 8x8x2 inch pan. Cover with Date Filling.

DATE FILLING:

¾ pound dates, cut in pieces
½ cup sugar
⅛ teaspoon salt

½ cup water
2 tablespoons lemon juice
½ cup nuts, chopped

Boil dates, sugar, salt and water until thick. Remove from range. Cool, and add lemon juice and nuts. Add remaining crumb mixture, pressing it down well. Bake at 375° F. about 40 minutes. Cut in squares. Yield: About 16 squares. Note: Store in ventilated cookie jar.

Alberta Brandt (Worden)

PUMPKIN BARS

4 eggs
1⅔ cups granulated sugar
1 cup cooking oil
1 16-ounce can pumpkin
2 cups flour
2 teaspoons baking powder
2 teaspoons ground cinnamon

1 teaspoon salt
1 teaspoon baking soda
1 3-ounce package cream
   cheese, softened
½ cup butter, softened
1 teaspoon vanilla
2 cups sifted powdered sugar

In mixing bowl, beat eggs, sugar, oil and pumpkin until light and fluffy. Stir together flour, baking powder, cinnamon, salt and soda. Add to mixture and mix thoroughly. Spread batter in ungreased 15x10x1 inch cookie sheet. Bake 25 to 30 minutes at 350° F. Cool. Frost with cream cheese icing.

CREAM CHEESE ICING:

Cream together the cream cheese and butter. Stir in vanilla. Stir in powdered sugar a little at a time. Beat well until mixture is smooth.

Beverly Dustmann (Dorsey)

If cookies are to be dipped in powdered sugar after baking, it is best to do so once while they are still warm and again after they have cooled.

PUMPKIN PIE SQUARES

1 cup flour
½ cup butter
½ cup quick cooking rolled
oats
½ cup brown sugar
1 1-pound can pumpkin
1 can evaporated milk
2 eggs
½ teaspoon ginger

¾ cup sugar
½ teaspoon salt
1 teaspoon cinnamon
¼ teaspoon cloves
½ cup chopped pecans
½ cup brown sugar
2 tablespoons butter

Preheat oven to 350° F. Mix flour, butter, rolled oats and brown sugar until crumbly. Press into ungreased 13x9x2 inch pan. Bake for 15 minutes. Mix pumpkin, milk, eggs, ginger, sugar, salt, cinnamon and cloves, and pour into crust. Bake for 20 minutes. Combine pecans, brown sugar and 2 tablespoons butter, and sprinkle over filling. Bake for 15 minutes longer.

Myra Campbell (Edwardsville)

RUM CAKES

1 cup powdered sugar
1 cup sifted flour
½ teaspoon salt
1 teaspoon baking powder
½ pound chopped candied
pineapple

½ pound chopped candied
cherries
1 pound chopped dates
4 eggs
1 teaspoon vanilla

Sift together sugar, flour, salt and baking powder. Combine with chopped fruit. Beat eggs well and add vanilla. Pour eggs over first mixture and blend well. Grease and flour one 9 inch square pan, one inch deep. Turn cake mixture into pan. Bake at 325° F. for 35 to 40 minutes. Ice with Rum Frosting. Cut cakes into one inch squares.

RUM FROSTING:

⅓ cup butter
1½ cups powdered sugar

Rum

Note: A month allows ample ripening time. However, if preferred, cakes may be made 5 to 10 days in advance and a small sponge soaked in rum stored in the box to speed ripening period.

Alberta Brandt (Worden)

LEMON LOVE NOTES

½ cup butter   1 cup flour
¼ cup powdered sugar

Mix together and press into 9-inch square pan. Bake 15 minutes at 350° F.

2 tablespoons lemon juice   1 cup sugar
Rind of one lemon   ½ teaspoon baking powder
2 eggs, beaten   2 tablespoons flour

Stir or sift together dry ingredients, add eggs and lemon. Mix well and pour on baked crust. Bake 25 minutes more. Sprinkle with powdered sugar and cut into squares. Makes about 16, depending on size of cut.

Ronnie Sommers (Godfrey)

Soft cookies will stay soft if stored in containers into which you place a quarter of an apple. Change the apple every other day to keep the cookies at their best.

CHOCOLATE SURPRISE

½ cup shortening   1¼ cups flour
1 cup sugar   ½ teaspoon salt
1 egg   ½ teaspoon baking soda
1 teaspoon vanilla   ½ cup cocoa
¼ cup milk   Marshmallows cut in half

Cream shortening and sugar, egg, vanilla and beat well. Add all remaining ingredients except marshmallows. Drop from teaspoon onto lightly greased cookie sheet. Bake 8 minutes at 350° F. Remove from oven and press ½ marshmallow, cut side down, into center of each cookie. Return to oven for two minutes more. After cookies are cool, cover marshmallow with frosting.

FROSTING:

2½ cups powdered sugar   5 teaspoons cocoa
3 tablespoons butter   5 teaspoons cream or milk
⅛ teaspoon salt

Mix all the above ingredients together and beat until smooth. Makes 3 dozen cookies.

Joan Thurmond (Highland)

SPARKLING ALMOND ROUNDS

¼ cup butter
½ cup shortening
1 cup sugar
¼ teaspoon almond extract
1 egg
1⅓ cups sifted flour

1¼ teaspoons baking powder
¼ teaspoon mace
¼ teaspoon cinnamon
¼ teaspoon salt
⅓ cup finely chopped,
    unblanched almonds

Brown butter in 1½ quart saucepan; remove from heat and add shortening, stirring to melt. Then blend in sugar and almond extract. Beat in egg with spoon. Mixture will thicken and become smooth. Mix in sifted dry ingredients and almonds. Use teaspoon measure to take out pieces of dough. Form small balls and drop into a dish of sugar; roll to coat well. (It's the sugar that gives the sparkle, the crackly-crisp top.) Place sugared balls about 2 inches apart on greased cookie sheet. Bake in moderate oven, 375° F., for about 10 minutes or until golden brown. Yield: About 4½ dozen 2-inch cookies. Keep crisp by storing in a canister or jar.

Alberta Brandt (Worden)

Almost all cookies can be frozen, unless the recipe indicates otherwise. Arrange cookies in a container lined with plastic wrap or foil and separate each layer of cookies with wrap or foil.

SPRINGERLE "ANISE" COOKIES

6 egg whites
1 pound powdered sugar
2 teaspoons baking powder

½ teaspoon anise oil
3½ cups flour

1. Beat egg whites very stiff; carefully fold in other ingredients.
2. Work in flour to make stiff dough.
3. Roll out dough, a third at a time, to a thickness of one-quarter inch.
4. Powdered sugar the Springerle board; press down firmly in dough so as to make clear designs; carefully lift off mold.
5. Cut along lines to separate designs. Lift each cookie and place one inch apart on greased cookie sheet.
6. Let cookies stand, uncovered, overnight, to air-dry.
7. Bake in slow oven 325° F. for 10 to 15 minutes.
NOTE: Cookies can be painted with food coloring and used as Christmas tree ornaments.

Norma Sparks (Collinsville)

FRESH APPLE COOKIES

½ cup shortening
1½ cups brown sugar
1 egg, unbeaten
2 cups unsifted flour
1 teaspoon soda

1 teaspoon cinnamon
¼ teaspoon nutmeg
1 cup peeled apples, grated
1 cup raisins
¼ cup milk

Mix shortening, sugar and egg until creamy. Add milk alternately with flour, starting and ending with flour. Add apples, raisins and nuts. Drop by teaspoon on cookie sheet. Bake at 350° F. for 10 to 15 minutes. Ice while still warm.

GLAZE:

2 cups powdered sugar
1 tablespoon margarine

½ teaspoon vanilla
3 tablespoons hot milk

Mix together and glaze cookies while still warm.

Martha Blom (Alhambra)

FRUIT CAKE COOKIES

¼ cup butter
½ cup brown sugar
⅓ cup tart jelly
2 eggs
2 teaspoons baking soda
1½ tablespoons milk
1½ cups sifted flour
½ teaspoon nutmeg
½ teaspoon cloves
½ teaspoon cinnamon

½ teaspoon allspice
1 pound chopped pecans
½ pound chopped candied
  cherries
½ pound chopped candied
  pineapple
½ pound chopped candied
  citron
1 pound raisins

Cream butter with sugar. Add jelly and eggs. Dissolve baking soda in milk. Add to creamed mixture. Sift flour with spices. Add half of flour mixture to shortening-sugar mixture. Add remaining half of flour to pecans and fruits. Add fruit mixture to batter and stir well. Drop from spoon onto a greased and floured baking sheet. Bake in 300° F. oven for 30 to 40 minutes. Ripen like fruit cake. Yield: About 12 dozen cookies.

Alberta Brandt (Worden)

CARAMEL NUT ICE BOX COOKIES

1 cup soft shortening or
   margarine
2 cups brown sugar (packed)
2 eggs
3½ cups sifted all purpose
   flour

½ teaspoon salt
1 teaspoon baking soda
⅔ cup chopped nuts

Mix thoroughly shortening, sugar and eggs. Sift together and stir in flour, salt and baking soda. Blend in nuts. Form into 2 rolls. Wrap in waxed paper. Chill overnight. Heat oven to 400° F. Cut in slices about ⅛ inch thick. Place slightly apart on greased baking sheet. Bake 8-10 minutes.

Mrs. William Kaufman (Alhambra)

CRISP HONEY COOKIES

½ cup butter or margarine
½ cup honey
1¾ cups flour
1 teaspoon baking soda

½ teaspoon cinnamon
¼ teaspoon ground cloves
⅓ cup wheat germ

Cream butter and honey. Sift together flour, baking soda, spices and mix in wheat germ. Combine dry ingredients with creamed mixture. *CHILL* about 1 hour. Roll on lightly floured board to about ⅛ inch thickness. Cut with cookie cutter. Bake on greased cookie sheets in 350° F. oven for 8 to 10 minutes. Cool on rack, then spread thinly with frosting. Yield—about 3 dozen.

Kay Losch (East Alton)

DIXIE'S CHOCOLATE COOKIES

½ stick butter
1 12-ounce package chocolate
   chips
1 can Eagle Brand sweetened
   milk

1 cup coarse nuts
1 cup flour

Melt butter and chocolate chips and cool slightly. Add milk and blend. Add nuts and flour and blend. Drop by teaspoonful on cookie sheet and bake at 350° F. for 10 minutes.

Ruth R. Rogier (Highland)

BOURBON BALLS

2½ cups finely crushed vanilla wafers
1 cup confectioner's sugar
2 tablespoons cocoa

1 cup finely chopped nuts
6 tablespoons corn syrup
¼ cup bourbon

Mix vanilla wafer crumbs, sugar, cocoa and nuts. Mix in remaining ingredients. Shape into balls size of walnut and roll in powdered sugar. Store in tightly covered can for two weeks.

Rhoda Brandt (Worden)

CHRISTMAS PUFFS

1 package yeast, compressed or dry
¼ cup water (lukewarm) for compressed, (warm) for dry
1 cup milk
¼ cup sugar
1 teaspoon salt

½ cup shortening
3¼ cups sifted enriched flour
1 egg
½ teaspoon vanilla extract
¼ cup candied cherries
¼ cup candied pineapple

Soften yeast in water. Scald milk. Add sugar, salt and shortening. Cool to lukewarm. Add 2 cups flour and beat well. Add softened yeast, egg and vanilla extract. Beat well. Add more flour to make a stiff batter. Beat thoroughly until smooth. Cover and let rise until bubbly (about 1 hour). Add fruit. Stir down, using wooden spoon. Drop batter by metal tablespoonfuls onto a bed of crumble mixture spread over a sheet of waxed paper. Toss batter lightly to cover completely with crumbs. Drop into well greased muffin pans which should be about one half full. Let rise in warm place until doubled in bulk (about 30 minutes). Bake at 375° F. for 20 to 25 minutes. Yield: About 2 dozen 3 inch puffs.

CRUMBLE MIXTURE:

½ cup enriched flour
½ cup bread crumbs
¼ cup sugar
1 teaspoon cinnamon

¼ cup butter
¼ cup finely chopped nut meats

Combine flour, bread crumbs, sugar, cinnamon and nuts. Cut or rub in butter until mixture is crumbly.

Alberta Brandt (Worden)

CHOCOLATE CHIP HONEY COOKIES

⅓ cup shortening
½ cup honey
1 egg, well beaten
1¼ cups, plus 2 tablespoons
  unsifted flour

½ teaspoon salt
½ teaspoon baking soda
1 6-ounce bag chocolate chips
1 teaspoon vanilla
½ cup chopped nuts

Cream shortening, add honey gradually and cream together until light and fluffy. Add egg and mix thoroughly. Add flour after sifting with soda and salt. Add chocolate chips, nuts and vanilla and mix well. Drop by teaspoonful on greased cookie sheet. Bake in 325° F. oven for 8 to 10 minutes. Makes 4 dozen. Note: the 2 extra tablespoons flour make a more rounded cookie.

Ruth R. Rogier (Highland)

DISH PAN COOKIES

1 cup white sugar
2 eggs
1 teaspoon vanilla
2 cups flour
1 cup coconut
½ cup maraschino cherries
½ teaspoon salt

1 cup brown sugar
1 teaspoon baking soda
1 cup oats
1 8-ounce package chopped
  dates
½ cup oil
½ cup nuts

Mix all together in large bowl. Drop on sheet. Bake at 350° F. for 10 to 20 minutes. Makes 7 dozen.

Mae Grapperhaus (Troy)

NEVER ENOUGH GINGER SNAPS

¾ cup shortening
1 cup sugar
¼ cup light syrup
1 egg, beaten
2 cups flour

2 teaspoons soda
1 teaspoon cinnamon or less
½ teaspoon cloves or less
1 teaspoon ginger

Cream shortening, sugar and egg, beat well. Add sifted dry ingredients, mix, roll into balls. Dip in sugar. Place on greased cookie sheet and bake at 350° F. for 10 to 15 minutes. Do not over bake. First they rise and then they fall and crack open.

Mildred Dustmann (Dorsey)

NIGHTY NIGHT COOKIES

2 egg whites, beaten stiff
¾ cup sugar

1 cup nuts
1 cup chocolate chips

Add sugar slowly to stiffly beaten egg whites. Fold in nuts and chocolate chips. Line cookie sheet with foil. Drop by teaspoonsful on sheet and press down a little. Bake at 350° F. for 10 minutes. Turn oven off. Say nighty night until the next morning.

Viola Huebener (Alton)

NUT ROLL

DOUGH:

2½ cups flour, unsifted
2½ teaspoons baking powder
½ cup sugar
1 teaspoon vanilla

1 egg
2 tablespoons milk
¼ pound butter

Make "well" in flour and baking powder that have been measured and sifted out on the table. Place egg, milk, vanilla and sugar in "well." Mix well. Cut butter into small pieces and work into dough and form a ball. Roll out to ¼ inch thickness.

FILLING:

½ pound pecans
½ cup sugar
½ teaspoon almond extract

Juice of ½ lemon
1 egg white, beaten
4 to 5 tablespoons water

Grind nuts and combine with egg white, sugar, almond flavoring, lemon juice and water. This filling is then spread thickly over the dough and then rolled up like a jellyroll. Place on a greased cookie sheet and shape it into a crescent.

TOPPING:

1 egg yolk
1 tablespoon milk

Powdered sugar

Brush with mixture of beaten egg yolk and milk. Bake at 400° F. for 30 to 35 minutes. When done, sprinkle with powdered sugar. When cool, slice and serve as a cookie.

Shirley Beck (Pocahontas)

POTATO CHIP COOKIES

1 pound margarine
1 cup sugar
3 cups flour
2 cups crushed potato chips

1 cup chopped pecans
1 teaspoon vanilla
Powdered sugar

Cream margarine and sugar. Add flour, then potato chips, nuts and vanilla. Shape dough into small balls, and place on ungreased cookie sheet. Flatten with fork dipped in cold water. Bake 325° F. for 20 minutes. Cool. Sift powdered sugar on top. Yield: 7 to 8 dozen cookies.

Ruth Brave (Granite City)

NO-BAKE CHOCOLATE COOKIES

2 cups sugar
½ cup milk
1 stick margarine
3 tablespoons cocoa
1 teaspoon salt

3 cups raw quick cooking
  oats
1 teaspoon vanilla
½ cup chopped nuts
1 cup flake coconut

Place sugar, milk, margarine and salt in large saucepan and bring to a boil. Remove from heat and stir in oats, vanilla, nuts and coconut. Quickly drop from teaspoon onto wax paper.

Mrs. Darlene Stille (Alhambra)

CHOCOLATE-OATMEAL DROP COOKIES

1 cup sugar
1 cup shortening (Crisco or
  similar)
2 eggs beaten
1 cup raisins, whole or
  chopped
1 cup milk

½ cup nutmeats, mixed with
  little flour
2 cups flour
2 cups quick oatmeal
2 tablespoons cocoa
1 teaspoon baking soda
1 teaspoon salt

Cream sugar, and shortening. Add beaten eggs; then oatmeal and raisins followed by milk and nut meats. Sift all other dry ingredients together; mix with wet mixture. Add more flour to make a stiff batter, if needed. Drop from a spoon on greased baking sheets. Bake 15 to 20 minutes in a 350° oven. Cookies are of a cake texture. Will burn if too hot. Lower temperature or decrease baking time.

Mrs. Richard M. Taylor (Brighton)

COCONUT OATMEAL COOKIES

2 cups sifted all-purpose flour
1 teaspoon Calumet baking
  powder
1 teaspoon salt
1 teaspoon baking soda
1 cup shortening
1 cup granulated sugar
1 cup firmly packed brown
  sugar

2 eggs
1 teaspoon vanilla
1 cup quick-cooking rolled
  oats
2 cups Angel Flake coconut
  or Cookie coconut

Sift flour with baking powder, salt and baking soda. Cream shortening and sugar. Add eggs and vanilla, beat well. Add flour mixture in four parts, beating just until smooth after each addition. Mix in rolled oats and coconut. Drop by teaspoonfuls onto ungreased baking sheets. If desired, sprinkle with additional coconut before baking. Bake at 375° F. for 9 to 12 minutes, or until golden brown. Makes 2½ dozen cookies.

Rhoda Brandt (Worden)

KATE'S OATMEAL COOKIES

1½ cups sugar
1 cup butter or shortening
2 eggs
½ teaspoon salt
1 teaspoon soda
¾ cup sweet milk
2 cups flour

2 cups Quaker rolled oats
1 teaspoon cinnamon
1 teaspoon ground cloves
1 cup chopped or ground
  raisins
1 cup broken nut meats (I like
  English walnuts)

Cream butter and sugar; add eggs and mix well. Beat until smooth. Dissolve soda in the milk and add. Mix flour, oats, salt, cinnamon, and cloves together; blend into mixture. Blend thoroughly and add nut meats and raisins, which have been dusted with flour. Drop by rounded teaspoonfuls on a well greased cookie sheet and bake in a hot oven, 400° F. for about 12 minutes or until nicely browned. Makes about 6 dozen cookies. Note: I sometimes add extra flour to make a more rounded cookie. Also, I refrigerate over night before baking. This gives the oats a chance to moisten before baking and add a better flavor and texture to the cookie.

Rose Marie Bauer (Granite City)

OATMEAL CRISPIES

1 cup soft shortening
1 cup brown sugar
1 cup white sugar
2 eggs, well beaten
1 teaspoon vanilla
1½ cups sifted flour

1 teaspoon baking soda
1 teaspoon salt
3 cups quick cooking oats
1 cup chopped nuts or
 coconut

Preheat oven to 350° F. Cream shortening and sugars. Add eggs and vanilla. Add dry ingredients. Blend in oats and nuts—dough will be stiff. Shape dough into two loaves about 2 inches in diameter. Chill. Slice ¼ inch thick and bake on greased cookie sheets for 10 to 12 minutes. Makes 6 dozen cookies.

Virginia Schuette (Staunton)

CHEWY OATMEAL COOKIES

1 cup sifted flour
1 teaspoon cinnamon
¾ teaspoon soda
½ teaspoon salt
¼ teaspoon nutmeg
¾ cup soft shortening

1⅓ cups packed brown sugar
2 eggs
1 teaspoon vanilla
2 cups uncooked oatmeal
1 cup raisins
½ cup chopped nuts

Sift flour, cinnamon, soda, salt and nutmeg together. Add shortening, sugar, egg and vanilla; beat until smooth. Stir in oatmeal and raisins and nuts. Drop by rounded teaspoons onto greased cookie sheets. Bake in preheated 350° F. oven for 12 to 15 minutes. Yield: 3½ dozen cookies.

Elsie Schrumpf (Highland)

MOLASSES COOKIES

½ cup margarine
½ cup sugar
½ cup brown sugar
1 egg
½ cup molasses
1 teaspoon baking soda
 (dissolved in ¼ cup hot
 water)

½ teaspoon cloves
½ teaspoon cinnamon
2½ cups flour
Dash of pepper
¼ teaspoon vanilla
Powdered sugar

Blend together in order listed. Bake at 375° F. for 8 to 10 minutes. Sprinkle with powdered sugar when cool.

Joan Thurmond (Highland)

304

BRER RABBIT MOLASSES COOKIES

2 cups sugar
½ cup Brer Rabbit molasses
1 cup butter
½ cup raisins or currants
½ cup chopped nuts
3 eggs, beaten
1 teaspoon baking soda,
  dissolved in a little cold
  water

½ teaspoon ginger
½ teaspoon cinnamon
½ teaspoon cloves
½ teaspoon allspice
3 cups flour

Mix ingredients as given. On floured cookie board, pat out dough with hands to ¼ inch thick. Cut with cookie cutter. Bake on cookie sheet at 375° F. for 10 minutes. Place cookies in jar with a slice of bread to soften. Seal jar.

Louise M. Kipp (Edwardsville)

Spritz cookies will not spread if they are pressed out on cold cookie sheets.

MONKEY FACES

2½ cups sifted flour
1 teaspoon soda
1 teaspoon salt
½ teaspoon ginger
½ teaspoon cinnamon
1 cup brown sugar

½ cup new-type shortening
1 teaspoon vinegar
½ cup buttermilk or sour milk
½ cup molasses
Raisins or currants for faces

Sift together flour, soda, salt, ginger, cinnamon. Add sugar and shortening. Combine vinegar, buttermilk or sour milk and molasses and add to flour mixture. Stir to combine ingredients, then beat 2 minutes. Drop by teaspoonfuls on ungreased baking sheets. Make faces with raisins or currants. Bake in 350° F. oven for 10 to 15 minutes. Yield: About 6 dozen cookies.

Alberta Brandt (Worden)

Placing cookies on foil on cookie sheets rather than directly on buttered cookie sheets usually makes them keep their shape better. The butter from the sheets may make cookies brown too quickly on the edges. (Foil may be wiped clean and reused again.) If greasing sheets, do not use oil or salted butter, as cookies may stick.

PEANUT BLOSSOMS

Sift together:
1¾ cups flour
1 teaspoon soda

½ teaspoon salt

Cream together:
½ cup shortening
½ cup peanut butter

½ cup sugar
½ cup brown sugar

Beat well and add (to creamed mixture):

1 egg
2 tablespoons milk

1 teaspoon vanilla
Chocolate candy kisses

Blend in dry ingredients. Shape by rounded teaspoonfuls into balls—roll in sugar and place on ungreased cookie sheet. Bake at 375° F. for 5 minutes. Remove from oven and place chocolate candy kiss on top of each cookie, pressing down so that cookie cracks around edge. Bake 2-5 minutes longer. Makes 3 dozen.

Carol Roseberry (Alton)

HONEY SPICE SNAPS

2¼ cups sifted all purpose
  flour
1½ teaspoons baking soda
½ teaspoon salt
1 teaspoon ginger
½ teaspoon cinnamon

¼ teaspoon cloves
1 cup firmly packed brown
  sugar
¾ cup solid shortening
1 unbeaten egg
¼ cup honey

Sift together flour, baking soda, salt, ginger, cinnamon, cloves and set aside. Cream shortening, add brown sugar and cream together. Blend in unbeaten egg and honey. Add the flour mixture to creamed mixture gradually and mix well. Chill dough. Shape dough into balls, using a rounded teaspoon for each. Dip half the ball into water and then into sugar. Place sugar side up on ungreased baking sheet. Bake at 350° F. for 12 to 15 minutes to a delicate brown. Yield: 4 dozen.

Kay Losch (East Alton)

Honey can be substituted for sugar in fruit cakes, steamed puddings, cookies, and candies with the result that these products will stay moist longer than if sugar is used. A general rule is to reduce the amount of liquid ¼ cup for each cup of honey used to replace sugar.

PEANUT BUTTER ROUND-UPS

1 cup shortening, softened
1 cup granulated sugar
1 cup firmly packed brown
  sugar
2 eggs

1 cup peanut butter
2 cups sifted flour
½ teaspoon salt
2 teaspoons baking soda
1 cup Quaker oats (uncooked)

Preheat oven to 350° F. Beat shortening and sugars together until creamy. Add eggs and beat well. Blend in peanut butter. Sift together flour, salt, baking soda. Add this to creamed mixture, mixing well. Stir in oats. Roll dough to form 1 inch balls. Place on ungreased cookie sheets. Flatten each cookie by pressing criss-cross with fork. Bake 12 minutes. Makes 6 dozen.

Ginger Schuette (Staunton)

FRUIT SNAPS

1½ cups sugar
1 cup shortening
3 eggs
½ cup molasses
3½ cups flour
1 teaspoon salt

1 teaspoon baking soda
1 teaspoon ground cloves
1 teaspoon cinnamon
1 cup raisins
1 egg, beaten

Preheat oven to 350° F. Cream together sugar and shortening, add eggs then molasses. Sift together dry ingredients and blend into creamed mixture. Add raisins. Drop by teaspoonful onto greased cookie sheet. Brush with beaten egg and place a pecan half in the middle of each cookie.

Amy Ellen Schaefer (Staunton)

SKILLET COOKIES

1 stick margarine
1 cup chopped dates
1 cup sugar
1 beaten egg

1 teaspoon vanilla
3 cups Rice Krispies
1 cup chopped nuts
Flake coconut

In a skillet, place margarine, dates, sugar and egg. Bring to a boil and boil for 3 minutes, stirring constantly. Remove from fire and add vanilla and Rice Krispies and nuts. Mix well. Drop by teaspoonfuls on flake coconut. Shape into cookies. Let stand until cool. Better next day.

Mrs. Lawrence Wall (New Douglas)

PECAN PIE COOKIES

DOUGH:

1 stick soft butter
1 3-ounce package cream
  cheese

1 cup all purpose flour

Mix. Make into balls about the size of walnuts. Press out with thumb to form shell in ungreased tea cake pans.

FILLING:

1 egg, beaten
¾ cup brown sugar
1 tablespoon butter, melted

1 teaspoon vanilla
Pinch of salt
1 cup nuts, chopped

Fill cups ⅔ full. Bake at 350° F. for 20 minutes. Turn immediately.

Donna Koenig (Edwardsville)

Transfer fragile cutout cookies from working surface to cookie sheets with a wide metal spatula to preserve their shape.

PEANUT BUTTER AND JELLY COOKIES

2¼ cups flour
½ cup sugar
½ cup brown sugar, firmly
  packed
½ teaspoon baking soda
½ teaspoon salt
½ teaspoon cinnamon
¼ teaspoon nutmeg

1 cup shortening
½ cup peanut butter
¼ cup applesauce
½ teaspoon vanilla
1 egg
1 cup rolled oats
3 tablespoons grape jelly

Lightly spoon flour into measuring cup. In a large bowl, combine all ingredients except 1 cup flour, oats and jelly. Mix well. Stir in reserved flour and oats. Shape into 1 inch balls. Place 2 inches apart on un-greased cookie sheets. Flatten in criss-cross pattern with fork dipped in sugar. Place ⅛ teaspoon jelly in center of each cookie. Bake 12 to 14 minutes in 350° oven.

Mrs. Louis A. Schmidt (Edwardsville)

Cool large or fragile cookies for a minute or two before removing from the cookie sheet unless the recipe indicates otherwise. Just-baked cookies are very tender and will become a bit firmer upon sitting.

GRANDMA'S EARLY AMERICAN COOKIE

2 cups sugar
3 teaspoons baking powder
¾ cup bacon fat drippings
3 eggs
3 tablespoons water

3½ cups sifted white flour
1 teaspoon ground nutmeg
½ teaspoon ground cloves
Dash of salt

Cream bacon fat and sugar together, then mix in a combination of beaten eggs, one cup of flour and the baking powder. Spices are added to the creamed mixture, with water and 2 cups of flour. The remaining ½ cup of flour is worked in until the dough is stiff enough to roll. Dough is rolled out in small portions on floured board, then cut into 2 inch circles and sprinkled with white or colored sugar, baked at 400° F. for 8 to 10 minutes or until brown as desired. Makes about 5½ dozen.

Margaret Turck Norwood (Collinsville)

Always place "drop" cookies about two (2) inches apart on cookie sheets to allow room for spreading.

GRANGER COOKIES

1 cup shortening, creamed
1 cup brown sugar

1 cup white sugar
2 eggs, beaten

Mix this all together. Combine the following ingredients and add to the above mixture.

2¼ cups flour
1 teaspoon baking powder

1 teaspoon baking soda

Add to the above:

2 cups rice krispies
2 cups corn flakes

½ cup oatmeal
½ cup coconut

Drop by teaspoonful on cookie sheet. Bake at 350° F. about 5 to 8 minutes, depending on size of cookie.

Frieda Paul (Staunton)

In a cake or cookie recipe that calls for other sweetening, the general rule is to reduce the amount of liquid one-quarter cup for each cup of honey used. Honey may be substituted for sugar cup for cup. When honey is substituted in baked goods, add ½ teaspoon baking soda to the recipe for every cup of honey used and bake at a lower temperature.

ROCKS

This is a favorite Christmas Cookie

⅔ cup margarine
1 cup brown sugar
1 tablespoon brandy
2 eggs
1 teaspoon baking soda
  dissolved in 1 tablespoon
  hot water

1 teaspoon cinnamon
1½ cups flour
1 pound dates, cut up
1 pound pecans, chopped

Cream margarine and sugar. Add eggs and brandy and mix well. Add cinnamon, then baking soda mixture, then flour. Mix in nuts and dates. Drop from teaspoonful onto greased baking sheet and bake at 350° F. for 10 to 12 minutes. Makes about 4 dozen. (Cookies can be sprinkled with powdered sugar.)

June Launhardt (Collinsville)

ROCKY ROAD COOKIES

1 cup chocolate morsels
½ cup butter or margarine
2 eggs
1 cup sugar
1½ cups flour

½ teaspoon baking powder
¼ teaspoon salt
½ teaspoon vanilla
1 cup chopped nuts
Miniature marshmallows

Melt ½ cup chocolate morsels and butter over low heat. Cool. Mix ½ cup chocolate morsels, eggs, sugar, flour, baking powder, salt, vanilla, nuts and melted chocolate mixture all together in mixing bowl. Drop dough by rounded teaspoonful on ungreased baking sheet 2 inches apart. Press one marshmallow into center of each. Bake at 400° F. for 8 minutes. Makes 4 dozen cookies.

Diane L. Martin (Edwardsville)

SWEETHEART COOKIES

1½ cups butter
1 cup sugar
2 egg yolks

3 cups flour
Powdered sugar
Jelly or candied cherry

Combine butter, sugar, yolks and flour. Shape into balls. Make print in ball with finger and put in jelly or candied cherry in center. Bake 10 minutes at 350° F. Roll in powdered sugar while warm.

Florence Dinwiddie (Roxana)

SUGAR COOKIES

1 cup butter
1 cup confectioners' sugar
1 cup white sugar
2 eggs
1 teaspoon cream of tartar

1 teaspoon vanilla
1 cup vegetable oil
1 teaspoon soda
½ teaspoon salt
4 cups flour

Thoroughly cream oil, sugars and butter. Add eggs and vanilla. Sift dry ingredients and stir. Chill about 1 hour. Roll dough into balls the size of nickel. Press down on a greased cookie sheet with a flat bottomed glass, dipped in sugar. Bake in 350° F. oven for 8 to 10 minutes or until very light brown. Makes 80 to 90 cookies. As an added decoration, sift powdered sugar on cooled cookie.

Florence Dinwiddie (Roxana)

VARIATION:

1 cup coconut

Donna Sievers (Staunton)

Butter cookies taste better after they have aged or mellowed. Store in a tightly covered container at room temperature up to about ten (10) days.

MOTHER'S SUGAR COOKIES

5 cups flour
1 cup sugar
1 teaspoon baking powder
1 teaspoon baking soda
½ teaspoon salt
¼ teaspoon nutmeg
1 cup butter

3 eggs
1 cup sugar
1 teaspoon vanilla
½ cup buttermilk
½ cup sugar for mix
¼ teaspoon cinnamon for mix

In large bowl sift flour, sugar, baking powder, soda, salt and nutmeg. Cut in butter. In another bowl beat eggs. Slowly add sugar. Add vanilla and buttermilk. Add egg mixture to the crumb mix; blend well, chill. Roll ¼ of dough at a time. Cut large cookies ⅛ inch or ¼ inch thick. Dip tops in sugar, cinnamon mix. Bake at 375° F. for 8 to 15 minutes. I usually save time by putting the sugar mix in a salt shaker and shake some on each cookie after the cookies are on the oiled baking sheet.

Cornelia Parrill (Edwardsville)

SUNFLOWER COOKIES

1 cup white sugar
1 cup brown sugar
1 cup shortening
2 eggs, beaten
1 cup coconut
1 cup sunflower nuts

1 teaspoon vanilla
1 teaspoon baking soda
½ teaspoon baking powder
½ teaspoon salt
2 cups flour
2 cups quick oatmeal

Cream shortening and sugar. Add eggs, coconut, sunflower nuts and vanilla. Drop by teaspoonsful on greased cookie sheet. Bake at 250° F. until delicately brown, about 20 minutes. Note: This may seem very low temperature but is correct.

Norma M. Hemann (New Douglas)

WALNUT SPICE KISSES

1 egg white
2 dashes salt
¼ cup sugar
1 teaspoon cinnamon

⅛ teaspoon nutmeg
⅛ teaspoon cloves
1 cup finely chopped walnuts
Walnut halves

Preheat oven to 250° F. Beat egg white with salt until stiff. Gradually beat in sugar mixed with spices. Fold in chopped nuts. Drop from teaspoon onto well greased cookie sheet. Top with a walnut half. Bake for 35 to 40 minutes. Yield: about 24 cookies.

Suzanne Blattner (Madison)

Always cover butter cookie dough while chilling in the refrigerator. This will prevent the dough from absorbing other flavors and from drying out.

When rolling out cookie dough, work with a small amount at a time so it does not become too soft. Use as little flour as possible on the cutting surface, but dip each cutter in flour to prevent sticking.

When rerolling the dough trimmings, do all the trimmings at one time to prevent too much handling and need for extra flour. Rerolled cookies will always be less tender.

COOKIES AND COOKIE BARS

COOKIES AND COOKIE BARS

COOKIES AND COOKIE BARS

CAKES

The abandoned Hitz bank of Alhambra tells a story of many of Adolph Hitz' donations to the community. The Hitz home for the elderly, the experimental farm used in prior years by the University of Illinois Extension Service. Farm Bureau was housed in this building during the formative years.

ANGELFOOD CAKE

1 cup sifted cake flour
1 cup powdered sugar
1½ cups egg whites
½ teaspoon salt

1 teaspoon cream of tartar
1 cup sugar
1 teaspoon vanilla

Sift flour and powdered sugar five times. Beat egg whites (these must be room temperature) with cream of tartar and salt until stiff, but not dry. Fold in the sugar and flavoring. Then carefully fold in the sifted flour and powdered sugar. Pour into a hot ungreased 10 inch tube pan, which has been heated in the oven while mixing the cake. Bake at 375° F. for 35 to 40 minutes or until done. Invert and let hang in the tube pan on the neck of a bottle for 1 hour to cool cake. Cake will shrink if removed from pan while warm.

Wilma Schoen (New Douglas)

YELLOW ANGEL FOOD

1 cup sugar
10 egg yolks
½ cup hot water

½ teaspoon salt
1 teaspoon baking powder
1⅔ cups cake flour

Beat yolks slightly. Add hot water. Beat 10 minutes; add sugar and fold in sifted dry ingredients. Bake at 350° F. for 1 hour. Invert pan until cool.

Amy Ellen Schaefer (Staunton)

FRESH APPLE CAKE

2 cups sugar
1 cup shortening or butter
4 eggs
2½ cups flour
½ cup cold water
1 tablespoon cinnamon

1 tablespoon nutmeg
1 teaspoon baking soda
1 teaspoon salt
1 cup nuts
2 cups fresh apples, chopped
fine

Mix sugar and shortening until creamy. Add eggs, then add water and vanilla. Sift flour, spices and salt together. Add to sugar mixture, then add apples and chopped nuts. Put in greased and floured pan, 9x13 inches. Bake at 350° F. for 45 to 50 minutes.

Georgia Engelke (Granite City)

319

CAKES

APPLE CAKE

1 cup salad oil
3 eggs
2 cups sugar
2 cups flour

1 teaspoon baking soda
1 teaspoon cinnamon
Pinch of salt
3 cups diced apples

Beat together oil, eggs and sugar. Sift together dry ingredients and add to sugar mixture. Add diced apples. Mix well. Bake in 9x13 inch ungreased pan for 1 hour at 325° F.

Mary Lou Sutton (Alton)

RAW APPLE CAKE

2 cups flour
2 cups brown sugar, firmly
   packed
½ cup butter
1 egg, beaten
1 cup nuts, chopped

1 cup sour cream
1 teaspoon vanilla
1½ teaspoons cinnamon
1 teaspoon baking soda
2 cups finely chopped apples

In a large bowl, combine flour, sugar and butter until crumbly. Add nuts and press 2 to 2⅔ cups crumbly mixture into a 9x13 inch ungreased cake pan. To the rest of the crumbly mixture, add cinnamon, egg, baking soda, salt, vanilla and sour cream. Mix well and add apples. Mix again. Pour over pressed, crumbly mixture and bake in a preheated 350° F. oven for 25 to 30 minutes or until a toothpick comes out clean. Top with your favorite topping or serve plain.

Melba Helmkamp (East Alton)

APPLE TART

1 egg
½ cup sugar
1 teaspoon baking powder

⅓ cup nuts
1 cup diced apples
½ cup flour

Cream egg and sugar, add flour and baking powder. Add nuts and apples. Pour in 9 inch greased pie tin. Bake at 375° F. for 25 to 30 minutes. Cut in wedges to serve.

Ruth Keller (Edwardsville)

320

APPLE PECAN CAKE

2 cups sugar
1½ cups vegetable oil
2 teaspoons vanilla
2 eggs, beaten
½ lemon, juice of
1 teaspoon salt

3 cups flour
1½ teaspoons baking soda
3 cups apples, chopped and
  peeled
1½ cups broken pecans

Mix together the sugar, oil, vanilla, eggs, lemon juice and salt. Add flour, baking soda and mix well. Add apples, pecans and mix. Pour into buttered bundt or 9x13x2 inch pan. Bake at 350° F. for 1 hour or until cake tester comes out clean.

Mildred Dustmann (Dorsey)

APPLESAUCE RING CAKE

½ cup butter
1 cup sugar
1 egg, slightly beaten
2 cups flour
1 teaspoon soda
½ teaspoon salt

½ teaspoon powdered cloves
1 teaspoon cinnamon
1 cup thick applesauce
½ cup chopped walnuts
½ cup chopped raisins
ice cream for topping

Preheat oven to 350° F. Cream butter and sugar; add beaten egg. Sift flour, soda and dry ingredients together. Dust the nuts and raisins with flour. Add flour mixture alternately with the applesauce to butter mixture. Blend well, add nuts and raisins. Pour into greased, medium size, ring mold. Bake about 45 minutes. When ready to serve, fill center with ice cream.

Suzanne Blattner (Madison)

BEET CAKE

3 eggs
1½ cups sugar
1 cup oil
1½ cups cooked beets, sieved
2 ounces chocolate

1¾ cups sifted flour
½ teaspoon soda
¼ teaspoon salt
1 teaspoon vanilla

Beat eggs and add sugar. Add oil, beets and melted chocolate. Add dry ingredients and bake 1 hour in 350° F. oven.

Mrs. Louvain Vieth (Edwardsville)

LOVELITE BANANA CAKE

2 eggs, separated	⅓ cup vegetable oil
1⅓ cups sugar	1 cup ripe bananas, mashed
2 cups flour	⅔ cup buttermilk or sour
1 teaspoon baking powder	cream
1 teaspoon salt	1 teaspoon vanilla
1 teaspoon soda	½ cup chopped nuts

Preheat oven to 350° F. Grease and flour loaf pan or 2 round pans. Beat egg whites until frothy. Gradually beat in ⅓ cup sugar and continue beating until very stiff and glossy. Measure flour by dip and level, blend remaining sugar, flour, baking powder, salt and soda. Add oil, mashed bananas, half of buttermilk and flavoring to flour. Beat 1 minute on medium speed, scraping sides. Add remaining buttermilk and yolks. Beat 1 more minute. Fold in whites then nuts. Pour into pan and bake 40 to 45 minutes.

Suzanne Blattner (Madison)

BLACKBERRY ROYAL BUNDT CAKE

1 18.5 ounce box of plain	3 eggs
white cake mix	½ cup cooking oil
1 3-ounce package blackberry	¾ cup Mogen David
gelatin	Blackberry Royal Wine

In large mixing bowl, stir together cake mix and gelatin until blended. Add eggs, cooking oil and blackberry wine. Blend on low speed of electric mixer until moistened, continue on medium speed for 2 minutes scraping sides of bowl. Pour batter into heavily greased bundt pan, and bake in preheated 350° oven for 1 hour, or until toothpick inserted in middle comes out clean. Cool thoroughly before inverting pan to remove cake.

BLACKBERRY ROYAL BUNDT CAKE GLAZE:

2 cups powdered sugar	½ cup Mogen David
	Blackberry Royal Wine

Mix sugar and wine in sauce pan on medium heat and bring to boil; ingredients should be thoroughly melted. Let glaze cool until it becomes the consistency of a thick syrup. Pour over cooled cake.

Oma Heepke (Edwardsville)

BURNT SUGAR CAKE

1¾ cups sugar
⅓ cup hot water
3 cups sifted cake flour
3 teaspoons baking powder
½ teaspoon salt

¾ cup butter or other
  shortening
3 eggs, unbeaten
1 teaspoon vanilla
⅔ cup milk

Prepare burnt sugar by placing ½ cup of the sugar in a heavy skillet, stirring constantly as sugar melts. When it becomes dark brown, remove it from the heat; add hot water very slowly and stir until dissolved. Cool. Sift flour, baking powder and salt together 3 times. Cream shortening; add remaining sugar (1¼ cups) gradually and cream until light and fluffy. Add eggs one at a time, beating thoroughly after each. Add vanilla and three tablespoons of the syrup and blend. Add dry ingredients and milk alternately beating until smooth. Pour into pans lined with wax paper and bake in 350° F. oven for 25 to 30 minutes. Makes two 9-inch layers. Good with a carmel icing.

Clara Beckmann (Granite City)

DEEP BUTTER CAKE

1 box yellow cake mix
1 stick butter or margarine,
  melted
1 egg

1 8-ounce package cream
  cheese
2 eggs
1 box confectioners' sugar

Mix first three ingredients with a fork. Press into bottom of a 9x13 inch greased baking dish. Blend next three ingredients with mixer. Pour over cake mix mixture. Bake at 350° F. oven for 40 minutes

VARIATION:
Add to cheese mixture your choice of:

1 cup of chopped nuts
1 cup of coconut

1 cup of chocolate chips
1 cup of raisins

TO MAKE COOKIES:

Press cake mixture into a large jelly roll pan; pour cheese mixture over top. Bake at 350° F. for 20 to 25 minutes.

Norma Lesko (Granite City)

BUTTER PECAN DELIGHT

1 butter pecan cake mix
  (Betty Crocker)
1 can Eagle Brand milk
15 miniature Heath Bars or
  6 regular, chopped

1 8-ounce Cool Whip
½ cup nuts, chopped
  (optional)

Bake cake according to directions. While hot, poke holes in cake with large tined fork. Pour Eagle Brand milk over top (milk is thick and you may have to force it into cake with spoon or knife). Cool and spread Cool Whip on top. Sprinkle chopped Heath Bars and nuts on top. Refrigerate.

Donna Price (Granite City)

DR. BIRD CAKE

3 cups sifted flour
1 teaspoon baking soda
1 teaspoon cinnamon
2 cups sugar
1 teaspoon salt
2 cups ripe bananas, mashed

1½ cups cooking oil
1 8-ounce can crushed
  pineapple with juice
1½ teaspoons vanilla
3 eggs

Measure and sift together the flour, baking soda, cinnamon, salt and sugar. Add bananas, oil, pineapple with juice, vanilla and eggs to the dry ingredients. Stir to blend. Do not beat. Pour into a greased 9 inch tube pan. Bake 350° F. for 1 hour 20 minutes.

Mrs. Verna Abert (New Douglas)

CREMÉ DE MENTHE CAKE

1 box white cake mix
6 tablespoons Cremé de
  Menthe

1 can Hershey's fudge
  topping (not syrup)
1 pint Cool Whip

Mix white cake mix as directed on package. Add 2-3 tablespoons Cremé De Menthe. Pour into 9x13 inch greased and floured pan and bake as directed on box. While warm, top with fudge topping. Chill in refrigerator until set. Top with Cool Whip to which 3 tablespoons Cremé de Menthe has been added. Store in refrigerator.

Pam Heepke (Edwardsville)

CARROT CAKE

1¼ cups oil	2 teaspoons cinnamon
2 cups sugar	4 eggs
2 cups flour	2 teaspoons baking powder
1 teaspoon salt	3 cups shredded carrots
1 teaspoon soda	1 cup chopped pecans

Beat together oil and sugar. Add flour, salt, soda, cinnamon, eggs and baking powder and beat for 3 minutes at medium speed. Stir in by hand shredded carrots and pecans. Bake in 13x9x2 inch pan, (greased and floured), for 1 hour at 350° F.

CREAMY FROSTING:

2¾ cups sifted powdered sugar	¼ cup white corn syrup
½ teaspoon salt	½ cup Crisco
1 egg	2 teaspoons vanilla

Combine sugar, salt and egg. Add Crisco and vanilla. Beat until creamy. Frost cooled cake.

Alice Stille (Alhambra)

CHOCOLATE CUSTARD DEVILS FOOD CAKE

4½ 1-ounce squares unsweetened chocolate, or 4½ tablespoons cocoa	¾ cup milk
	2 *small*, well beaten eggs
	1 cup sugar

Combine chocolate, milk, eggs and sugar; mix well and cook over low heat until thick. Cool.

¾ cup shortening	½ teaspoon salt
1½ cups sugar	1½ teaspoons baking soda
3 egg yolks, well beaten	1½ cups milk
3 cups flour	1½ teaspoons vanilla

Cream shortening and sugar, add egg yolks and mix well. Add sifted dry ingredients alternately with milk and vanilla. Stir in chocolate custard mixture. Bake in preheated 350° F. oven for 25 to 30 minutes. Makes three 8-inch layers.

Gracie Koeller (Godfrey)

FOAMY CHOCOLATE CAKE

1 cup shortening
2 cups sugar
3 eggs, separated
3 squares chocolate
1 cup sweet milk
½ cake dry yeast

¼ cup warm water
½ teaspoon salt
2¾ cups cake flour
1 teaspoon baking soda
3 tablespoons hot water
1½ teaspoons vanilla

Cream together, sugar and shortening; add yolks and chocolate. Then add yeast, dissolved in ½ cup warm water and ½ teaspoon salt. Add flour and milk alternately. Add beaten egg whites. Let stand in mixing bowl overnight. In the morning, add 1 teaspoon baking soda, dissolved in 3 tablespoons hot water. Add vanilla. Bake in 9x13 inch baking pan, in 350° F. oven for 40 to 45 minutes. Will not be bitter. Very light texture.

Mrs. Richard M. Taylor (Brighton)

COCONUT SOUR CREAM CAKE

¾ cup Crisco
1½ cups sugar
¾ cup sour cream
1 teaspoon vanilla
3 cups sifted cake flour
¾ teaspoon baking soda

2 teaspoons baking powder
¾ teaspoon salt
1¼ cups milk
1 3½-ounce package flaked
    coconut
4 egg whites

Cream shortening and sugar until light and fluffy. Blend in sour cream and vanilla. Add combined flour, soda, baking powder and salt to creamed mixture alternately with milk, mixing well after each addition. Stir in ¾ cup coconut. Fold in stiffly beaten egg whites and pour into 3 greased and floured 9-inch cake pans or one 9x12 inch pan. Bake at 350° F. for 30 to 35 minutes or until cakes test done. Cool ten minutes before removing from pans. Frost and sprinkle with remaining coconut.

FLUFFY VANILLA FROSTING:

¾ cup Crisco
½ teaspoon vanilla
⅛ teaspoon salt

6 cups sifted powdered sugar
1 egg white
2 to 3 tablespoons milk

Cream Crisco and blend in vanilla and salt. Add powdered sugar alternately with egg white and milk, beating until light and fluffy

Rhoda Brandt (Worden)

CHERRY UPSIDE DOWN CAKE

⅓ cup butter
1 cup chopped walnuts
2 cups drained, pitted
  cherries, cooked
⅔ cup butter or other
  shortening

2 cups sugar
2 eggs
1 teaspoon vanilla
⅔ cup milk
2½ cups cake flour
3 teaspoons baking powder

Heat butter in large, heavy frying pan, sprinkle with ½ cup sugar, nuts and cherries; set aside while mixing cake batter. Cream butter, add 1½ cups sugar and cream thoroughly. Add eggs one at a time and beat two minutes. Add milk and vanilla alternately with sifted flour and baking powder. Pour batter over mixture in skillet and bake at 350° F. for 50 to 60 minutes. Turn out immediately on a large plate and serve warm with a sauce made with cherry juice.

SAUCE:

1⅓ cups cherry juice
1 tablespoon cornstarch

⅔ cup sugar
⅔ cup whipping cream

Put one cup cherry juice in saucepan with sugar and bring to boil, thicken with cornstarch which has been mixed smooth with remaining juice. Boil five minutes, stirring constantly, then cool. Before serving, whip cream, add cherry syrup and serve with cake.

Rhoda Brandt (Worden)

CHERRY CHOCOLATE CAKE

2 cups flour
¾ cup sugar
¾ cup vegetable oil
2 eggs
2 teaspoons vanilla
1 teaspoon baking soda
1 teaspoon cinnamon

⅛ teaspoon salt
1 21-ounce can cherry pie
  filling
1 6-ounce package semi-sweet
  chocolate morsels
1 cup chopped nuts

Preheat oven to 350° F. In large bowl, combine flour, oil, sugar, eggs, vanilla, baking soda, cinnamon and salt; mix well. Stir in cherry pie filling, chocolate morsels and nuts. Pour into greased, floured 9-cup bundt pan or 10 inch tube pan. Bake at 350° F. for 1 hour. Cool 10 minutes; remove from pan. Cool completely and sprinkle top with confectioners' sugar, if desired.

Ronnie Sommers (Godfrey)

CHIFFON BLACK FOREST TORTE

In a large bowl mix:

1¾ cups Gold Medal flour
1¾ cups sugar
1¼ teaspoons baking soda
1 teaspoon baking powder
⅔ cup Chiffon soft-type
margarine

4 1-ounce squares Bakers
unsweetened chocolate,
melted and cooled
1¼ cups water
1 teaspoon vanilla
3 eggs

Preheat oven to 350° F. and bake for 15 to 18 minutes. Combine first 8 ingredients in a large bowl and beat at low speed to blend, then beat 2 minutes at medium speed. Add eggs and beat 2 minutes more. Pour about 1 cup plus 1 tablespoon of batter into four 9-inch round cake pans that have been greased and floured. Layers will be thin. Cool slightly and remove from pan. Cool on cake rack.

CHOCOLATE FILLING:

1½ 4-ounce bars Bakers
German sweet chocolate
¾ cup Chiffon margarine

½ cup nuts
1 9½-ounce Cool Whip

Melt chocolate in pan over low heat, stirring to keep from burning. Cool and blend in margarine. Stir in nuts. Spread first layer with ½ Cool Whip. Repeat layers ending with cream on top. Do not frost sides. Make chocolate curls with remaining ½ bar of chocolate and decorate top completely. Wrap sides with Saran Wrap. Refrigerate or freeze. Freezes very well.

Lois Beckmann (Granite City)

RHUBARB UPSIDE DOWN CAKE

4 cups raw rhubarb, cut up
1 cup sugar
1 small box dry strawberry
Jello

1 box lemon-yellow cake mix
Whipped cream for topping

Butter a 13x9x2 inch pan. Mix together rhubarb, sugar and dry Jello. Put into pan. Mix box cake according to package directions. Pour over rhubarb mix. Bake at 350° F. for 50 to 60 minutes. Turn upside down immediately when done. Serve with whipped cream.

Rose Schrage (Edwardsville)

CRUSADERS' CAKE

1 18½-ounce package yellow cake mix	4 eggs
1 4-ounce package vanilla instant pudding mix	1 teaspoon cinnamon
	½ teaspoon ground ginger
1 cup beer	½ teaspoon ground cloves
½ cup salad oil	½ teaspoon ground cardamon
	¼ teaspoon ground allspice

In a large mixing bowl, blend all ingredients. Beat at medium speed for 2 minutes. Pour into a greased and floured 10 inch tube pan. Bake in moderate oven 350° F. about 50 to 60 minutes. Cake springs back in center when done. Cool right side up in pan about 25 minutes; remove to wire rack to cool thoroughly.

LEMON GLAZE:

1½ cups unsifted confectioners' sugar	¼ teaspoon grated lemon peel
2 tablespoons softened butter or margarine	1 to 2 tablespoons lemon juice

Blend all ingredients until smooth. Spread on top of cooled cake allowing glaze to drip down sides of cake. Decorate with lemon slices. This Crusaders' cake, a lemon spice cake, includes beer and the flavorings of most of the spices the Crusaders brought to Europe—all but the pepper! And has the added convenience of using modern mixes so you can prepare it with ease and the confidence that it will turn out well every time!

Rose Marie Bauer (Granite City)

Eggs are easiest to separate when cold, but whites reach their fullest volume if allowed to stand at room temperature for 30 minutes before beating.

If a given recipe calls for cake flour and you wish to substitute general purpose flour, you will allow two (2) level (not heaping) tablespoons of flour less per cup than the recipe calls for.

Leave a plastic measuring spoon in your baking powder, one in your instant coffee jar, corn starch and many dry ingredients, saves washing and also very handy, especially instant coffee.

CRUMB CAKE

2 cups brown sugar
2½ cups flour, sifted

Pinch salt
½ cup shortening (Crisco)

Mix the above ingredients until like crumbs. Take out ¾ cup crumbs for the topping. Add to the remaining crumbs:

2 eggs
1 cup buttermilk
1 teaspoon baking soda,
   dissolved in milk

1 teaspoon vanilla

Beat well. Put in loaf pan which has been greased and floured. Spread crumbs on top. Bake in 350° F. oven for 45 to 55 minutes or until tester inserted in center comes out clean.

Ruth R. Rogier (Highland)

COCONUT CAKE

2½ cups sifted cake flour
1⅔ cups sugar
1 teaspoon salt
3½ teaspoons baking powder
⅔ cup Crisco

1¼ cups milk
3 eggs
1 teaspoon vanilla
7 minute frosting
½ cup coconut

Combine flour, sugar, salt and baking powder in large bowl. Add Crisco and ¾ cup milk. Beat 2 minutes. Add eggs and remaining ½ cup milk and vanilla. Beat 2 minutes longer. Pour equal amounts in 2 greased and papered 9 inch pans. Bake 350° F. oven for 35 to 40 minutes. Frost with 7 minute frosting and dust with coconut.

7 MINUTE FROSTING:

2 egg whites
5 tablespoons water
1½ cups sugar

1½ teaspoons light corn syrup
1 teaspoon vanilla

Combine egg whites, water, sugar and syrup in top of double boiler. Beat with electric mixer on high speed, continue beating rapidly over boiling water for seven minutes or until frosting will stand in peaks. Remove from heat and add vanilla. Beat again. Spread on cake.

Norma Albrecht

GERMAN CHOCOLATE STREUSEL CAKE

1 package swiss chocolate
  cake mix
1 package instant vanilla
  pudding
2 tablespoons Crisco oil
1½ cups water

2 eggs
½ cup flour
½ cup brown sugar
¼ cup flaked coconut
2 tablespoons butter, melted

Preheat oven to 375° F. Blend cake mix, pudding mix, oil, water and eggs. Beat 2 minutes, medium speed. Do not over-mix. Spread ¾ of batter evenly in greased and floured tube pan. Combine remaining streusel ingredients. Sprinkle ⅔ cup of this mixture over batter in pan. Spread remaining batter over streusel, top with remaining streusel. Bake 40 to 50 minutes at 375° F. Cool right side up 25 minutes. Remove from pan and drizzle on glaze topping.

Delores Geiger (Alhambra)

SOUR CREAM DEVIL'S FOOD CAKE

2 eggs
2 cups sugar
1 cup sour cream
1 teaspoon vanilla
¼ teaspoon salt

½ cup cocoa
½ cup boiling water
2 cups flour
1 teaspoon baking soda

Beat eggs and add sugar and mix well. Add vanilla to sour cream. Add water to cocoa and mix. Add to egg mixture. Then add flour and sour cream alternately. Beat 2 minutes. Pour into loaf pan, bake 45 minutes in 350° F. oven; or use 2 8-inch layer pans lined with waxed paper, and bake in 350° F. oven for 25 minutes. Cool and frost with French pastry frosting.

FRENCH PASTRY FROSTING:

2 tablespoons butter
2 tablespoons hot cream

1 teaspoon vanilla
1¼ cups powdered sugar

Mix all the frosting ingredients together and beat until creamy. This will frost loaf cake or the tops of the layer cake.

Eva Koeller (Godfrey)

DATE SANDWICH CAKE

1 cup brown sugar
½ cup butter
1½ cups flour
1 teaspoon baking soda
1 cup quick oatmeal
1 package pitted dates,
    chopped

½ cup sugar
1 cup boiling water
Whipped cream or ice cream
    for topping

Mix like pie crust, using no liquids; brown sugar, butter, flour, baking soda and oatmeal. Spread half of mixture in 8x8 inch buttered baking pan. Boil together until thick; dates, ½ cup sugar and 1 cup boiling water. Cool. Spread over crumb mixture and spread remaining crumb mixture on top. Bake in a slow oven 250° F. for 30 minutes. Cool. Cut into serving squares; top with whipped cream or ice cream. Very rich. Increase recipe 1½ times for a 9x13 inch pan.

Mrs. Richard M. Taylor (Brighton)

DUMP CAKE

1 #2-can crushed pineapple
1 can cherry pie filling
1 box yellow cake mix

2 sticks butter or margarine
½ cup pecans, chopped

Spread pineapple on bottom of pan, spoon cherry pie filling over the pineapple. Sprinkle cake mix over pineapple and cherries. Cut the butter in pats and cover the cake mix with them. Sprinkle nuts on top and bake 1 hour at 350° F. in a 9x13x2 inch pan; or 325° F. in a glass baking pan.

Mildred Dustmann (Dorsey)
Janice Bradley (Marine)

Variation:

Instead of using the cherry pie filling try varying it by using a can of vanilla, butterscotch or other flavor of pie filling.

Velma Ernst (Alhambra)

FRENCH COFFEE CAKE

1 stick margarine
1 cup sugar
2 eggs
2 teaspoons baking powder
1 teaspoon soda
2 cups flour
1 cup buttermilk or sour milk
½ teaspoon salt

1 teaspoon vanilla
2 apples
1 cup sugar for topping
1 teaspoon cinnamon for
 topping
½ cup chopped nuts for
 topping

Cream margarine, sugar and eggs. Sift flour, baking powder and salt together. Dissolve soda in buttermilk. Add flour mixture and buttermilk alternately to creamed mixture. Add vanilla. Pour ⅔ batter in floured 9x13 inch pan. Slice apples thinly and put over batter and ½ of sugar. Pour remaining batter over apples and the remaining sugar mix over the top. Bake at 350° F. for 30 minutes.

Martha Blom (Alhambra)

FRUIT CAKE

1½ cups raisins
1½ cups chopped dates
2 cups sugar
2 cups boiling water
5 tablespoons shortening
3 cups flour

1 teaspoon baking soda
2 teaspoons cinnamon
1 teaspoon cloves
½ teaspoon salt
1 cup chopped nuts

Place in a saucepan; raisins, dates, sugar, water and shortening. Simmer gently for 30 minutes. Cool. Sift together flour, baking soda, spices and salt. Sift into cooled mixture, adding 1 cup floured chopped nuts. Pour into two loaf pans. Bake 1½ hours at 325° F. Add candied fruit, if desired.

Suggestion: Heavily grease inside of baking pans; line with trimmed pieces of medium weight brown paper bag. Grease lining before pouring batter. Peel from baked cake when cool enough to handle. Crust will not be hard.

Mrs. Richard M. Taylor (Brighton)

GENTLEMAN'S DELIGHT

1 box Jiffy yellow cake mix
1 3¾-ounce package instant
  pudding
1 8-ounce package cream
  cheese, softened

1 16-ounce can crushed
  pineapple, drained well
1 large container Cool Whip
½ cup chopped nuts

Bake cake as directed in 9x13 inch pan. Prepare instant pudding, whip until thick, then add softened cream cheese. Blend well and spread over cooled cake in pan. Spoon drained pineapple over pudding mix, patting down lightly. Spread Cool Whip over entire cake and sprinkle with nuts. Refrigerate 3 hours.

Marie Nungesser (Highland)

NUT TORTE

3 egg whites
⅛ teaspoon cream of tartar
½ cup white sugar
1 teaspoon vanilla
¾ cups finely crushed graham
  cracker crumbs
2 tablespoons pecan pieces

1½ bananas, sliced ⅛ inch
  thick
1 cup whipping cream,
  whipped
2 tablespoons toasted
  almonds
Maraschino cherries

Sift together ½ cup white sugar and ½ cup brown sugar. Add slowly to egg whites beating after each addition of sugar. Beat until egg whites are stiff and glossy; thoroughly mix in 1 teaspoon vanilla. Combine ¾ cup finely crushed graham cracker crumbs and 2 tablespoons pecan pieces and sprinkle little at a time over egg whites folding gently after each addition. Place batter into heavily greased 8 inch cake pan 2 inches deep; bake in preheated 350° F. oven for 30 minutes. (Will be light in color when done.) Cool in pan. Arrange banana slices on top of cooled torte which has been removed from pan. Whip 1 cup whipping cream and decorate top and sides of torte. Garnish with two tablespoons of toasted almonds, sliced bananas and Maraschino cherries.

Virginia Herrmann (Edwardsville)

ITALIAN CREAM CAKE

1 stick butter or margarine
½ cup Crisco
2 cups sugar
5 eggs, separated
1 teaspoon baking soda

2 cups flour
1 cup buttermilk*
1 teaspoon vanilla
1 cup chopped nuts
1 cup coconut

Cream butter, Crisco and sugar. Add egg yolks, beat well. Sift flour and baking soda. Add alternately with buttermilk, flour first and last. Add vanilla. Stir in nuts and coconut. Fold in stiffly beaten egg whites. Bake in three greased and floured 9 inch cake pans, at 350° F. for 25 minutes or until done.

*To make buttermilk: add 3 tablespoons lemon juice to 1 cup milk.

ICING:

1 8-ounce package cream
   cheese
½ cup Crisco

1 box powdered sugar
1 teaspoon vanilla
1 tablespoon milk

Mix all ingredients. Spread between layers and on top and sides.

Sharon Schlaefer (St. Jacob)

MAYONNAISE CAKE

1 cup mayonnaise
1 cup boiling water
1 teaspoon vanilla
2 cups flour

1½ cups sugar
4 tablespoons cocoa
2 teaspoons baking soda

Stir the above ingredients together well. Bake at 350° F. until tester inserted in middle comes out clean.

ICING:

5 tablespoons flour
1 cup milk
2 sticks butter

1 cup sugar
1 teaspoon vanilla

Cook flour and milk together until thick. Remove from heat and cool. Add butter, sugar and vanilla and beat until fluffy.

Pat Bojkovsky (Glen Carbon)

GRAHAM CRACKER CAKE

1 stick butter
1 cup brown sugar, firmly
  packed
4 eggs, separated
1 teaspoon vanilla

1 teaspoon almond flavoring
2 cups graham cracker
  crumbs
2 teaspoons baking powder
1 cup milk
½ to ¾ cup chopped nuts

Preheat oven to 350° F. Cream butter and sugar, add egg yolks and mix well. Add flavoring. Mix baking powder with graham crumbs and add alternately with milk. Beat eggs whites until stiff and gently fold in with chopped nuts. Bake 30 minutes.

Suzanne Blattner (Madison)

JEWISH COFFEE CAKE

1 package white cake mix
1 package instant vanilla
  pudding
4 eggs
8 ounces sour cream
1 cup oil

2 teaspoons vanilla
¾ cup sugar
2 teaspoons cocoa
1 teaspoon cinnamon
½ cup chopped nuts

Put together in bowl and mix well; cake mix, pudding, eggs, sour cream, oil and vanilla. Mix together; sugar, cocoa, cinnamon and nuts. Put half of cake mixture in greased bundt or angel food pan. Sprinkle half of sugar and nut mixture and swirl through. Pour remaining cake mixture over this and sprinkle rest of sugar mix on top. Bake at 350° F. 50 to 55 minutes.

Alice Stille (Alhambra)

LEMON MERINGUE CAKE

1 package yellow cake mix	4 eggs, separated
½ cup softened butter	2 tablespoons butter
1 egg, slightly beaten	1 tablespoon grated lemon
1⅓ cups sugar	rind
½ cup cornstarch	½ cup fresh lemon juice
¼ teaspoon salt	¼ teaspoon cream of tartar
1¾ cups water	½ cup sugar

Preheat oven to 350° F. Stir the cake mix, butter and egg together and press the dough into a 9x13 inch pan. Set aside. Combine the sugar, cornstarch, salt and water in a saucepan over low heat and stir constantly until boiling. Add the egg yolks quickly and cook (stirring constantly) until thick. Stir in butter, lemon rind, lemon juice and pour everything over the cake dough in the pan. Beat the egg whites together with the cream of tartar until frothy. Gradually add the ½ cup of sugar and beat at high speed until stiff peaks form. Spread this mixture over the lemon filling and bake in a preheated oven 25 to 30 minutes. Cool and refrigerate one hour before serving.

Reita Sparrowk (Bethalto)

PINEAPPLE-COCONUT FRUITCAKE

1½ cups diced candied	½ cup butter
pineapple	1 cup sugar
1½ cups light raisins	4 eggs
1 7-ounce package flaked	½ cup pineapple juice
coconut	2½ cups sifted flour
1 cup chopped walnuts or	1 teaspoon baking powder
pecans	½ teaspoon salt

Combine pineapple, raisins, coconut and pecans. Cream butter and sugar until fluffy. Add eggs, beating well after each one. Stir in pineapple juice. Sift flour, baking powder and salt; add to sugar mixture. Fold into fruit mixture. Spoon into 7 greased and floured 10½ or 12 ounce cans. Bake at 300° F. for 1½ hours. Cool. Remove from cans. Wrap separately in brandy-soaked cheese cloth. Overwrap in foil. Store in cool place at least 2 weeks. Remoisten once or twice. Delicious at holiday time.

Rose Schrage (Edwardsville)

ORANGE PINEAPPLE CAKE

1 Duncan Hines butter cake mix
1 can mandarin orange sections with juice
3 eggs
1 stick butter

1 package instant vanilla pudding
1 can crushed pineapple with juice
1 9-ounce container Cool Whip

Mix together cake mix, orange sections with juice, eggs and butter. Beat 4 minutes. Pour into 2 9-inch round greased cake pans. Bake at 350° F. for 35 minutes. Mix together pudding, pineapple and juice as for making instant pudding. Fold in Cool Whip. Ice layers and store in refrigerator until served.

Pauline Shafer (East Alton)

FRESH PEACH DELIGHT

1 yellow cake mix
1 quart fresh peaches
½ cup sugar
8-ounce package cream cheese

½ cup sugar
½ 9-ounce carton frozen whipped cream
1 envelope unflavored gelatin
½ cup water

Add sugar to fresh peaches and allow to stand several hours or overnight. Bake yellow cake in 15x10½x1 inch pan. Cool. Drain and heat peach juice. Dissolve gelatin in ½ cup water and add to hot peach juice. Allow to set to consistency of egg whites. Whip and add ½ carton whipped cream. Beat cream cheese, ½ cup sugar and ½ carton cream. Spread on cooled cake and chill. Cover with whipped gelatin, peach juice which has peaches added and whipped cream. Refrigerate several hours.

Ruth Brave (Granite City)

PEACH CAKE

2 cups sugar
2 cups flour
2 teaspoons soda

½ teaspoon salt
2 eggs
2½ cups peaches, drained

Mix all together with mixer. Bake at 350° F. for 30 to 35 minutes in a 9x13 inch pan. Do not grease pan.

ICING:

1 stick margarine
⅔ cup Milnot
1 teaspoon vanilla

¾ cup sugar
1 cup nuts, chopped

Cook margarine, milnot, vanilla and sugar for 10 minutes. Add nuts. Ice cool cake.

Dorothy M. Westerhold (Edwardsville)

PINEAPPLE MARLOE

1 pound marshmallows
1 cup milk
1 pint whipping cream, chilled
1 cup drained, crushed pineapple

1 3-ounce box cherry Jello
1 cup chopped walnuts
¼ cup melted butter
½ pound or 3⅓ cups vanilla wafers, crushed

Make Jello according to directions on box. Cut in two-inch squares. Combine vanilla wafers with ¼ cup melted butter. Melt marshmallows in milk in double boiler; cool. Whip the whipping cream and add vanilla; add to marshmallow mixture. Also, add pineapple to marshmallow mixture. Refrigerate the pineapple before using. Use 13x9 inch pan (deep pan). Line bottom of pan with one-half of the vanilla wafer crumb mixture. Sprinkle with ½ cup of the chopped walnuts. Use ½ of whipped cream mixture for next layer. Then make layer of Jello pieces, all of the Jello. Then again, the remaining half of whipped cream mixture. Top with remaining ½ of crushed vanilla wafers and sprinkle top with remaining crushed nuts. Refrigerate.

Alberta Brandt (Worden)

EASTER POUND CAKE

1 lamb mold cake pan or 1 Easter rabbit or 2 chicken mold cake pans. (Remainder may be poured into loaf pan.)

½ cup butter
4 eggs
3 cups flour
1 cup milk

2 cups sugar
1 teaspoon vanilla
1 teaspoon baking powder

Sift dry ingredients. Cream sugar and butter. Add dry ingredients, vanilla, milk and add eggs one at a time. Bake molds 35 minutes on one side then turn on other side and bake for 35 minutes at 350° F. (Grease and flour pan very well before pouring batter into mold.)

Mae Grapperhaus (Troy)

RHUBARB CAKE

1 cup brown sugar
½ cup white sugar
½ cup shortening
1 cup buttermilk
2 cups flour
1 teaspoon baking soda

2 teaspoons vanilla
1½ cups finely chopped
 rhubarb
2 teaspoons cinnamon
½ cup sugar

Mix rhubarb and ½ cup sugar and let stand for awhile. Mix in order given and pour in a greased 9x13x2 inch pan. Sprinkle 2 teaspoons cinnamon and ½ cup sugar mixed together on top. Run a fork through several times so sugar mix is moist. Bake at 350° F. for 40 minutes.

Mrs. Lawrence Wall (New Douglas)

RHUBARB UPSIDE DOWN CAKE

¼ cup butter
1 cup brown sugar
2 cups diced rhubarb
¾ cup sugar
¼ cup butter
1 egg, well beaten

1½ cups sifted flour
3 teaspoons baking powder
½ teaspoon salt
½ cup milk
1 teaspoon vanilla
Whipped cream for topping

Combine ¼ cup butter and brown sugar. Cook slowly in a heavy iron, 9-inch skillet until thick and smooth. Remove from heat; add diced rhubarb. Set aside. Cream together sugar and butter; add egg and beat well. Sift together flour, baking powder and salt. Add alternately with milk to creamed mixture. Add vanilla. Pour batter over rhubarb and bake in a slow oven, 325° F. for 50 minutes. Invert over a large plate, cool. Cut wedges. Serve with whipped cream for topping.

Mrs. Richard M. Taylor (Brighton)

SEVEN-UP CAKE

1 lemon cake mix
¾ cup oil
1 box instant lemon pudding

4 eggs
1 10-ounce bottle Seven-Up
(instead of water)

Bake according to box directions of cake. Makes 3 layers.

ICING:

3 eggs
1 small can crushed
pineapple, drained

1½ cups sugar
1 stick butter
1 cup coconut

Cook first 4 ingredients until thick and add a cup of coconut.

Pat Bojkovsky (Glen Carbon)

SAUERKRAUT CAKE

⅔ cup butter or margarine
1½ cups sugar
3 eggs, beaten
1 teaspoon vanilla
2¼ cups all-purpose flour
½ cup cocoa

1 teaspoon baking powder
1 teaspoon baking soda
¼ teaspoon salt
1 cup water
⅔ cup sauerkraut, rinse,
    drain and chop

Blend together the butter and sugar. Beat in the eggs and vanilla. Sift dry ingredients together. Add alternately with water. Stir in sauerkraut. Turn into two 8-inch cake pans (or one 9x13 inch pan). Bake until center springs back when lightly touched. Bake at 350° F. for 30 minutes. Ice with Mocha whipped cream or a powdered sugar icing.

Viola Huebener (Alton)

SPICY APPLE GINGERBREAD

2½ cups sifted flour
1 teaspoon baking soda
¾ teaspoon salt
2 teaspoons cinnamon
2 teaspoons ginger
1 teaspoon ground cloves
1 stick butter
½ cup sugar

½ cup brown sugar
3 eggs, beaten
1 cup dark molasses
¼ cup hot water
1 cup buttermilk
½ cup chopped apples
1 teaspoon lemon juice

Sift together flour, soda, salt and spices. In separate bowl, cream butter and sugars until light and fluffy. Beat in eggs, then molasses and water. Gradually add dry ingredients alternately with buttermilk, mixing thoroughly after each addition. Fold in apples and lemon juice. Pour batter into 2 greased loaf pans. Bake 350° F. for 35 to 40 minutes.

Velma Ernst (Alhambra)

TROPICAL CAKE

1 package yellow cake mix
⅓ cup oil
3 eggs
1 cup liquid (pineapple juice and water)
½ cup coconut
½ cup chopped nuts
2 tablespoons margarine

1 15-ounce can crushed pineapple
2 or 3 bananas, mashed
1 teaspoon baking soda
½ teaspoon vanilla
½ teaspoon almond or lemon extract

Drain pineapple; reserve juice. Melt margarine, add nuts and coconut. Spread evenly on the bottom of a greased and floured 13x9x2 inch pan. In a large mixer bowl, blend cake mix, oil, eggs, baking soda, extracts and liquid. Beat until well mixed. Add the bananas and mix well. Pour in pan. Strew the pineapple evenly over the cake mixture. Bake at 350° F. for 45 to 50 minutes. Serve with Cool Whip.

Mildred Roemelin (Moro)

AUNT RUBY TURCK'S WHISKEY CAKE

1 Yellow cake mix
1 package instant vanilla pudding
½ cup salad oil

4 eggs
1 cup coconut
1 cup ground nuts
1 cup water

Mix above ingredients together. Bake at 350° F. for 50 minutes. Use tube pan.

TOPPING:

½ cup melted butter
½ cup sugar

½ cup whiskey

Mix together. Spoon on cake while warm. Wrap in foil for three days before serving.

Brenda Norwood Dusek (Collinsville)

CHOCOLATE ZUCCHINI CAKE

½ cup soft margarine
½ cup vegetable oil
1¾ cups sugar
2 eggs
1 teaspoon vanilla
½ cup sour milk
2½ cups unsifted flour

4 tablespoons cocoa
½ teaspoon baking powder
1 teaspoon baking soda
½ teaspoon cloves
½ teaspoon cinnamon
2 cups finely diced zucchini
¼ cup chocolate chips

Cream margarine, oil and sugar. Add eggs, vanilla and sour milk. Beat well with mixer. Mix together all dry ingredients. Add to creamed mixture. Beat well with mixer. Stir in diced zucchini. Spoon batter in greased and floured 9x12 pan. Sprinkle top with chocolate chips. Bake at 325° F. for 40 to 45 minutes.

Hilda Brakhane (Edwardsville)

ZUCCHINI CARROT CAKE

2 eggs
1 cup sugar
1 cup oil
1¼ cups flour
1 teaspoon baking powder
1 teaspoon baking soda

1 teaspoon cinnamon
½ teaspoon salt
1 cup grated carrots
1 cup grated zucchini,
    drained
½ cup chopped nuts

Beat eggs with sugar until frothy. Gradually beat in oil. Add flour, baking powder, baking soda, cinnamon and salt. Beat at high speed for 4 minutes. Stir in carrots, zucchini and nuts and pour into greased 9 inch square pan. Bake at 350° F. for 35 minutes.

CREAM CHEESE FROSTING:

1 3-ounce package cream
    cheese
3 tablespoons margarine

1 teaspoon vanilla
2 cups powdered sugar

Beat softened cream cheese, margarine and vanilla. Slowly add powdered sugar and beat until smooth.

Janice Bradley (Marine)

344

CUPCAKE WITH SURPRISE

1 box chocolate cake mix

Mix as directed

SURPRISE MIXTURE:

1 6-ounce bag chocolate chips
1 egg
½ cup confectioners' sugar

1 teaspoon vanilla
1 8-ounce package
    Philadelphia cream cheese

Mix egg, sugar, vanilla and cheese. When mixed, add chocolate chips. Drop 1 teaspoon of mixture into center of cup cake. Bake as suggested on cake mix. Frost if desired.

Viola Huebener (Alton)

TRULY DIFFERENT CUP CAKES

4 squares semi-sweet
    chocolate
2 sticks margarine
¼ teaspoon butter flavored
    extract
1 teaspoon vanilla extract

1¾ cup sugar
1 cup flour
¼ teaspoon baking powder
4 eggs
1½ cups chopped pecans

Melt together the chocolate and margarine and let cool. Add butter flavoring and vanilla; blend, *don't beat*. Blend together sugar, flour, baking powder and eggs; add to first mixture and blend, *don't beat*. Add pecans. Line cup cake pan with paper liners ⅔ full. Bake in 325° F. oven for 30 minutes.

Gracie Koeller (Godfrey)
Virginia Herrmann (Edwardsville)

CAKES

CAKES

PIES

Glen Carbon caught the spirit of '76 and constructed a covered bridge at the west end of Main Street.

EASY PIE CRUST

2 cups flour
¾ cup shortening
¾ teaspoon salt

6 tablespoons cola or 7-up or
Pepsi

Put in large plastic sealed bowl. Shake until it forms a ball. Roll as for any pie crust. Enough for 9 inch double crust.

Barbara Floyd (Edwardsville)

LAZY CRUST

1 stick margarine
1 cup flour
⅔ cup milk
¼ teaspoon salt or dash of
  salt

1 teaspoon baking powder
1 cup sugar
4 cups fruit (approximately)

Melt margarine in 9x13 inch pan. Mix next 4 ingredients and spoon over margarine. Mix sugar with fruit and put on top of batter. Bake at 350° F. until golden brown, about 30 minutes. You can use cherries, peaches, apples, plums, blackberries or any other fruit. Use 1 teaspoon cinnamon for apples. It's like a cobbler.

M. L. Maedge (Highland)

VINEGAR PIE PASTRY

Refrigerate or freeze

4 cups flour (all purpose)
1 tablespoon sugar
2 teaspoons salt
1¾ cups shortening

½ cup water
2 tablespoons cider vinegar
1 egg

In a large bowl, combine flour, sugar and salt with pastry blender. Cut shortening until mixture resembles coarse crumbs. Combine water, vinegar and egg and beat with fork. Pour into flour mixture. Mix well until pastry holds together. (Dough will be sticky.) Cover and chill at least 2 hours. Divide dough into 4 or 5 balls. Wrap tightly and refrigerate up to 2 weeks or freeze up to 2 months. Makes enough for 4 or 5 single crust pies.

Gracie Koeller (Godfrey)

NO ROLL PIE CRUST

Put in pie pan:

1½ cups flour
1½ teaspoons sugar
1 teaspoon salt

½ cup oil
2 tablespoons milk

Combine oil and milk in shaker and pour over flour, use fork to mix and shape in pan. Prick with fork and bake at 425° F. for 12 to 15 minutes.

Mrs. Hilda Brakhane (Edwardsville)

NEVER FAIL PASTRY

5 cups flour
1 tablespoon sugar
1 tablespoon salt

1 egg
Ice water
1 pound lard

Sift flour, blend in sugar and salt. Cut in lard. Put egg in a measuring cup; beat; add enough ice water to fill cup. Add to lard and flour mixture. Blend well. You will have enough pastry for five double pies. It will keep in refrigerator for three weeks.

Lillian Brokaw (Granite City)

GRANDMA NOLLAU'S CRUMB APPLE PIE

Prepare crust for a single 9 inch pie.

7 to 8 apples thinly sliced

CRUMB TOPPING:

⅔ cups white sugar
⅓ cup brown sugar

⅓ cup flour
½ stick soft margarine

In a bowl, mix the sugars and flour together and add margarine. Mix well. Spread ⅓ cup of crumb topping mixture in bottom of pie shell. Put in apple slices, heaping them high. Spoon the remaining topping mixture onto the apples. Make a small hole in the topping (center of the pie) and pour in ¼ cup milk. Close hole. Sprinkle with cinnamon. Bake at 350° F. for 1 hour.

June Launhardt (Collinsville)

APPLE PIE TOPPING

PIES

¼ cup brown sugar
2 tablespoons flour
3 tablespoons Karo blue label syrup

2 tablespoons softened margarine
¼ cup chopped pecans

Mix together. Spread on top crust of baked pie. Return to oven for 10 minutes or until topping is bubbly.

Alice Stille (Alhambra)

SHORTBREAD CRUST FOR FRUIT PIE

½ pound butter
½ cup sugar
½ cup cornstarch

2 cups flour
Pinch salt

Cream butter and sugar until white and fluffy. Sift together cornstarch, flour and salt. Add gradually to the creamed mixture. Knead until smooth. Press into pie plate. Prick with a fork. Bake 325° F. for 30 minutes or until done.

Gracie Koeller (Godfrey)

PINEAPPLE-GLAZED APPLE PIE

1½ cups unsweetened pineapple juice
¾ cup sugar
7 medium apples, peeled, cored, wedged
3 tablespoons cornstarch

1 tablespoon butter
½ teaspoon vanilla
¼ teaspoon salt
1 baked 9-inch pie shell, cooled

In large saucepan combine 1¼ cups pineapple juice and the sugar. Bring to boiling; add apple wedges. Simmer, covered, 3 to 4 minutes or until apples are tender. With slotted spoon, lift apples from pineapple liquid; set apples aside to drain. Blend remaining ¼ cup pineapple juice slowly into cornstarch; add to hot pineapple liquid in saucepan. Cook and stir until mixture thickens and bubbles; cook 1 minute more. Remove from heat. Stir in the butter, vanilla and salt. Cover and cool 30 minutes without stirring. Pour half the pineapple mixture into the baked pie shell, spreading to cover bottom. Arrange apples atop. Spoon remaining mixture over apples. Cover and refrigerate till chilled. May be garnished with whipped cream.

Marina Brugger (East Alton)

353

MOCK APPLE PIE

2 cups water
1½ cups sugar
2 teaspoons cream of tartar
1 stick butter

22 Ritz crackers
1 lemon
Cinnamon to taste
1 deep dish pie crust

Bring water, sugar and cream of tartar to boil. Add butter and Ritz crackers. Boil 2 minutes. Add the juice of lemon donna and cinnamon and put in unbaked pie shell. Bake at 350° F. for 25 minutes. Note: If desired, serve with Cool Whip.

Suzanne Blattner (Madison)

HEAVENLY CHERRY PIE

1 envelope unflavored gelatin
¼ cup cold water
1 can cherry pie filling
½ cup flaked coconut
½ cup chopped nuts
½ teaspoon vanilla

¼ cup powdered sugar
1 cup heavy cream or Dream Whip
1 9-inch baked graham cracker crust

Soften gelatin in cold water. Add ¼ cup water to cherry pie filling. Bring to a boil. Remove from heat and add softened gelatin, stirring until dissolved. Chill. When slightly congealed, whip until fluffy, add coconut, nuts and flavoring. Beat powdered sugar into whipped cream. Fold half of whipped cream into gelatin fruit mixture and spoon into pie shell. Cover pie with remaining whipped cream and chill thoroughly.

Wilma Ernst (Alhambra)

CHERRY CUSTARD CRUSTLESS PIE

4 eggs
1 cup sugar
½ cup flour
2 cups milk
1 cup coconut

6 tablespoons butter
½ teaspoon salt
2 teaspoons vanilla
Top with ¾ cup cherries

Preheat oven to 350° F. Put all ingredients except cherries, in blender. Blend for 10 seconds at a time—3 times. Pour into buttered and floured 10 inch pyrex pie pan. Carefully stir in cherries. Bake for 50 minutes. Chill.

Donna Sievers (Staunton)

CPR PIE

Prepare crust for a single 9-inch pie.

3 eggs, beaten
1½ cups sugar
3½ tablespoons margarine,
  melted
1½ tablespoons vinegar

¾ cup sweet shredded
  Coconut
¾ cup chopped Pecans
¾ cup Raisins

To the beaten eggs, add the remaining ingredients in the order listed. Pour into pie shell. Bake at 350° F. for 25 to 30 minutes. The pie may be shakey when removed from the oven but will settle.

June Launhardt (Collinsville)

CUSTARD PIE

4 eggs
½ cup self-rising flour
1½ cups sugar
¼ cup melted butter

2 cups milk
2 cups flaked coconut
¼ teaspoon nutmeg
1 tablespoon rum flavoring

Beat eggs. Mix flour with sugar and nutmeg. Add to eggs with remaining ingredients. Blend until well mixed. Pour into a 10 inch pie pan. Bake at 350° F. for 35 minutes or until done.

Reita Sparrowk (Bethalto)

IMPOSSIBLE PIE

4 eggs
½ cup flour
¼ teaspoon salt
2 cups milk
1 teaspoon vanilla
¼ cup butter

1 cup sugar
½ teaspoon baking powder
1 cup coconut (I use fruit
  instead of coconut,
  sometimes)

Put all ingredients into blender at once. Blend until mixed. Pour into 10 inch pie pan. Bake 1 hour at 350° F.

Evelyn Keilbach (Highland)
Mrs. Eileen Becker (Moro)

Note: ½ cup of Bisquick may be substituted in place of the ½ cup flour and ½ teaspoon baking powder.

Janice Bradley (Marine)

355

COCONUT CREAM PIE

1 9-inch pie shell, baked
⅓ cup sugar
¼ teaspoon salt
5 tablespoons cornstarch
1 tablespoon butter

3 egg yolks, well beaten
3 cups milk, scalded
¼ cup shredded coconut
1 teaspoon vanilla flavoring
¼ teaspoon nutmeg

Prepare and bake pie shell. Combine sugar, salt and cornstarch with butter. Blend thoroughly. Stir into yolks. Gradually pour milk over egg mixture, stirring constantly, until thick. Remove from heat and stir in remaining ingredients. Cool. Pour into pie shell. Top with 3 egg meringue. Sprinkle with coconut. Bake in oven, 325° F., for 15 to 20 minute, until coconut is lightly browned.

THREE EGG MERINGUE:

3 egg whites
¼ teaspoon cream of tartar

6 tablespoons sugar

Beat egg whites and cream of tartar to a stiff foam. Gradually add sugar, 1 tablespoon at a time. Beat until meringue is thick but not dry. Swirl on cold filling. Bake at 325° F. for 15 minutes.

Mary Jane Gass (Granite City)

SOUR CREAM RHUBARB CRUMB PIE

3 cups rhubarb, cut up
1 cup sour cream
1¼ cups sugar
1 egg, beaten

3 tablespoons flour
½ teaspoon salt
1 teaspoon vanilla
1 unbaked pie shell

Mix well and pour in unbaked pie shell. Bake 15 minutes at 400° F. Bake another 25 minutes at 350° F. Then add crumb topping and bake another 15 to 20 minutes.

CRUMB TOPPING:

⅓ cup sugar
⅓ cup flour
¼ cup margarine

1 teaspoon cinnamon or
  nutmeg
Pinch of salt

Mix together and sprinkle on pie.

Melba Helmkamp (East Alton)

EASY CHEESE PIE

2 8-ounce packages cream
  cheese
¼ cup sugar
2 teaspoons lemon juice

½ teaspoon vanilla
3 eggs
1 9-inch pie crust or graham
  cracker crust

Heat oven to 325° F. Combine cream cheese, sugar, lemon juice and vanilla. Mix well until blended. Add eggs, one at a time, mixing well after each addition, about 3 minutes. Pour into crust and bake for 30 minutes. Chill.

Ruth Holman (Granite City)

OATMEAL PIE

3 eggs
⅔ cup white sugar
1 cup brown sugar
⅔ cup uncooked oatmeal

⅔ cup grated coconut
1 teaspoon vanilla
½ cup milk
2 tablespoons butter

Mix well and pour into unbaked 10 inch pie shell and bake 30 minutes at 375° F.

Mrs. Louvain Vieth (Edwardsville)

PEAR PIE

6 firm (medium) pears
½ cup sugar
3 tablespoons cornstarch

3 tablespoons lemon juice
1 teaspoon grated lemon peel
1 10-inch unbaked pie shell

Preheat oven to 400° F. Combine pears, peeled, cored and sliced, with sugar, cornstarch, lemon juice and peel. Mix gently but thoroughly. Spoon into unbaked pie shell. Add topping.

TOPPING:

½ cup flour
½ cup sugar
½ teaspoon cinnamon

½ teaspoon ginger
⅓ cup butter

Combine flour, sugar and spices in small bowl. Cut in butter with pastry blender; sprinkle evenly over top of pie. Bake for 45 minutes at 400° F.

Florence Highlander (Hamel)

LEMON CREAM PIE

FILLING:

¾ cup plus 2 tablespoons
   sugar
3 tablespoons cornstarch
3 tablespoons flour
¼ teaspoon salt

1¾ cups water
2 eggs
juice of 2 lemons
grated rind of 1 lemon

MERINGUE:

2 egg whites
4 teaspoons water

4 tablespoons sugar

Measure flour and cornstarch, then sift with the sugar and salt. Add water and cook in double boiler until thick and clear. Stir in slightly beaten egg yolks and cook 1 minute. Remove from heat and add lemon juice and grated rind, fill 10 inch baked pie shell. Cover with meringue made by beating together until foamy, 2 egg whites and 4 teaspoons of cold water, add 4 tablespoons sugar and beat until stiff. Bake in 325° F. oven for 16 minutes or until golden brown.

NOTE: The 2 teaspoons of water to each egg white gives more volume and makes a more tender meringue. Measure flour before sifting.

Eva Koeller (Godfrey)

STRAWBERRY RHUBARB PIE

1½ cups sugar
3 tablespoons quick cooking
   tapioca
¼ teaspoon salt
¼ teaspoon nutmeg
1 pound rhubarb, cut in ½
   inch pieces (3 cups)

1 cup sliced, fresh
   strawberries
1 tablespoon butter
2 crust unbaked pastry recipe
Currant jelly, optional

In large bowl combine sugar, tapioca, salt and nutmeg. Add rhubarb and strawberries; mix well to coat fruit. Let stand about 20 minutes. Spoon fruit mixture into pastry-lined 9-inch pie plate. Dot with butter. Moisten pastry edge. Top with lattice crust; flute edge. Bake in hot oven 400° F. for 35 to 40 minutes. If desired, decorate lattice top with additional sliced fresh strawberries dipped in melted currant jelly.

Ruth Ann Henke (Staunton)

GRANDMA'S CUSTARD PUMPKIN PIE

3 cups pumpkin
1 can condensed milk
2 teaspoons cinnamon
½ teaspoon cloves

8 eggs
1½ cups sugar
½ teaspoon nutmeg
Pinch of salt

Beat eggs, milk and pumpkin with mixer. Add sugar and spices and mix again. Bake in two unbaked pie shells for ten minutes at 450° F. and about 45 minutes to one hour at 400° F. Done when knife inserted in middle comes out clean.

Donna Koenig (Edwardsville)

GRAPE PIE

2 pie crusts
4 cups Concord grapes
1 cup sugar
3 tablespoons flour

Dash salt
1 tablespoon lemon juice
1 tablespoon butter
¼ teaspoon cinnamon

Preheat oven to 400° F. Remove skins from grapes and put in bowl. Put the grapes in pan over medium heat and boil until seeds look free of pulp. Strain well and add to grape skins. Add sugar which has been mixed with flour and cinnamon and salt. Add lemon juice, stir well and put in pie crust. Dot with butter and cover with crust. Bake about 40 minutes.

Suzanne Blattner (Madison)

FRUIT PIE

1½ cups sugar
½ cup cornstarch (packed)
Dash salt
1 #2-can crushed pineapple

1 #2-can sour bing cherries
1 teaspoon vanilla
4 bananas, diced
1 cup pecans

Drain pineapple and bing cherries, save juice and add water to make 2 cups liquid. Pour liquid into a pan and add dry ingredients and cook until thick. Remove from heat and add pineapple and cherries. Add vanilla. Let cool. Then add bananas and pecans. Pour into shortbread crust and store in the refrigerator. When ready to serve, top with real whipped cream or Cool Whip.

Gracie Koeller (Godfrey)

MILLIONAIRE PIE

1 unbaked pie shell (9 inch,
   rather deep)
1 cup sour cream
1 cup raisins
1 cup sugar
1 cup nutmeats

1 cup coconut
1 teaspoon cinnamon
3 beaten eggs
½ teaspoon salt
½ teaspoon nutmeg
½ teaspoon cloves

Mix eggs and sour cream together. Mix spices and sugar together. Combine everything and put in unbaked pie shell. Bake in 350° F. oven for 45 minutes.

Mrs. George P. Eckert (Collinsville)

PECAN PIE

1 cup corn syrup
1 tablespoon butter
⅛ teaspoon salt
3 eggs
½ cup sugar

1 teaspoon vanilla
1 cup chopped pecans
Whipped cream for topping
1 unbaked pie shell

Put all together and mix with rotary beater. Put in unbaked pie shell and bake slowly for 1 hour at 300° F. Serve with whipped cream topping.

Pamela Nungesser (Highland)

Blender useful to smooth applesauce and pumpkin for pie.

RHUBARB MERINGUE PIE

3 cups frozen rhubarb, cut in
   small pieces
3 egg yolks
1 stick butter

1 cup sugar
3 rounded tablespoons flour
1 baked pie shell
Meringue topping

Put butter in pan and melt, then add rhubarb, egg yolks, sugar and flour. Cook about 10 to 15 minutes. If too thick add a little milk. Pour into baked pie shell and put meringue on top.

Virginia Herrmann (Edwardsville)

STRAWBERRY PIE

1 envelope or 1 tablespoon
  unflavored gelatin
Dash salt
1 cup sugar

1¾ cups water
Few drops red food coloring
4 cups sliced strawberries
1 baked 9-inch pie shell

In a heavy sauce pan, combine gelatin, salt and sugar. Add water. Cook stirring constantly until gelatin is dissolved. Cool. Add food coloring. Chill until partially set. Fold in berries. Pour into pie crust and chill until firm. Trim with whipped cream.

Mrs. Edward Barth (Brighton)

STRAWBERRY PIE

1 cup sugar
1½ cups water
2½ tablespoons cornstarch
1 3-ounce box strawberry
  Jello

1 quart fresh strawberries,
  sliced
1 9-inch baked pie crust

Combine sugar, water and cornstarch. Cook until thick and clear. Add gelatin and cool slightly. Add sliced strawberries. Pour into a 9-inch baked pie crust. Refrigerate. Serve with whipped cream.

Lorraine Gremaud (Granite City)

PIES

DESSERTS

Western Military Academy fell victim to inflation and is now used by the Baptist Church as the Mississippi Valley Christian School. Tennis courts are used by the Alton Tennis Club

ANGEL PARADISE

1 cup sugar
1 cup boiling mixture of
water and juice from
drained pineapple
2 tablespoons plain gelatin
4 tablespoons cold water for
soaking gelatin
1 cup orange juice (use fresh
only)

Juice of 1 lemon
Dash salt
1 8¾-ounce can crushed
pineapple
1 4-ounce bottle maraschino
cherries, drained
1 pint whipping cream
2 1-pound angel food cakes
(may be bought)

Pour mixture of boiling water and juice from drained pineapple over sugar. Soaked gelatin is added and mixture is stirred until dissolved. After orange and lemon juices and dash of salt are stirred in, the completed mixture is chilled until partially thickened. Brown crust from cake is removed and discarded. Cake is broken into bite size pieces. Cherries are chopped and added to gelatin mixture along with the drained pineapple. The whipping cream is folded in last. Line a large mixing bowl with waxed paper and fill with alternate layers of cake pieces and filling mixture. Cake layer is on bottom and top. A flat plate is placed on top in order to slightly compress the layers and the filled bowl is refrigerated for 24 hours. Cake is unmolded onto serving plate and is frosted with sweetened whipped cream and flavored with the vanilla, then thickly sprinkled with coconut.

TOPPING:

1 pint whipping cream
Vanilla to taste

Sugar to taste
7 ounces flaked coconut

Marge Norwood (Collinsville)

BAKED CHEESECAKE

1 package crescent rolls
3 8-ounce packages cream
cheese
1 8-ounce carton sour cream

1 cup sugar
5 eggs
1 tablespoon vanilla
Cinnamon

Lay crescent rolls in bottom of 9x13 inch pan. Beat all ingredients together until creamy. Pour over rolls. Sprinkle with cinnamon. Bake at 350° F. for 45 minutes.

Donna Koenig (Edwardsville)

ANGELFOOD PUDDING

Bake cake the day before or buy an angel food cake

1 package lemon Jello
2 cups liquid, drained
   pineapple juice and water
1 20-ounce can chunk
   pineapple, drained

1 package miniature, colored
   marshmallows
1 package Dream Whip

Heat liquid and mix with Jello. Chill. Whip Jello when it has thickened. Prepare Dream Whip according to package directions. Mix with Jello, pineapple and marshmallows. Break cake into small pieces and put into 9x13 inch pan. Pour Jello mixture over cake and refrigerate over night.

Mrs. Edward Barth (Brighton)

EASY PUDDING

2 egg yolks
¾ cup sugar
1¾ cups milk
1 tablespoon flour

1 tablespoon cornstarch
1 tablespoon milk
1 teaspoon vanilla

Heat milk. Mix sugar, flour, cornstarch (add 1 tablespoon of milk to make moist) and beat in egg yolks. Add this mixture to the hot milk. Stir until bubbles appear, cooking over medium heat. Cool.

VARIATION: Add 1 tablespoon cocoa for chocolate pudding. Add 1 tablespoon flour or cornstarch extra for pie filling.

Norma Hemann (New Douglas)

CHERRY PARTY DESSERT

1 large container Cool Whip
1 can Eagle Brand condensed
   milk
1 16-ounce can crushed
   pineapple, drained

1 #2 can cherry pie filling
1 cup nuts, chopped
1 cup coconut, optional

Stir together in a large mixing bowl. Chill in serving dish. A quick, pretty dessert that can be frozen.

Mrs. Verna Abert (New Douglas)

APPLE DUMPLINGS

2 quarts apples, peeled and
   quartered
2 cups water
1 teaspoon vanilla
½ to ¾ cup sugar

1 tablespoon butter
1 cup biscuit mix
⅓ cup milk
2 tablespoons sugar
Cinnamon

Place apples in saucepan with the water. Add vanilla and sugar. Cover and cook. Add butter, set aside. For dumplings, mix together biscuit mix, milk and 2 tablespoons sugar. Moisten a tablespoon in the juice first, then spoon biscuit mixture onto juice and apples, making approximately six dumplings. Cover and simmer for 10 minutes. Sprinkle with cinnamon.

Mrs. Donna Sievers (Staunton)

CHEESE CUP CAKES

3 8-ounce packages cream
   cheese
1 cup sugar
5 eggs
1 teaspoon vanilla

1 cup sour cream
½ cup sugar
½ teaspoon vanilla
1 1-pound can of Cherry pie
   filling

Preheat oven to 350° F. Mix together the cream cheese, 1 cup sugar, eggs and 1 teaspoon vanilla. Pour into cup cake tins lined with papers. Fill ½ to ¾ full. Bake 40 minutes. Mix sour cream, ½ cup sugar and ½ teaspoon vanilla. Put a teaspoonful on top of each cake. Add a teaspoon pie filling and bake 5 minutes more. Makes about 24 cup cakes.

Myra Campbell (Edwardsville)

CHEESECAKE

2 8-ounce packages cream
   cheese
3 eggs
½ cup sugar

½ teaspoon almond extract
½ pint sour cream
2 tablespoons sugar
1 teaspoon vanilla

Blend together cream cheese, eggs, ½ cup sugar and extract. Put into 9 inch pie plate and bake ½ hour at 350° F. Remove from oven. Turn oven to 300° F. Mix well together, sour cream, sugar and vanilla. Pour into sunken shell. Bake at 300° F. for 10 minutes.

Sharon Schlaefer (St. Jacob)

COOL WHIP CAKE

First Layer:

Mix together
½ cup margarine
1 cup flour

½ cup nuts

Spread in 9x13 inch oblong pan. Bake 15 minutes at 350° F.

Second Layer:

Mix together
1 8-ounce package cream
  cheese

1 cup powdered sugar
1 medium carton Cool Whip

Spread over first layer when it is cool.

Third Layer:

Cook
1 large package vanilla
  pudding in

2½ cups milk

Let cool before adding to the above.

Fourth Layer:

Spread can of cherry pie filling over third layer.

Fifth Layer:

Add
1 medium Cool Whip
1 cup shredded or angel flake
  coconut

Maraschino cherries

The Maraschino cherries are for decoration and can be omitted if so desired. Chill well. Very tasty.

Mary K. Willaredt (Granite City)

CHERRY CHEESECAKE

CRUST:

2½ cups vanilla wafers,
  crushed

½ cup chopped nuts
1 stick margarine, melted

Combine all ingredients and press into oblong baking dish, 9x13x2 inches.

FILLING:

3 8-ounce packages cream
  cheese
1 cup sugar

3 eggs
½ teaspoon vanilla

Cream the cheese and sugar. Add eggs, one at a time, beat well. Add vanilla. Spoon onto crust. Bake 20 minutes at 375° F. Remove from oven.

Beat:

1 pint sour cream
3 tablespoons sugar

¼ teaspoon vanilla

Spoon on top of cheese filling. Bake 5 minutes at 500° F. Remove from heat, cool. Spoon on 1 can cherry pie filling. Chill before serving.

Mildred Dustmann (Dorsey)

CHERRY SLICES

1 cup margarine, creamed
1¾ cups sugar
4 eggs
1 teaspoon vanilla
3 cups flour

1½ teaspoons baking powder
½ teaspoon salt
1 21-ounce can cherry pie
  filling (may use other fruit
  fillings)

Preheat oven to 350° F. Add sugar to margarine and beat well. Add eggs, one at a time, beating well after each addition. Add vanilla. Sift flour, baking powder and salt. Add dry ingredients gradually and beat well. Spread about ⅔ of batter into 11x17 inch pan, greased and floured, keeping ⅓ for top. Spread fruit filling on batter. Place remaining batter on top by spoonfuls, spreading best you can. Bake 30-40 minutes. Frost with confectioners' sugar if desired.

Ginger Schuette (Staunton)

UNBAKED CHEESE CAKE

1 8-ounce package cream
  cheese
1 cup white sugar
1 teaspoon vanilla
1 3-ounce box lemon Jello

1 cup boiling water
1 can Milnot (large)
1 tablespoon lemon juice
Graham cracker crust

Cream the cream cheese with the sugar and vanilla. Prepare Jello with hot water and let thicken. Mix with the cheese mixture and whip well with mixer. Whip Milnot until thick and firm and fold into cheese mixture with the lemon juice. Pour into graham cracker crust and chill.

GRAHAM CRACKER CRUST:

20 graham crackers, crushed
¾ stick margarine, melted

¼ cup sugar

Mix above ingredients together and pat into 9x13 inch pan.

Mrs. Lawrence Wall (New Douglas)

CONFECTION STRAWBERRIES

5 tablespoons butter
1 cup sugar
2 eggs
1½ cups chopped dates
Pinch salt

1 teaspoon vanilla
2½ cups rice cereal
1 cup pecans, chopped
Red sugar

Melt butter over low heat in electric skillet, add eggs and sugar beaten together. Stir the mixture to blend. Chopped dates are added and heat is increased to 340° F. Continue mixing as mixture melts. This will require about 10 minutes, after which the heat is turned off and add salt and vanilla. Mixture should be a thick molted mass, soft enough to saturate the rice cereal and nuts and still be thick enough to be shaped into individual strawberries. Drop these into red sugar immediately after forming, roll to coat all sides, then set aside to cool. Makes 40 large or 50 small pieces. Make green strawberry top out of green paper and attach with green toothpick.

Virginia Herrmann (Edwardsville)

SHARON'S RUM CHEESE CAKE

1¼ cups graham cracker
   crumbs
¼ cup sugar
6 tablespoons butter or
   margarine, melted
1 envelope unflavored gelatin
½ cup sugar
½ cup Bacardi light rum

1 tablespoon grated lime peel
½ cup lime juice
4 eggs, separated
2 8-ounce packages cream
   cheese, softened
½ cup sugar
1 cup heavy cream

Combine crumbs, ¼ cup sugar and butter or margarine: reserve 3 tablespoons crumb mixture. Press remaining crumbs in bottom of 9-inch springform pan: chill. Meanwhile, combine gelatin and ½ cup sugar in medium saucepan: stir in rum, lime peel and juice. Beat egg yolks and blend into rum mixture. Cook over medium heat, stirring constantly, until slightly thickened, about 8 minutes; remove from heat. Beat in cream cheese until smooth. Set aside. Beat egg whites until foamy; gradually beat in remaining ½ cup sugar; beat until stiff peaks form. Now whip cream to soft peaks. Fold egg whites and whipped cream into rum mixture. Turn into crumb-lined pan; sprinkle with reserved crumbs. Cover and chill several hours, or until firm. (Makes 12 servings)

Mrs. Oma Heepke (Edwardsville)

THE BEST APPLE CRISP

5 pounds Jonathan apples
1 cup sugar

2 or 3 teaspoons cinnamon
¼ cup water

TOPPING:

1½ cups flour
1 cup sugar

Pinch of salt
2 sticks margarine

Preheat oven to 350° F. Grease a 9x13x2 inch pan. Peel and slice apples and place in pan. Combine sugar, cinnamon and pour over apples. Sprinkle with water. Then blend flour, sugar, salt, and margarine with pastry blender. When crumbly, spread over apples. Bake about 1 hour or until golden brown.

Beverly Meyer (Edwardsville)

CHEESE TARTS

2 8-ounce packages cream
  cheese
2 eggs
½ cup sugar
2 teaspoons vanilla

24 vanilla wafers
1 #2 can cherry pie filling
Prepared whipped cream
  topping

Soften cheese and beat with eggs, sugar and vanilla for 5 minutes. Place 24 liners in muffin tins and put vanilla wafer in each. Divide cheese mixture into them. Bake 350° F. for 12 minutes. Cool. Spoon cherries on top and garnish with cream.

Ruth Brave (Granite City)

GREEN CRÈME-DE-MENTHE SHERBET RING

3 pints lemon sherbet
⅓ cup green crème-de-menthe

1 quart fresh strawberries
Confectioners' sugar

Let sherbet stand in refrigerator 30 minutes to soften slightly. Turn into large bowl and beat with mixer until smooth but not melted. Quickly stir in crème-de-menthe until well blended. Put in 5½ cup ring mold. Freeze until firm. Wash strawberries, drain, do not hull. Refrigerate. To serve, invert ring mold on round, chilled platter. Place strawberries in center of mold. Dust lightly with confectioners' sugar. Serve immediately. Serves 8.

Frances Runyon (Wood River)

DANISH PUFF

1 cup flour
½ cup butter
2 tablespoons water
1 cup water
½ cup butter

1 cup flour
3 large eggs
1 teaspoon almond extract
Icing, cherries, nuts

Mix flour, butter, 2 tablespoons water as for pie crust. Divide into 2 balls. Form each ball into a 3x12 inch oblong. Place on cookie sheet.

Then heat 1 cup water and butter to boiling and add flour all at once. Stir together until it clears the sides of the bowl. Add the eggs, one at a time, beating after each one. Add the almond extract. Divide and spread over the bottom layer, spreading not quite to the edge. Bake at 350° F. for 55 minutes. Decorate with white icing, cherries and nuts.

Mrs. Charlene Bandy (Moro)

DATE PUDDING

3 eggs
1 cup sugar
1 cup nuts, chopped
1 cup dates, chopped

1 cup bread crumbs
2 teaspoons baking powder
1 teaspoon vanilla
Whipped cream

Beat eggs. Add sugar and beat to mix. Stir in remaining ingredients. Pour into 9x13 inch greased and floured pan. Bake 350° F. for 25 minutes. Refrigerate overnight. Serve with whipped cream.

Ruth Brave (Granite City)

FRUIT PIZZA

¾ cup softened butter
⅓ cup powdered sugar
1½ cups flour
8 ounces softened cream
   cheese
½ cup sugar
1 teaspoon vanilla

1½ cups any fruit, cherries,
   berries, peaches, etc.
1 tablespoon cornstarch
½ cup fruit juice (pineapple)
¼ cup sugar
1 tablespoon lemon juice

Ahead of time, soften cream cheese and butter. For crust; mix butter, ⅓ cup sugar and flour with beaters until crumbly. Press into greased 12 inch pizza pan. Bake at 300° F. until edges turn slightly brown. Cool.

SAUCE: Mix softened cream cheese, ½ cup sugar, vanilla and spread evenly over crust.

TOPPING: Arrange any combination of fruit on cream mixture. Use sliced bing cherries, strawberries, blueberries, pineapple, peach slices, mandarin orange slices, melon balls, etc.

GLAZE: Combine cornstarch, fruit juice, sugar, lemon juice and mix in a saucepan and heat to boiling until thick. Cool slightly. Spoon glaze over all fruit to preserve color. Keep refrigerated.

NOTE: If using canned peaches, substitute the syrup for the juice and omit sugar.

Carol Russell (Bethalto)

CREAM PUFFS

1 cup water	2 large cartons whipped
½ cup butter	cream or vanilla cream
1 cup flour	pudding, prepared as
4 eggs	directed
	Powdered sugar

Heat oven to 400° F. Heat water and butter to rolling boil. Stir in flour and stir vigorously over low heat about 1 minute or until mixture forms a ball. Remove from heat. Beat in eggs, all at once. Continue beating until smooth. Drop dough by scant ¼ cupfuls, 3 inches apart onto ungreased sheet. Bake 35 to 40 minutes or until puffed and golden color. Cool away from draft. Cut off tops. Pull out any filaments of soft dough. Carefully fill puffs with filling. Whipped cream or vanilla pudding. You may ice or sprinkle on powdered sugar.

ICING:

1 ounce unsweetened	1 cup confectioners' sugar
chocolate	2 tablespoons hot water
1 teaspoon butter	

Heat chocolate and butter over low heat. Gradually add sugar and the hot water. Pour over tops of cream puffs.

Mrs. Lylah Hock (Cottage Hills)

RHUBARB CRUNCH

1 cup sifted flour	1 cup sugar
1 cup uncooked quick	2 tablespoons cornstarch
oatmeal	1 cup water
1 cup brown sugar	1 teaspoon vanilla
½ cup soft margarine	Red food coloring (if using
1 teaspoon cinnamon	green rhubarb)
4 cups raw diced rhubarb	

Preheat oven to 350° F. Mix the first five ingredients until crumbly. Place ½ of this mixture in a greased 9 inch square pan. Cover the crumb mixture with diced rhubarb. Cook the sugar, cornstarch and water until thick and clear, stirring constantly. Pour over rhubarb and crumb combination, top with remaining crumbs. Bake for 1 hour. Cut into squares and serve warm. May top with a scoop of ice cream or whipped cream.

Mrs. Virginia Schuette (Staunton)

RHUBARB TORTE

1 cup butter
2 cups flour
4 tablespoons sugar
5 cups finely cut rhubarb
6 eggs, separated
2 cups sugar
7 tablespoons flour

¼ teaspoon salt
1 cup cream (Milnot)
¾ cup sugar
¼ teaspoon salt
¼ teaspoon cream of tartar
1 teaspoon vanilla

Preheat oven to 350° F. Mix until crumbly butter, flour and sugar and pat into a 9x13 inch pan. Bake at 350° F. for 10 minutes. Mix together rhubarb, egg yolks, sugar, flour, salt and cream. Pour over crust. Now bake at 350° F. for 45 minutes, until custard is set.

MERINGUE: beat the 6 egg whites till stiff, gradually add ¾ cup sugar, ¼ teaspoon salt, ¼ teaspoon cream of tartar and vanilla. Continue beating until stiff. Spread over the torte and bake at 350° F. for 15 minutes or until lightly browned.

Roleen Henke (Staunton)

CO CO CREAM DESSERT

1 cup flour
½ cup butter
2 tablespoons sugar
½ cup walnuts or pecans,
  chopped
1 cup coconut, toasted in
  oven (set aside)
1 8-ounce package cream
  cheese

1 cup confectioners' sugar
1 8-ounce container Cool
  Whip
2 packages coconut cream
  pudding
3 cups milk

Mix first four ingredients and press into a 9x13x2 inch pan. Bake 15 minutes at 350° F. Cool. Beat cream cheese and confectioners' sugar until creamy, then fold in 1 cup Cool Whip. Spread on cooled crust. Cook pudding and milk until thick and let cool completely. Then spread over cheese layer. Top with rest of Cool Whip. Add toasted coconut to garnish.

Dottie Suhre (Alhambra)

VARIATION: Add one more 8-ounce package cream cheese and substitute instant lemon pudding for coconut pudding.

Mildred Dustmann (Dorsey)

CHOCOLATE TEMPTATION

1 cup powdered sugar
½ cup margarine
2 squares Baker's chocolate, melted
3 eggs, separated

½ cup nuts, chopped
½ pound vanilla wafers, rolled fine
Whipped cream

Melt chocolate and margarine. Add powdered sugar; mix until creamy. Add egg yolks. Beat egg whites and add to mixture; add nuts. Line bottom of Pyrex dish with half vanilla wafer crumbs. Pour in filling and top with remaining crumbs. Refrigerate for several hours. Serve with whipped cream. Will serve 4. Note: to double recipe, do not double vanilla wafers.

Unknown

TAPIOCA CREAM

2 egg yolks, slightly beaten
2 cups milk
2 tablespoons sugar
2 tablespoons quick-cooking tapioca

¼ teaspoon salt
1 teaspoon vanilla
2 egg whites
¼ cup sugar

Mix egg yolks, milk, 2 tablespoons sugar, tapioca and salt in sauce pan. Cook over low heat, stirring constantly, until mixture boils. Remove from heat. Cool. Stir in vanilla. Beat egg whites until frothy. Gradually beat in the ¼ cup sugar. Continue beating until stiff and glossy. Fold into mixture in the sauce pan. Put into dessert dishes and serve with cream or fruit juice. Serves 6.

Carleen Paul (Worden)

RITZY TORTE

3 egg whites
1 cup sugar
20 crushed Ritz crackers
½ cup chopped nuts

1 large banana
1 8-ounce container Cool Whip
¼ cup chopped nuts

Beat egg whites until stiff and then beat in sugar. Add Ritz crackers and ½ cup nuts. Spread in square pan. Bake 30 minutes in 350° F. oven. Let cool, then cover with sliced banana and Cool Whip. Top with ¼ cup chopped nuts.

Louise Eckert (Collinsville)

APRICOT DELIGHT

1 6-ounce package apricot
  Jello
2 cups boiling water
2 cups cold water
1 #2 can crushed pineapple,
  drained

2 large bananas, sliced
1 cup miniature
  marshmallows

Dissolve Jello in water. When partially set, add remaining ingredients. Pour into 9x13 inch Pyrex dish. Chill, and when set, pour topping over above.

TOPPING:

1 cup pineapple juice
2 tablespoons cornstarch
½ cup sugar

2 eggs, slightly beaten
¼ teaspoon salt
1 tablespoon butter

Mix the topping ingredients together and cook until thick. Cool. Blend in 1 cup whipped Dream Whip.

Donna Sievers (Staunton)

FOUR LAYER DELIGHT

1 stick margarine
1 cup flour
½ cup chopped nuts
1 cup confectioners' sugar
1 6-ounce package cream
  cheese
1 package Dream Whip
  (mixed by directions)

2 3-ounce packages chocolate
  instant pudding
4 cups milk
1 package Dream Whip
  (mixed by directions)
1 cup chopped nuts

Mix margarine, flour and ½ cup chopped nuts. Press into 13x9 inch baking dish. Bake at 350° for 15 minutes. Cool.

For second layer, combine confectioners' sugar, cream cheese and 1 package prepared Dream Whip. Pour over first layer. Refrigerate.

For third layer, mix chocolate pudding and milk. Pour over second layer.

For fourth layer, combine prepared Dream Whip and chopped nuts. Spread over third layer and refrigerate to chill well until ready to serve.

Marcia Fontana (Troy)

NO BAKE HEATH BAR DESSERT

1 package Lorna Doone
  cookies
1 stick butter
2 packages instant vanilla
  pudding

2 cups milk
1 quart butter pecan ice
  cream
1 large container Cool Whip
8 Heath bars, crushed

Crush cookies and mix with melted butter. Spread in a 9x13 inch pan. Mix instant pudding and milk and beat with mixer. Add ice cream and pour over crust. Let set in refrigerator for 30 minutes. Top with Cool Whip. Sprinkle crushed Heath bars on top. Hint: let ice cream melt a little before mixing. Freeze Heath bars before crushing.

Carol Russell (Bethalto)

NUTS IN A T-SHIRT

1 cup flour
1 3-ounce package cream
  cheese
¼ pound butter
¾ cup brown sugar

1 cup crushed pecans
1 egg
1 teaspoon vanilla
1 tablespoon melted butter

Cream well, flour, cream cheese and ¼ pound butter. Form into 24 small balls. Refrigerate one hour. Press into miniature cup cake pans. Mix together brown sugar, pecans, egg, vanilla and 1 tablespoon butter for filling. Put filling in center of cup cakes and bake 20 minutes at 375° F. Yield 24.

Louise Eckert (Collinsville)

STRAWBERRY DELIGHT

3 cups hot water
1 6-ounce package
  Strawberry Jello
1 pint whipping cream or
1 package Dream Whip
  prepared

1 quart sliced strawberries,
  sweetened and drained
Angel food cake

Break cake into pieces and put into a 13x9x2 inch pan. Mix Jello with 3 cups hot water and let set slightly. Mix strawberries and whipped cream with Jello and pour over cake. Do not stir. Let stand in refrigerator until ready to serve. Cut in squares to serve.

Helen Ernst (New Douglas)

EMMA JEAN'S PERSIMMON PUDDING

1 egg	1 teaspoon baking soda
2 cups milk	½ teaspoon salt
2 cups persimmon pulp	½ teaspoon allspice
2 cups flour	1 teaspoon cinnamon
1 cup sugar	

Beat together egg and milk; add all other ingredients, beating until well blended. Pour into buttered 2-quart baking dish (11¾x7½x1¾ inches). Bake in 325° F. oven for 1¼ hours. Serves 6.

Carolyn Losch (East Alton)

STRAWBERRY ANGEL DELIGHT

1 cup flour	1 quart frozen strawberries
½ cup brown sugar	(at least partially thawed to
½ cup margarine	separate easily)
½ cup pecans, chopped	3 cups whipped cream
4 tablespoons lemon juice	(or Dream Whip)
13 ounce jar marshmallow	
cream	

Combine flour and sugar, cut in margarine, add nuts. Press into 9x13 inch pan. Bake at 350° F. for 20 minutes. Cool. Gradually add lemon juice to marshmallow cream until well blended. Stir in strawberries. Fold in whipped cream, pour over crumb crust and freeze. One additional cup of whipped cream and ¼ cup nuts may be put on before freezing or as garnish or can be omitted. Yields 15 to 18 servings.

Irma Henkhaus (Alhambra)

STRAWBERRY VANILLA PUDDING

4½ to 5 cups angel cake cubes	1 3-ounce package strawberry
1 3 or 3¾-ounce package	gelatin
instant vanilla pudding mix	1½ cups boiling water
1 cup milk	1 10-ounce package frozen
1 pint vanilla ice cream	strawberry slices

Place angel cake cubes in 7x11 inch baking dish. In mixing bowl, combine instant pudding and milk; add ice cream. Beat at low speed until well blended. Pour over cake cubes. Set aside until firm. Dissolve gelatin in boiling water; add frozen strawberries. Stir until gelatin begins to thicken. Pour over pudding; do not stir. Chill until set.

Reita Sparrowk (Bethalto)

PUMPKIN-MARSHMALLOW SQUARES

50 large or 6 cups miniature
   marshmallows
1 16-ounce can pumpkin
1 teaspoon cinnamon
⅔ teaspoon nutmeg
¼ teaspoon allspice
¼ teaspoon ginger
Dash cloves

¼ teaspoon salt
3 cups whipped dessert
   topping (2 envelopes of
   Dream Whip)
2 cups crushed graham
   crackers
½ cup butter or margarine

In a large heavy sauce pan, at low heat, combine first eight ingredients and stir until smooth. Take off heat and cool at least 15 minutes, but while still warm, add 3 cups of whipped topping. While mixture is cooling, mix graham crumbs and butter together and take out ½ cup for topping. Pat remaining crumbs into a 9x13 inch pan. Pour pumpkin mixture over crumbs. Top with one cup or more of whipped cream and top with crumbs or omit cream and just sprinkle with reserved crumbs. Refrigerate several hours or over night. Cut into squares. Yields 15 to 18 servings.

Irma Henkhaus

STRAWBERRY DESSERT

2⅔ cups pretzels, crushed
3 tablespoons sugar

¾ cup butter

Cream the sugar and butter together. Add crushed pretzels and press in a greased 13x9x2 inch pan. Bake at 350° F. for 10 minutes and cool.

2 3-ounce packages
   strawberry Jello

2 cups hot water
1 pint frozen strawberries

Mix together and chill until slightly set.

1 8-ounce package cream
   cheese
1 cup sugar

1 9-ounce container Cool
   Whip

Cream together and spread cheese mixture over cooled pretzels covering to edges. Spread Jello mixture over this and chill.

JoAnn Brase (Edwardsville)

RICE PUDDING

½ cup rice
3 cups water
1½ teaspoons salt
1 can Eagle brand milk

2 eggs
1 teaspoon vanilla
¼ teaspoon nutmeg

Mix rice, water, and salt in a 2 quart saucepan, cover and bring to a boil. Reduce heat and simmer 15 minutes. Stir in milk. Beat eggs and add slowly to rice. Return to medium heat and stir constantly. Remove from heat and add vanilla and nutmeg. Serve warm or chilled.

Mrs. Cheryll Sievers (Staunton)

VANILLA WAFER CAKE

1 cup butter
2 cups sugar
6 eggs
1 12-ounce package vanilla
  wafers

½ cup milk
1 7-ounce package flaked
  coconut
1 cup chopped pecans

Crush vanilla wafers and set aside. Cream butter and sugar. Add eggs, one at a time, beating after each addition. Add crushed vanilla wafers alternately with milk. Fold in coconut and pecans. Pour into greased (solid shortening) and floured bundt pan, tube pan or 2 loaf pans. Bake 275° F. for 1 hour 40 minutes. Will be very brown. Cool in pan 20 minutes. Sprinkle with powdered sugar when cool. Freezes well.

Ruth Brave (Granite City)

BANANA SPLIT CAKE

2 sticks margarine
2 cups crushed graham
  cracker crumbs
2 eggs
2 cups powdered sugar

1 #2 can crushed pineapple
5 bananas, thinly sliced
1 large container Cool Whip
Nuts and cherries for topping

Melt 1 stick margarine and mix with crumbs. Press into a 9x13 inch pan. Beat eggs and powdered sugar; add 1 stick margarine. Spread over crumbs, cover with banana slices. Spread pineapple on top, then cover with Cool Whip. Add a few nuts and cherries, if desired.

Mrs. Cletus Hediger (Highland)
Myra Campbell (Edwardsville)

BREAD PUDDING

1 cup dark brown sugar	3 eggs, beaten
1 cup raisins	2 cups milk
3 slices bread, buttered	1 teaspoon vanilla
generously, cut into cubes	Pinch salt

Put in double boiler in order, brown sugar, raisins, bread cubes. Mix slightly beaten eggs with milk, vanilla and salt. Pour over bread. Don't stir. Simmer 1 hour.

Norma Meyer (Edwardsville)

PERFECT PEACH COBBLER

4 cups sliced peaches	½ teaspoon salt
1 tablespoon lemon juice	1 beaten egg
1 cup all-purpose flour	6 tablespoons butter
1 cup sugar	

Place peaches on bottom of 10x6x1½ inch baking dish. Sprinkle with lemon juice. Add ½ cup sugar to peaches and mix. Sift together dry ingredients. Add egg—toss with fork until crumbly. Sprinkle over peaches. Drizzle with butter. Bake at 375° F. for 35 to 40 minutes, or until slightly browned. Top with cinnamon ice cream, if desired; (1 pint vanilla ice cream, softened and ¾ teaspoon cinnamon.)

JoAnn Brase (Edwardsville)

PUMPKIN PIE CAKE

4 eggs, slightly beaten	1 teaspoon salt
2 cups pumpkin or 1 16-ounce	1 can Milnot (13 ounce)
can	1 box yellow cake mix
1½ cups sugar	2 sticks butter or margarine,
2 teaspoons pumpkin pie	melted
spice	1 cup chopped nuts

Mix first 6 ingredients in order listed. Pour into ungreased 9x13x2 inch pan. Sprinkle cake mix over filling. Pour melted butter over top of cake mix. Sprinkle with chopped nuts. Bake at 350° F. for one hour or until knife comes out clean when inserted at center. Serve warm or cold; plain or with whipped cream. Note: Keeps well frozen.

Norma Lesko (Granite City)
Reita Sparrowk (Bethalto)

YUM YUM CAKE

Mix:

2 cups flour
2 cups sugar
2 eggs

2 teaspoons baking soda
2 cups crushed pineapple and
juice

Pour into greased and floured oblong pan (9x13). Bake at 350° F. for 30 to 45 minutes. Cool.

TOPPING:

Boil 5 minutes
1 cup sugar
1 stick margarine
1 small can evaporated milk

1 cup coconut
1 cup chopped nuts

Spread on top of cake. (Very easy and delicious)

Judy Ernst

DESSERTS

DESSERTS

CANDY

The first governor of the Illinois territory built and lived in this home on Buchanan Street, Edwardsville. Ninian Edwards, a Kentuckian, was appointed governor by Madison.

CARAMELS

2 cups sugar
1 cup light corn syrup
A pinch of salt

¾ teaspoon vanilla
1 pint cream
½ cup butter

Mix sugar, syrup, salt, vanilla and one half of the cream. Cook to 220° F. Add remaining cream. Remove from heat, add butter, return to heat. Cook to 254° F. Stir constantly. Pour into buttered 8½x11-inch pan. Cool until lukewarm and not sticky. Cut into squares; wrap with waxed paper. Yield: 75 pieces.

Kathy Klein (New Douglas)

CHOCOLATE COVERED CHERRIES

3 cups sugar
½ cup white syrup
⅔ cup water
2 egg whites
Vanilla

1 box Baker's bitter chocolate
¼ bar parawax
10 ounce jar of maraschino
   cherries

Cook sugar, syrup and water for about 5 minutes or until it forms a hard ball immediately when dropped into a cup of cold water. Using the mixer, beat the egg whites until stiff. While the mixer is going, pour the hot mixture slowly into the beaten egg whites. Add 1 teaspoon vanilla. Keep beating until firm enough to form balls. Cherries should have been drained and patted dry with paper towel. Shape candy around each cherry, being sure to completely cover each cherry. Cool completely or overnight. Melt the chocolate and parawax in a double boiler. Dip the candy into the hot chocolate. Place candy on wax paper to cool. Using powdered sugar on your hands to form balls makes it a little less sticky to handle.

Nellie Dauderman (Alhambra)

CRACKER JACK

⅓ cup sorghum
2 tablespoons butter
1 cup sugar
⅔ cup water

2 tablespoons vinegar
¼ teaspoon baking soda
4-5 gallons of warm popcorn

Boil in four-quart pan to crack stage the first five ingredients. Beat in ¼ teaspoon baking soda. Pour over four to five gallons of warm popcorn. Use a very large pan or roaster to stir this up in.

Abby Daugherty (Granite City)

BUTTERSCOTCH CLUSTERS

1 package (6 ounce)
  butterscotch chips
¼ cup light corn syrup
¼ cup margarine

1 teaspoon vanilla
2 cups Cheerios
1 cup peanuts

Heat butterscotch chips, corn syrup, margarine and vanilla in a 2-quart saucepan over low heat, stirring constantly until butterscotch is melted and mixture is smooth. Remove from heat, stir in Cheerios and peanuts until well coated. Drop mixture by rounded teaspoonfuls onto waxed paper. Refrigerate until firm, about 25 minutes. Refrigerate any leftover candies. Makes about 3 dozen.

Suggestion: If you set the mixture on low heat and stir in Cheerios and peanuts, it mixes better. Also, drop the mixture into cupcake liners. May also add a few sunflower seeds or coconut for variety.

Melba Helmkamp (East Alton)

CINNAMON NUTS

1 cup sugar
½ teaspoon cinnamon
⅛ teaspoon cream tartar

¼ cup boiling water
½ cup walnut meats
½ teaspoon vanilla

Mix sugar, cinnamon, cream of tartar and water in saucepan. Boil until it reaches 246° F. on candy thermometer. Add nuts and cool slightly. Add vanilla and stir until mixture sugars and coats the nuts and turn onto waxed paper.

Gracie Koeller (Godfrey)

PEANUT SQUARES

2 sticks butter or margarine
1 1-pound box powdered
  sugar, sifted
1 cup peanut butter

1⅓ cups crushed graham
  crackers (fine)
1 12-ounce package chocolate
  chips

Melt butter or margarine and add peanut butter and stir well. Add powdered sugar and crushed graham cracker crumbs. Mix well, then press in a 9x13-inch pan. Melt the chocolate chips and pour on top. When cool, cut into squares.

Myrna Strohmeier (Edwardsville)

CHERRY-MARSH CANDY

2 cups sugar
⅔ cup evaporated milk
½ cup butter
12 large marshmallows
6 ounce package cherry
   chips

1 teaspoon vanilla
12 ounce package chocolate
   chips
6 ounces milk chocolate
⅔ cup peanut butter
12 ounces crushed peanuts

Boil sugar, milk and butter five minutes. Add marshmallows, cherry chips and vanilla. In another pan, melt chocolate chips, milk chocolate, peanut butter, then add peanuts. Put one half of chocolate mixture in 9-inch x 13-inch buttered pan. Pour cherry mixture over first layer of chocolate. Let set for a minute. Spread remaining chocolate on top. When set, cut into squares.

Dorothy Marti (Pocahontas)

DIVINITY

1½ cups granulated sugar
½ cup light corn syrup
¼ cup hot water
½ teaspoon white vinegar
Few drops food coloring
   (optional)

1 stiffly beaten egg white
½ teaspoon vanilla
½ cup broken nut meats

Combine sugar, corn syrup, water, vinegar and food coloring, cover; place over moderate heat, heat to boiling. Remove cover after 5 minutes. Cook to very hard boil stage (260° F.). Remove from heat, cool slightly. Add gradually to stiffly beaten egg white, beating constantly until very stiff. Let cool, stirring occasionally. Stir in vanilla and nut meats. Drop from buttered teaspoon onto buttered cookie sheet. Makes 30 pieces.

Oma Heepke (Edwardsville)

POPCORN BALLS

1 cup white syrup
½ cup sugar

1 package Jello
5 quarts popped corn

Boil syrup and sugar. Add Jello, stir well. Pour over popcorn and when cool enough to handle, form into balls.

Suzanne Blattner (Madison)

PEANUT BUTTER SWIRL FUDGE

2 cups granulated sugar
⅔ cup milk
½ 7-ounce jar of Marshmallow
    Creme
1 cup smooth or chunky
    peanut butter

1 teaspoon vanilla
½ cup semi-sweet chocolate
    pieces, melted

Combine sugar and milk. Bring to a boil and cook at a boil to soft-ball stage (234° F.). Remove from heat and stir in marshmallow creme, peanut butter and vanilla. When smooth and blended spread evenly into a buttered 8-inch square pan. Spoon melted chocolate over fudge and swirl into fudge. While still warm, cut into 1-inch squares. Cook until set and then separate into pieces.

Gert Pfeiffer (Edwardsville)

PEANUT FLAKE CANDY

1 package (6-ounce) semi-
    sweet chocolate chips
⅔ cup chunky peanut butter

3 cups Corn Flakes
½ cup chopped pecans

Melt chocolate pieces over low heat. Add peanut butter and stir well. Stir in Corn Flakes and peanuts. Drop by teaspoonful onto greased cookie sheet. Chill in refrigerator until firm. Makes 4 dozen.

Oma Heepke (Edwardsville)

PEANUT BRITTLE

2 cups granulated sugar
½ cup boiling water
⅔ cup white corn syrup
2 cups raw peanuts

1⅓ tablespoons butter
1⅓ teaspoons vanilla
1⅓ teaspoons baking soda
⅔ teaspoon salt

Dissolve sugar in boiling water. Add corn syrup and cook until the mixture will spin a thread, 230° F. Warm the peanuts in oven while syrup is cooking. Add the warm peanuts when syrup reaches 230° F. Continue cooking and stir constantly until syrup reaches 290° F. Remove from heat, add salt, soda, vanilla and butter. Stir as fast as you can with wooden spoon. Spread on a buttered cookie sheet as thinly as possible. When cold, break into pieces. Yield: 2 pounds.

Judy Klein (New Douglas)

OVEN CARAMEL CORN

8 or 9 quarts popped corn
2 cups brown sugar
1 cup margarine

1 teaspoon salt
½ cup white syrup
1 teaspoon soda (baking)

Boil all ingredients, except for popped corn and soda, five minutes, mixing well and stirring occasionally. Remove from heat and add soda. Stir in quickly. Pour over popped corn, mixing well. Put in two large flat pans and place in oven at 250° F. for 1 hour, stirring 2 or 3 times. Store in tightly closed container (this is important). I put it in freezer. Tastes just like Cracker Jacks. Peanuts can be added or any other nuts.

M. L. Maedge (Highland)

PEANUT CLUSTERS

1 cup sugar
1 package (3 or 4 ounces, not instant) chocolate or vanilla pudding and pie filling

½ cup evaporated milk
1 tablespoon butter
1 cup salted peanuts
¼ teaspoon vanilla

Blend sugar with pudding in saucepan. Add milk and butter. Stir and cook over medium heat until mixture comes to a boil. Lower heat and boil gently for 3 minutes, stirring constantly. Remove from heat and stir in peanuts and vanilla. Beat until thick and creamy (about 8 minutes). Drop from teaspoon onto waxed paper. Let cool until set. Yield about 3 dozen pieces.

Brenda Norwood Dusek (Collinsville)

PEANUT BRITTLE

2 cups white sugar
1 cup white syrup
½ cup water
2 cups raw peanuts

2 tablespoons butter
2 teaspoons baking soda
1 teaspoon vanilla

Using candy thermometer, cook to hard boil. Add raw peanuts. Stir well. Add butter. Cook to hard crack stage. Take off heat and add baking soda and vanilla. Stir soda in well. This will foam up some, so have large enough pan. Pour out on well-buttered cookie sheet to harden. Makes large amount.

Mrs. Grover J. Norwood (Collinsville)
Mrs. Gerald Dusek

OLD FASHIONED PEANUT BRITTLE

2 cups granulated sugar	2 cups raw peanuts
1 cup dark corn syrup	¼ teaspoon salt
½ cup water	1 teaspoon vanilla
2 tablespoons butter	3 teaspoons baking soda

Combine sugar, syrup, water and butter in heavy 3-quart saucepan. Cook slowly, stirring, until sugar dissolves. Cook to soft ball stage on candy thermometer (238° F.). Then add peanuts and salt to syrup mixture. Cook to hard crack stage (290° F.), stirring constantly. Take off fire and add vanilla, stir in well, add baking soda. Stir well as it will foam up and then stir again. Pour onto well greased platter or cookie sheet, and with forks stretch out as much as possible. Then lift edges and turn over and stretch out more. When cool, break up in pieces. Must do the thinning or stretching process while mixture is still hot.

Louise Eckert (Collinsville)

PECAN PRALINES

Mix together in saucepan:

1 cup brown sugar	¾ cup Pet milk, diluted with
2 cups white sugar	½ cup water
3 tablespoons white corn syrup	

Cook to the boiling point, stirring constantly. Continue cooking, stirring occasionally, to 236° F. or until a few drops form a soft ball when dropped into cold water. Remove from heat.
Cool at room temperature, without stirring, until lukewarm or until hand can be held comfortably on bottom of pan.

Stir in:

2 teaspoons maple flavoring   1½ cups pecans

Beat until candy holds its shape. Drop rapidly from a spoon onto waxed paper to form patties about 4 inches in diameter. Wrap in waxed paper. Makes 1 dozen.

Grace Burian (Edwardsville)

PECAN CHEWS

½ pound soft caramels
2 tablespoons cream
1¼ cups pecan halves

½ pound Hershey's chocolate
bar

Melt caramels and cream. Let mixture cool a little. Arrange pecans on cookie sheet and drop by ½ teaspoonfuls on top of pecans. Melt chocolate and coat caramels.

Lois Beckmann (Granite City)

PECAN ROLLS

1 1-pound box powdered
   sugar, scant
1 jar Marshmallow Creme
1 package Kraft caramels

¼ pound butter
1 to 2 cups chopped pecans

Work in scant 1 pound of powdered sugar into marshmallow creme. Form into 6 or 7 rolls. Wrap individually and freeze. Melt in a double boiler, one package of caramels and ¼ pound butter. When melted, stir well and dip logs in caramel mixture. Roll logs in chopped pecans. (The logs will be frozen and stiff so they handle well; they can be rewrapped and frozen again and taken out just prior to use. They slice well when partially frozen.)

Florence Highlander (Hamel)

MILLION DOLLAR FUDGE

4½ cups sugar
1 stick butter
1 can Pet Milk (13 ounces)
¼ teaspoon salt
2 8-ounce Hershey bars
2 13-ounce jars Marshmallow
   Creme

1 12-ounce package chocolate
   chips
1 cup nuts
1 teaspoon vanilla

Cook first 4 ingredients to soft ball stage. Remove from burner and add other ingredients. Beat with a wooden spoon for about 30 minutes. Pour into two buttered 9x13-inch pans. Score with wet knife into one-inch squares. Turn out and break apart when cool.

Abby Daugherty (Granite City)

CRUNCHY FUDGE SANDWICHES

6 ounce package (1 cup)
butterscotch morsels
½ cup peanut butter
4 cups Rice Krispies cereal
6 ounce package (1 cup) semi-
sweet chocolate morsels

½ cup confectioners sugar
2 tablespoons butter
1 tablespoon water

Melt butterscotch morsels with peanut butter in heavy saucepan over low heat, stirring until blended. Stir in Rice Krispies. Press half of mixture into buttered 8-inch square pan. Chill. Set aside remainder of mix. Stir over hot water, chocolate morsels, sugar, butter and water until chocolate melts. Spread over chilled mixture. Top with reserved mixture. Chill. Cut into 1½-inch squares. Yield: 25 pieces.

Mary Lou Sutton (Alton)

SURPRISE FUDGE

1 pound butter
1 pound Velveeta cheese
4 pounds powdered sugar

1 cup cocoa
1 tablespoon vanilla
½ cup chopped nuts

Mix all ingredients together with a mixer and spread about ½ to ¾-inch thick into several pans of your choice and let cool. Cut into 1-inch pieces.

Carleen Paul (Worden)

ROCKY ROAD CANDY

1 12-ounce package semi-
sweet chocolate morsels
1 14-ounce can Eagle Brand
milk
2 tablespoons butter or
margarine

1½ to 2 cups chopped nuts of
your choice
1 10½-ounce package
miniature marshmallows

In top of double boiler, melt chocolate morsels with Eagle Brand milk and margarine. Remove from heat. In a large bowl, combine nuts and marshmallows. Fold in melted chocolate mixture. Spread into a wax paper lined 13x9-inch pan.
Chill 2 hours or until firm. Remove from pan, pull off waxed paper and cut into small squares. Store in a covered container.

Beckie Schrumpf (Highland)

CHINESE PEANUT CRUNCHIES

1 6-ounce package semi-sweet
  chocolate chips
1 tablespoon vegetable
  shortening
½ cup peanut butter

2 tablespoons confectioners
  sugar
3 cups Chinese chow mein
  noodles
1 cup salted peanuts

Melt chocolate and shortening over hot water. Stir in peanut butter
and sugar. Stir in noodles and peanuts. Drop while still warm by teaspoonfuls on wax paper. Chill until firm. Makes 4 dozen.

Gert Pfeiffer (Edwardsville)

NUTTY FUDGE

2 cups granulated sugar
3 tablespoons cocoa
½ cup evaporated milk
½ cup butter

½ cup peanut butter
2 cups quick rolled oats
1 teaspoon almond extract

Combine sugar, cocoa, milk and butter in a saucepan over low heat.
Stir until butter melts, then cook for 2 minutes. Add peanut butter,
rolled oats and almond extract and stir to mix well. Pour into a lightly
greased 9x9x1½-inch pan. Refrigerate overnight and cut into 1½-inch
squares. Makes 3 dozen.

Oma Heepke (Edwardsville)

ENGLISH TOFFEE

1 pound sugar
1 pound butter
½ teaspoon salt
¼ pound finely chopped
  almonds

¼ pound milk chocolate,
  melted
¼ pound finely chopped
  English walnuts

Use a 4-quart pan. Melt butter over low heat, add sugar and salt. Raise
heat and allow to come to a boil, stirring. Add almonds and insert
thermometer and cook to 278° F., stirring constantly and vigorously.
When candy is nearly done, it will be light brown and almonds will
smoke. Pour in strip on marble slab or cold greased cookie sheet. Lay
off immediately into bars with tableknife. Add a coating of melted
milk chocolate and sprinkle with chopped walnuts. Break into pieces
when cool.

Kay Losch (East Alton)

MINTS

½ stick butter, melted
15 drops oil of peppermint
2-3 tablespoons water

1 1-pound box powdered
  sugar
Food coloring

Melt butter; add oil of peppermint and water. Add powdered sugar and mix well. When mixed, divide into 4 parts and color each part (pink, green, yellow and blue). Roll into small balls about the size of a big marble. Flatten with heel of hand on cookie sheet. Put cross marks on top with a fork.

Oma Heepke (Edwardsville)

NAPOLEON CREMES

½ cup butter
¼ cup sugar
¼ cup cocoa
1 teaspoon vanilla
1 egg, slightly beaten
2 cups finely crushed graham
  cracker crumbs
1 cup flaked coconut

½ cup butter
3 tablespoons milk
1 3¾-ounce package vanilla
  instant pudding
2 cups sifted powdered sugar
1 6-ounce package chocolate
  chips
2 tablespoons butter

Combine first 4 ingredients in top of double boiler. Cook over simmering water until butter melts. Stir in egg. Continue cooking and stirring until mixture is thick, about 3 minutes. Blend in crumbs and coconut, press into 9-inch square pan. Cream butter well, stir in milk, pudding mix and sugar. Beat until fluffy. Spread evenly over crust. Chill until firm. Melt chocolate and butter over simmering water in top of double boiler. Cool slightly and spread over pudding layer. Chill. Cut through chocolate layer before it is completely cool to prevent cracking. Finish cutting candy when served.

Connie Plocher (Pocahontas)

HEAVENLY HASH CANDY

1 pound milk chocolate
18 large marshmallows, diced

1 cup nuts, chopped

Melt the chocolate in a double boiler. Line a 6x10-inch pan with wax paper. Pour ½ of the chocolate in pan. Put marshmallows and nuts on top. Press down. Pour rest of chocolate on top of this. After cooled, cut into squares.

Nellie Dauderman (Alhambra)

PANOCHE WALNUTS

1 cup brown sugar (packed
  firmly)
¼ teaspoon salt
¼ teaspoon cinnamon
1 teaspoon grated orange rind

6 tablespoons cream
1 teaspoon vanilla
2½ to 3 cups English walnut
  halves

Combine first 5 ingredients in saucepan and cook stirring frequently until it reaches 236° F. Remove from heat and add vanilla and the walnut halves. Stir until mixture coats all the nuts. Turn out on waxed paper and separate nuts.

Gracie Koeller (Godfrey)

POPCORN CAKE

3 poppers full popcorn
1 cup sugar
⅓ cup white syrup
¼ cup butter

¾ teaspoon salt
¾ teaspoon vanilla
⅓ cup water
Colored sugars (optional)

Cook ingredients together over low heat. Remove at 270° F. or when it gets thicker but not too thick. Add vanilla last and stir. Pour popped corn into liquid. Butter hands well. Put into angel pan. Cool. Remove and slice like you would cake.

Mae Grapperhaus (Troy)

RICE KRISPIES CANDY

⅓ cup syrup (dark or light)
½ cup brown sugar (packed)
½ cup peanut butter (chunky
  is best)

3 cups Rice Krispies

Combine syrup and sugar, stir over moderate heat until it bubbles. Remove from heat. Blend in peanut butter and add Rice Krispies. Stir until coated. Press into greased square pan. Cool 20 minutes. Cut in squares.

Rose Schrage (Edwardsville)

ROCKY MOUNTAIN CANDY

32-36 ounces white bark
2 cups chunky peanut butter
2 cups mini marshmallows
  (colored or white)

2 cups Rice Krispies
12 ounce jar dry roasted
  peanuts

Preheat oven to 200° F. Melt bark in a large pan in 200° F. oven. Add peanut butter, mix well. Add marshmallows, Rice Krispies and peanuts. Mix well. Drop by teaspoon onto wax paper. Allow to cool. Makes large amount. Freezes well also.

Ginger Schuette (Staunton)
Florence Highlander (Hamel)

CANDY

CANDY

CANNING

The county museum is housed in the Weir Mansion, North Main Street, Edwardsville.

APPLE BUTTER

(Pressure Cooker Type)

| 1 gallon cut up apples with peel | 4 cups sugar |

Mix together. Let set all morning or overnight until juice is formed. Add in small cheesecloth bag:

| 2 sticks cinnamon | 1 star anise |

Pressure cook 25 minutes at 15 # pressure. Let pressure cool down by itself. Put through ricer, reheat and seal in jars. Makes 4 pints or 2 quarts.

Rose Schrage (Edwardsville)

STOVE TOP APPLE BUTTER

Wash, cut and core apples. Do not peel. Add 2 cups sugar to 1 gallon apples. Let stand overnight with sugar. Pour into a heavy pot, cook on low heat for four to five hours. (Do not stir while cooking.) Stir when done. Rice through sieve or food processor. Return to stove and add about 2 cinnamon sticks to 1 gallon apples and a few drops of anise oil. Cook and stir until thick.

Esther Schuette (Staunton)

HOME-MADE APPLE PIE FILLING

10 cups water	1 teaspoon salt
4½ cups sugar	2 drops yellow food coloring
1 cup cornstarch	5½ pounds apples, peeled,
2 teaspoons cinnamon	cored and sliced
¼ teaspoon nutmeg	3 tablespoons lemon juice

In a large saucepan blend sugar, cornstarch, cinnamon, nutmeg and salt. Stir in water. Cook and stir until mixture comes to a boil and thickens. Add lemon juice and food coloring. Remove from heat. Fill hot jars to the neck with apples. Add hot thickened syrup to the neck. Add lids and process in hot water bath for 20 minutes. Makes seven quarts.

Donna Sievers (Staunton)
Lucille Brase (Edwardsville)

BANANA PEPPERS IN OIL

Bake peppers in shallow pan (1 layer) in oven 350° F. until skins pop and turn slightly brown. Pack in clean quart jars.

To each quart jar add:

2 tablespoons oil	1 teaspoon salt
1 clove garlic	

Heat equal parts of vinegar and water to boiling. Pour over peppers and seal.

Helen Miller (Granite City)

PICKLED BEETS

2 quarts sliced beets	2 cups water
1 cup sugar	2 cups vinegar

Select young and tender beets, wash, leave 2 inches of stem and boil until tender, about 15 minutes. Pour off hot water and cool with cold water; rub off skins. Slice about ¼ inch thick. Make a syrup of the sugar, water and vinegar. Boil 10 minutes. Add 1 quart of beets, bringing back to boil and boil 1 or 2 minutes. Seal in sterilized jars. Repeat for remaining sliced beets.

Eva Koeller (Godfrey)

CHILI SAUCE

7 or 8 pounds tomatoes	2 teaspoons cinnamon
(½ peck)	1 teaspoon cloves
2 cups chopped celery	1 tablespoon mustard seed
2 cups chopped onion	2 cups vinegar
2 cups chopped green pepper	1½ teaspoons salt
2 cups sugar	

Peel tomatoes (dip tomatoes in boiling water for a minute and skins will slip off easily). Remove seeds, chop the tomatoes into large pieces, drain well. Add celery, onions and peppers, cook 20 minutes. Add remaining ingredients and cook slowly until thick, stirring frequently for 1 to 1½ hours. (There will still be some juice, the celery, etc. should be a little crisp when finished cooking.)

NOTE: Cut celery and onion at least ¼ inch pieces or it will cook too soft.

Eva Koeller (Godfrey)

PICKLED BEETS

Cook beets until tender. Dip into cold water. Peel off skins. Make syrup:

2 cups sugar
2 cups vinegar
1 tablespoon cinnamon
2 cups water

1 teaspoon allspice
2 tablespoons Realemon juice
1 teaspoon cloves

Pour over beets and simmer 15 minutes. Pack into jars and seal.

Mrs. Norman Henke (Staunton)

PICKLED SPICED BEETS

8 quarts small beets
2 cups vinegar
2 cups water
2 cups sugar

1 teaspoon allspice
1 tablespoon cinnamon
1 teaspoon cloves
1 lemon, thinly sliced

Select small beets, cook until tender, dip in cold water and peel off skins. Make the syrup. Combine the remaining ingredients and bring to a boil. Add the beets to this syrup and simmer 15 minutes. Pack into sterilized jars and seal.

Wilma Becker (Moro)

HOT DOG RELISH

4 cups ground onions
1 medium head cabbage,
    ground (about 4 cups)
10 green tomatoes, ground
12 sweet green peppers
6 red sweet peppers
½ cup salt

6 cups sugar
1 tablespoon celery seed
2 tablespoons mustard seed
1½ teaspoons turmeric
4 cups vinegar
2 cups water

Mix the first six ingredients together and let stand for several hours. Drain and rinse through two clear waters. Combine sugar, celery seed, mustard seed, turmeric, vinegar and water. Pour vegetable mix into this mixture and heat to boiling; then simmer three minutes. Put into pint jars and seal. Makes eight pints. (Very good)

Mrs. Lawrence Wall (New Douglas)

BREAD AND BUTTER PICKLES

12 unpeeled medium sized
  cucumbers
6 onions (medium size)
⅓ cup salt
ice cubes
1 quart vinegar (add a little
  water)

2 cups sugar
1 teaspoon mustard seed
1 teaspoon turmeric
1 teaspoon celery seed
½ teaspoon black pepper

Salt cucumbers and onions together, layer with ice cubes, finishing with a layer of ice on top, let stand 3 hours or overnight in cool place covered so ice does not melt. Drain. Boil vinegar, water, sugar, and spices together 10 minutes, then add the drained cucumbers and onions, small batches at a time, and heat just to boiling. Seal in sterilized jars. Makes at least 6 pints.

NOTE: The one minute cooking time keeps the pickles crisp and green. Wait at least a month before sampling, so pickles can "pickle." The ice-salt mixture helps make the pickles extra crisp. Cooking one quart at a time, also keeps them crisp.

Mary Jane Koeller (Godfrey)

COLESLAW FOR FREEZING

1 medium cabbage head,
  shredded
1 carrot, grated

1 green pepper, chopped
1 teaspoon salt

Mix salt with cabbage, let stand 1 hour. Squeeze out excess moisture. Add carrot and pepper. While cabbage is standing, make the following dressing:

1 cup vinegar
¼ cup water
1 teaspoon whole mustard
  seed

1 teaspoon celery seed
2 cups sugar

Combine ingredients and boil 1 minute. Cool to lukewarm, pour over slaw mixture, put into containers, cover and freeze. This thaws in just a few minutes for serving, and leftover slaw can be refrozen easily.

VARIATION: May add 2 stalks chopped celery.

Wilma Brase (Edwardsville)
Linda Meyer (Staunton)

BREAD AND BUTTER PICKLES

1 gallon sliced cucumbers   ½ cup salt
8 small onions

Wash cucumbers. Slice cucumbers and onions and mix with salt. Cover with chopped ice and let stand 3 hours. Drain off liquid and any ice that is left.

MAKE SYRUP OF:

5 cups sugar   ½ teaspoon ground cloves
5 cups of *mild* white vinegar   1½ teaspoons turmeric
2 tablespoons mustard seed   1 teaspoon celery seed

Put syrup over cucumbers and mix. Cook the mixture until scalding hot. Do not boil. Put in sterilized jars and seal. Makes 9 pints.

Gracie Koeller (Godfrey)

DILL PICKLES—FRESH KOSHER STYLE

30 to 36 cucumbers,   6 tablespoons salt
  3 to 4 inch size   Fresh or dried dill
3 cups vinegar   1 or 2 cloves garlic, sliced
3 cups water   1 tablespoon mustard seed

Wash cucumbers. Make a brine of vinegar, water and salt. Bring to a boil. Place a generous layer of dill, ½ to 1 clove garlic (sliced) and ½ tablespoon mustard seed in bottom of clean quart jar. Pack cucumbers till jar is half full, then add another layer of dill. Complete packing cucumbers in jar. Fill jar to ½ inch from top with boiling brine. Seal. Process 5 minutes in boiling water bath.

Mrs. Ella Bentrup (Staunton)

PICKLED OKRA

4 pounds okra   1 cup water
¾ cup salt   10 pods red pepper
4 cups vinegar   10 cloves garlic

Wash okra, pack in jars. Add 1 pepper and 1 clove garlic to each jar. Heat vinegar, water and salt to boiling. Pour over okra and seal. Process in hot water bath for 5 minutes. Let stand 8 weeks before using. If desired, you can add mustard seed or celery seed to hot vinegar.

Helen Miller (Granite City)

DILL PICKLES

3 quarts water
1 cup canning salt
1 quart distilled vinegar
1 head dill

1 hot red pepper
1 garlic bud
Alum

Have cucumbers at room temperature. Wash and dry. Pack in jars and add dill, pepper, and garlic, also add a pinch of alum to each jar. Heat vinegar, salt and water to boiling or until salt is dissolved. Pour over pickles in jars and seal.

Beverly Dustmann (Dorsey)

DILL PICKLES WITH BANANA PEPPER

3 quarts water
1 quart white vinegar
1 cup salt
Pickles

Dill for each jar
1 banana pepper per jar
1 clove garlic per jar
Pinch of alum per jar

Heat the water, vinegar and salt to boiling. Pack pickles and dill with one banana pepper and one clove garlic in each jar. Pour boiling solution over pickles but do not seal. Let stand for five minutes. Pour solution back into pot and reheat. Add a pinch of alum to each packed jar. Pour hot solution over pickles and seal.

Helen Brase (Worden)

CRISP PICKLE SLICES

4 quarts medium-sized
   cucumbers, sliced and
   unpeeled
6 medium white onions, sliced
3 cloves garlic, crushed
1 green pepper, cut in strips
1 sweet red pepper, cut in
   strips

⅓ cup salt
3 cups white vinegar
5 cups sugar
1½ teaspoons turmeric
1½ teaspoons celery seed
2 tablespoons mustard seed

Combine cucumbers, onions, garlic, peppers and salt. Cover with cracked ice and mix thoroughly. Let stand 3 hours, drain well. Combine remaining ingredients in large kettle and drained cucumbers. Heat to boiling point. Pack in hot, sterilized jars. Seal at once. Makes 8 pints.

Wilma Brase (Edwardsville)

CROSS-CUT PICKLE SLICES

6 pounds (4 quarts) cucumbers
⅓ cup salt
1½ cups onion
2 large cloves garlic
2 trays ice cubes

4½ cups sugar
1½ teaspoons turmeric
1½ teaspoons celery seed
2 tablespoons mustard seed
3 cups white vinegar

Wash cucumbers, drain. Slice ⅛ to ¼ inch thick. Add garlic and onion. Add salt and mix. Cover with ice cubes. Let stand 3 hours, drain. Remove garlic. Combine sugar, spices, vinegar. Heat to boiling. Add cucumbers and onions. Heat 5 minutes. Pack hot in clean pint jars to ½ inch from top. Adjust lids. Process in boiling water for 5 minutes. Start to count processing time as soon as water in canner returns to boiling. Remove jars and seal tight.

Mrs. Ella Bentrup (Staunton)

FREEZER CUCUMBERS

7 cups sliced cucumbers
1 cup chopped onion
1 tablespoon salt
1 cup vinegar

2 cups sugar
1 teaspoon celery seed
½ teaspoon mustard seed

Sprinkle salt on cucumbers and onions; let set three to four hours. Boil vinegar, sugar, celery seed and mustard seed. Cool and pour over drained cucumbers. Place in glass bowl and refrigerate for 3 days. Then freeze in small containers.

Dorothy Marti (Pocahontas)

ICE WATER PICKLES

3 quarts white vinegar
3 cups sugar
1 cup salt

6 pounds of medium sized
cucumbers (cut in half)

Soak cucumbers in ice water and salt for 3 hours. Drain. In clean quart jars layer the following (bottom, middle, top) between cucumbers:

1 teaspoon mustard seed
2 onion slices

2 celery sticks

Bring vinegar, sugar to boil. Fill to ½-inch from top. Seal.

Ella Bentrup (Staunton)

REFRIGERATOR CHIP PICKLES

7 cups thin sliced unpeeled
cucumbers
1 cup thin sliced onion

1 green pepper, chopped
1 tablespoon salt

Let stand 2 hours. Drain.

1 cup vinegar
2 cups sugar

1 teaspoon celery seed

Bring to boil. Cool. Pour over sliced cucumbers. Set in refrigerator two or three days. Put in plastic containers and freeze. Have juice cover pickles. To use, put in refrigerator a day before serving.

Evelyn Keilbach (Highland)

SWEET PICKLE STICKS

9 medium cucumbers
  (4½ inches long)
6 cups boiling water
2⅓ cups cider vinegar
2¼ cups sugar

2 tablespoons salt
1 tablespoon celery seed
3¼ teaspoons turmeric
¾ teaspoon mustard seed

Select fresh, firm cucumbers. Wash and cut into sticks. Pour boiling water over and let stand overnight. Drain, pack solidly into clean jars. Combine remaining ingredients and boil 5 minutes. Pour boiling liquid over cucumbers in jars. Screw lids tight. Process in boiling water bath 5 minutes.

Darlene Stille (Alhambra)

SWEET PICKLE STICKS

1 gallon cucumbers, washed
  and cut in strips
2⅓ cups cider vinegar
2 tablespoons salt

3¼ cups sugar
1 tablespoon celery seed
3½ teaspoons turmeric
3 teaspoons mustard seed

Place cucumber strips in large pan and pour boiling water over. Let stand overnight. The next morning, drain and place in jars. Place remaining ingredients in large saucepan and boil for 5 minutes. 1 gallon firmly packed cucumbers will yield 6 pints or 3 quarts of pickles.

VARIATION: May slice cucumbers ¼-inch thick rather than strips.

Edna Suhre (Alhambra)

SWEET PICKLES

7 pounds pickles, 3 inches or smaller in length	1 pint salt 1 gallon cold water

Put pickles in a jar with brine made of one pint salt and one gallon cold water. Let stand four days, then pour brine off, cover with clear water. Let stand three days. Wash and split pickles regardless of size. Put in a kettle and add:

1 slightly rounded teaspoon alum	2 cups vinegar Enough water to cover

Let simmer for two hours (not boil). Pour off liquid, put pickles back in jar. Heat:

6 cups vinegar	1 ounce whole allspice
6 cups sugar	1 ounce stick cinnamon

Pour over pickles and let stand overnight. Next morning pour off liquid, bring to boil, pour over pickles again. Let stand overnight. The third day pack pickles in jars and pour the vinegar mixture boiling hot over pickles and seal.

Mrs. Don Wilkening (Edwardsville)

INDIA RELISH

12 cups peeled and chopped tomatoes	4 cups vinegar
3 cups chopped celery	½ cup mustard seed
2 cups chopped onions	2 chopped red peppers
¼ cup salt	1 teaspoon ground cinnamon
3 cups brown sugar	¾ teaspoon ground allspice
	¾ teaspoon ground cloves

Combine tomatoes, celery, onions and salt. Let stand 2 hours. Prepare home canning jars and lids according to manufacturer's instructions. Add vinegar, brown sugar, mustard seed, red peppers, cinnamon, allspice and cloves to tomato mixture. Cook until the mixture is thickened. Carefully fill hot jars one at a time, leaving ¼ inch head space. Wipe jar rim clean, place lids on and screw band down evenly and firmly. Place closed jars in canner. Repeat for each jar. Process pint and half pints 15 minutes in a boiling water bath container. Yields 10 pints.

Mrs. George P. Eckert (Collinsville)

10 DAY SWEET PICKLES

**7 pounds cucumbers, 3 inches
long**

Place in stone jar, cover with brine made of:

1 pint salt   **1 gallon cold water**

Let stand four days. Then pour off brine and cover with clean cold water and let stand three days. Then wash and split at ends of pickles almost half-way (each pickle) put them in kettle or pot. Add:

2 cups vinegar   **Slightly rounded teaspoon
Enough water to cover   alum
Handful of green grape leaves**

Simmer for two hours. Pour off liquid and put pickles back in stone jar. Heat:

6 cups sugar   **1 ounce whole allspice
4 cups vinegar**   **1 ounce cinnamon stick**

Pour this over pickles and let stand overnight. Next day, pour off liquid and bring to boil. Pour over pickles again. The third day pack pickles in jar and add vinegar mixture, boiling hot and seal.

Helen Brase (Worden)

RELISH

2½ cups cucumbers   **1 cup onions
1½ cups carrots**   **2 teaspoons salt**

Grind vegetables, stir in salt. Let stand 3 hours. Drain.

1 cup vinegar   **1½ teaspoons mustard seed
2 cups sugar**   **1½ teaspoons celery seed**

Bring to a boil and add ground vegetables. Simmer 20 minutes. Put into hot sterile jars and seal. Makes 2½ pints.

Mildred Roemelin (Moro)

CANADIAN HOT DOG RELISH

Grind:

8 cups cucumbers   2 pounds onions
5 green peppers

Pour nine cups water and one half cup salt over this and set overnight.
Drain.

Simmer one hour:

2 tablespoons mustard seed   6 cups sugar
1 tablespoon turmeric   Enough vinegar to cover
2 tablespoons celery seed

Mix together:

2 tablespoons cornstarch   Dab of water

Add all ingredients, including cucumber mixture and cook until glossy.
Can in jars.

Donna Koenig (Edwardsville)

CUCUMBER RELISH

1 gallon cucumbers, washed,   1 quart crushed ice
  ground without seeds   ½ cup salt

Mix above and place in refrigerator for 3 hours or overnight. Drain,
then add:

8 small white onions   2 green peppers, seeded and
                                  ground

Make syrup of:

5 cups vinegar   ½ teaspoon turmeric
5 cups sugar   ½ teaspoon ground cloves
2 teaspoons mustard seed   1 teaspoon celery seed

Add vegetables. Heat slowly with very little stirring. Scald well but
do not boil. Put in jars and seal at once. Makes about 10 pints. Good
with hot dogs or in tuna or chicken salad.

Alice Stille (Alhambra)

PEPPER RELISH

2 dozen bell peppers (use
  some red)
½ dozen onions
1 bunch celery

3 cups sugar
3 tablespoons salt
1 pint white vinegar, 5%

Use coarse blade and grind all vegetables. Cover with boiling water, let set 5 minutes. Drain thoroughly. Add sugar, salt and vinegar. Boil 5 minutes. Pour into sterilized jars and seal. Good on sandwiches or use with mayonnaise for chicken or tuna salad.

Ruth Brave (Granite City)

ZUCCHINI SQUASH RELISH

10 cups ground, peeled
  squash
2 large onions, chopped
1 red pepper, chopped
1 green pepper, chopped
5 tablespoons salt
6 cups sugar
½ teaspoon nutmeg

1 teaspoon turmeric
3 tablespoons cornstarch
1 teaspoon dry mustard
½ teaspoon pepper
2 teaspoons celery seed
½ teaspoon baking soda
2½ cups vinegar

Mix together squash, onions, red and green peppers, salt. Let stand overnight. Then put in cold water and drain well. Mix together sugar, nutmeg, turmeric, cornstarch, dry mustard, pepper, celery seed, baking soda. Add to squash mixture with vinegar. Cook 30 minutes, stirring often. Put into clean jars and seal tight.

Doris Keck (Alhambra)

TOMATO SAUCE

Chop peck of tomatoes or more, remove core and spots. Cook until tender, put through blender to get all the pulp. (If you like peppers and onions, add cooked ones at this time, four of each.) Press through cone strainer. Drain through jelly bag (cheesecloth) for 1 to 2 minutes. Put back into container immediately from bag. Fill jars, add 1 teaspoon of mixture of 2 parts sugar, 1 part salt; or ½ teaspoon salt only to each pint jar. Process per instructions on canner. Using the cheesecloth bag for 1 or 2 minutes eliminates cooking or skimming to remove some of the water and does it in a hurry.

Florence Rapp (Edwardsville)

MINCE MEAT

8 pounds apples	3 teaspoons cinnamon
6 pounds cooked beef	2 teaspoons nutmeg
4 pounds raisins	2 tablespoons cloves
2 pounds currants	2 tablespoons allspice
5 pounds brown sugar	2 tablespoons salt
2 quarts cider	1 pound tallow
1 quart fruit juice	

Dice apples and beef and about a pound of tallow, add all remaining ingredients. Cook in a large roaster for about one hour on medium heat. Put in quart containers and freeze.

Mrs. Don Wilkening (Edwardsville)

FREEZER TOMATO SAUCE

20 large tomatoes, washed, cored and cut in chunks	½ cup chopped parsley
4 large onions, chopped	3 tablespoons sugar
4 large carrots, pared and shredded	2 tablespoons salt
	¼ teaspoon pepper

Place in large kettle. Bring to boil stirring often, lower heat and simmer 30 minutes, or until thickened. Cool, then measure 3 cups at a time into blender and whirl at high speed about 1 minute. Pour into freezer containers.

Lorene Genczo (New Douglas)

TOMATO SOUP FOR CANNING

1 peck ripe tomatoes	¼ cup salt
1 bunch celery	1½ cups sugar
4 medium onions	3 sticks butter
4 whole cloves	1 cup flour

Cook tomatoes, celery, onions and cloves until soft. Run through ricer. Put in large pan and add salt and sugar. Melt butter and blend in flour, add to juice. Cook 5 to 10 minutes or until slightly thickened. While still very hot, put in jars and seal. Be very sure jar rims are clean or soup will spoil.

Mary Alice Cooper (Dorsey)

GRAPE JELLY

Wash grapes then drain. Mash with potato masher. Boil for 20 minutes. Put in jelly bag and let drip overnight. Measure juice, and for every cup of juice, measure equal amount of sugar. Put sugar in oven 350° F. until hot. Bring juice to boil and cook for 10 minutes. Spoon in hot sugar and stir until dissolved. Pour into jars and seal.

Ella Bentrup (Staunton)

GRAPE JUICE

2 cups grapes   Boiling water
¾ cup sugar

Wash and drain grapes. Put in quart jar. Add sugar and enough boiling water to fill jar to within ½ inch from the top, seal. Process 10 minutes in boiling water (Cold Packer), or you can bring water to boiling and turn off and let stand overnight or until cold. You may double the recipe and use half gallon jars instead. Then when you open jar, add about ½ jar of water or water to suit your taste.

Ruth R. Rogier (Highland)

RHUBARB JAM

5 cups rhubarb, cut fine   1 3-ounce package strawberry
3 cups sugar   gelatin
1 3-ounce package strawberry
  Kool Aid

Put sugar over rhubarb and let set overnight. Cook over low heat until soft. Remove from heat and add gelatin and Kool Aid. Mix well until all powder is dissoved. Pour into pint jars and seal.

Mrs. Hilda Brakhane (Edwardsville)

STRAWBERRY PRESERVES

4 cups strawberries, mashed   1 teaspoon alum
6 cups sugar

Boil berries and sugar for 10 minutes. Remove from heat and add alum. Stir 5 minutes. Let cool and put in sterile jars or jelly glasses and seal. You can also let it stand overnight and can the next morning. Very good.

Rosa Klueter (Edwardsville)

QUICK EASY RHUBARB JAM

5 cups rhubarb, cut up
5 cups sugar
1 20-ounce can crushed
   pineapple

1 large strawberry or
   raspberry Jello

Mix together the first three ingredients and let stand overnight. Then boil 20 minutes. Stir in Jello. Boil 1 minute and seal in sterile jars. Approximately 4 pints.

Norma Hemann (New Douglas)

YELLOW TOMATO PRESERVES

8 cups yellow tomatoes,
   peeled and cut up
4 cups crushed pineapple

6 cups sugar
2 lemons, sliced thin
¼ teaspoon salt

Combine all ingredients and cook until thick. This will take about 45 minutes. Pour into sterilized jars and seal with paraffin.

Irene Starkey (Moro)

CANNING

CANNING

ACCOMPANIMENTS AND MISCELLANEOUS

Stand in the shadow of this tomb and you can almost hear Elijah Lovejoy declare Freedom of the Press is guaranteed by our Constitution, just as the freedom and dignity of man is granted by God.

BEER BATTER
(for deep fried chicken)

1 cup flour
1 can warm beer
½ cup cream

2 eggs
½ teaspoon salt
1 teaspoon cinnamon

Put all ingredients into a large bowl and beat until batter consistency. Dip chicken into batter and deep fry. Enough for 15 chicken wings. Real good.

Mrs. George P. Eckert (Collinsville)

BEER BATTER

1 12-ounce can beer

1½ cups flour

Mix together, let stand four hours. Will be thick and ready to dip onion rings or other vegetables or fish in to fry. Fry at 350° F. until golden brown and drain.

Kay Losch (East Alton)

CHIPS AND CHEESE

Tostitos or Doritos
Cheddar cheese, grated

Taco sauce for dip (optional)

Place Tostitos in single layer on plate. Sprinkle with cheese. Place in microwave oven at Full power for 35 seconds.

Optional:
Oven method: Place Tostitos in single layer on cookie sheet. Sprinkle with cheese. Place in preheated oven at 350° F. for 5 minutes.

Donna Price (Granite City)

CRUNCHY BREAKFAST BARS

1 6-ounce package (1 cup)
  semisweet chocolate pieces
¾ cup peanut butter

4 cups granola or 3 cups oat
  cereal

Place chocolate in 2-quart bowl. Heat uncovered, at high for 3 to 4 minutes or until melted. Stir in peanut butter until smooth. Fold in granola. Turn onto waxed paper lined 8x8x2-inch pan; chill. Store in refrigerator. Makes 36 bars.

Karen Mueller (East Alton)

BREAD DRESSING

1 loaf bread
1½ sticks butter or margarine
5 medium onions
1½ cups diced celery
6 eggs
1 teaspoon poultry seasoning

1 teaspoon salt
¾ teaspoon pepper
4 cups chicken broth or 4
   chicken bouillon cubes
   dissolved in 4 cups water

Cut day old bread into cubes. Sauté onion and celery in butter or margarine. Whip eggs and add to chicken broth. Add salt, pepper, poultry seasoning and mix together. Bake 1½ hours in a 350° F. oven.

Louvain Vieth (Edwardsville)

CHICKEN DRESSING

6-7 slices bread, toasted and
   broken into pieces
Liver from chicken
Gizzard from chicken
Heart from chicken
2 cups water
1-2 chicken bouillon cubes
2-3 stalks celery, cut fine

2 eggs, beaten
Salt to taste
Pepper to taste
Poultry seasoning, optional
Raisins, optional
Nuts, optional
Small onion, chopped

Cook chicken liver, gizzard and heart in 2 cups water until done. Cut into small pieces. Add 1-2 bouillon cubes to the water. Mix the celery, eggs and bread together with the water and meat mixture. Salt and pepper to taste. Add raisins and nuts, if desired, and onion. Let set in bowl for about 1 hour or overnight in the refrigerator. Grease a 9-inch pie pan very good with butter all around. Put dressing in pie pan. Have plenty of broth on dressing when you put it in the pan. If you don't have enough, dissolve a bouillon cube in 1 cup hot water and add to dressing. Bake for 1 hour in 350° F. oven until brown. You can make this the night before and then the flavor will draw through.

NOTE: For a 9x13-inch pan you must increase the following:

10-12 slices of bread
1 cup or more celery

3 eggs

Verna Kasubke (New Douglas)

DUMPLINGS

1½ cups flour
¼ cup Crisco
½ teaspoon salt

¼ cup milk
1 egg

Cut flour, Crisco, and salt in mixing bowl until it looks like cornmeal. Add milk and egg. Roll out on floured board and cut into strips. Let dry for 30 minutes before placing over one boiled and deboned chicken. Cook for 20 minutes without taking the lid off the pan.

Georgia Engelke (Granite City)

MOM'S DROP DUMPLINGS

1 egg
2 cups flour
½ teaspoon baking powder

½ teaspoon salt
¾ cup milk

Combine all ingredients and if needed add more liquid. The dough should be soft and beaten well, until it becomes elastic. In a pot of boiling water, add salt and a few drops of cooking oil. Drop dough by teaspoons into boiling water. Cook about 15 to 20 minutes until it rises to the top. Drain well before serving.

Helen Eich (Edwardsville)

HOME-MADE NOODLES

2 egg yolks or 1 whole egg
2 tablespoons cream or
  canned milk

1 tablespoon Mazola oil
¼ teaspoon salt
1 cup flour

Beat eggs, cream and Mazola oil. Sift flour and salt together. Add egg mixture to flour mixture. Mix well. You may need more flour to make them stiff. Then roll real thin and cut as you want them, and cook at once for about 15 minutes. You do not have to let them dry.

Wilma Schoen (New Douglas)

REUBEN TREET SANDWICH

For each sandwich, arrange slices of Swiss cheese on rye bread. Top with slices of fried Treet and ¼ cup well-drained sauerkraut. Add second slice of bread which has been spread with mustard. Grill in melted butter.

JoAnn Brase (Edwardsville)

GREEN TOMATO SANDWICH SPREAD

1 quart ground green tomatoes	1 quart mayonnaise
	1 cup salt
1 quart ground green and red peppers	1 quart vinegar
	1 quart sugar
1 quart ground onions	

Cover tomatoes, peppers and onions with salt and let stand overnight. Drain and add vinegar and sugar. Cook 25 minutes and add mayonnaise. Seal in jars and chill in refrigerator. Use in 3 or 4 days.

Mrs. Don Wilkening (Edwardsville)

HAM AND CHEESE SANDWICHES

SAUCE:

½ stick butter, melted	2 tablespoons salad mustard
2 tablespoons grated onion	1 tablespoon poppy seeds

Ham	Swiss cheese

On bun, put on slice of Swiss cheese and ham and one generous tablespoon of sauce, wrap in foil. Make ahead of time and refrigerate.

Virginia Herrmann (Edwardsville)

SPAGHETTI SAUCE

2 pounds ground beef	2 cups water
1 cup chopped onion	1 teaspoon sugar
2 cloves garlic, minced	1 teaspoon salt
3 tablespoons butter or cooking oil	1½ teaspoons oregano
	½ teaspoon Italian seasoning
2 6-ounce cans tomato paste	1 bay leaf
2 8-ounce cans tomato sauce	2 tablespoons parsley

In a dutch oven, combine onions, meat and garlic. Cook until meat is browned and onion is tender. Drain off excess fat. Add remaining ingredients. Simmer *uncovered* for approximately 2½ to 3 hours or until the sauce is thick. Stir occasionally. Remove bay leaf. Serve over hot spaghetti. This sauce is also good on lasagna. Mushrooms may be added the last 15 minutes of cooking.

Virginia Herrmann (Edwardsville)

FRENCH FRIED ONION RINGS

1 large onion
½ cup milk (more or less)
1 cup buttermilk pancake mix

4 tablespoons yellow corn
meal

Preheat electric skillet to 350° F. with ½ inch oil. Slice onions approximately ¼-inch thick. Separate rings and remove membrane. Dip in milk, then in mixture of pancake mix and corn meal. Dip rings back into milk and again into the dry mixture. Onion rings may be prepared ahead and left to dry before frying. Fry onions in oil for a minute or two on each side. Turn only once.

Dottie Suhre (Alhambra)

GOLDEN ONION RINGS

1 cup pancake mix
¼ cup cornmeal
¼ teaspoon salt

1 cup milk
1 large onion

Combine pancake mix, cornmeal, salt and milk. Beat until smooth. Peel onion. Cut into ¼-inch slices and separate into rings. Dip onion rings into batter. Allow excess batter to drain off. Fry rings in deep fat until golden brown. Drain on paper towels to remove excess fat and serve at once.

Doris Gvillo (Edwardsville)

NO SALT-SEASONING SPICE MIX

3½ teaspoons paprika
2 teaspoons ground mustard
½ teaspoon oregano
1 teaspoon garlic powder
1½ teaspoons thyme
1 teaspoon curry powder
1 teaspoon onion powder
1 teaspoon ground celery
  seeds or leaves

½ teaspoon dried rosemary
½ teaspoon Italian herb
  seasoning
3 teaspoons dried parsley
¼ teaspoon lemon pepper
¼ teaspoon ground ginger
1 teaspoon herb seasoning

Mix all ingredients together. Use in place of salt for flavoring meats and soups. Store in shaker jar.

Helen Eich (Edwardsville)

MARINADE (FLANK STEAK)

½ cup cooking oil
¼ cup soy sauce
2 tablespoons vinegar

3 tablespoons honey
1½ teaspoons garlic salt

Beat 15 minutes in blender.

Diane Mindrup (Edwardsville)

MUSTARD SAUCE

1 cup dry mustard
2 eggs, beaten

1 cup vinegar
1 cup sugar

Combine mustard and vinegar, mix well and let stand and soak overnight. Next morning, in a double boiler, add the 2 beaten eggs and the sugar. Cook gently stirring frequently until thick and smooth. Yield: 1⅔ cups. Store in jar in refrigerator. Will keep almost indefinite period of time. Use on meats, cheeses, etc.

Florence Dinwiddie (Roxana)

PINEAPPLE CASSEROLE

1 20-ounce can pineapple
   chunks
2 slices bread

1 stick margarine
2 tablespoons flour
1 cup sugar

Drain pineapple chunks. Cut the bread into cubes. Melt margarine. Add flour and sugar and juice drained from the pineapple. Boil for five minutes. Place pineapple chunks and bread into casserole. Pour boiled mixture over pineapple and bread. Bake in a 350° F. oven for ½ hour. NOTE: This is excellent with ham or any pork dish.

Doris Gvillo (Edwardsville)

HOT ZUCCHINI SAUCE

4-5 cloves of garlic
1 stick butter
2 green chili peppers,
   chopped (or more to taste)

2 pounds zucchini squash,
   sliced unpeeled
2 14½-ounce cans creamed
   corn

Sauté garlic in butter. Add chopped peppers, zucchini and corn. Use as a sauce on steaks or as a side dish. Good anytime. Freezes well for about a year.

Brenda Norwood Dusek (Collinsville)

HERMAN STARTER

2 cups all-purpose flour
2 cups warm water

1 package (¼-ounce) Active
Dry yeast

In glass or plastic bowl, mix flour, water and yeast with wooden spoon. (Do not use metal container or spoon.) Let stand overnight in a warm place. In the morning, feed Herman one batch of Herman Food (recipe follows). (You'll feed him another batch of Herman Food on the fifth day and another batch on the tenth day, when the process starts again.)

HERMAN FOOD:

1 cup flour
1 cup milk

½ cup sugar

Mix flour, milk and sugar; makes one batch of Herman Food. Mix Herman Food with Herman Starter (the mixture will be lumpy). Cover bowl loosely with plastic wrap and store mixture in refrigerator. Stir daily. On the fifth day, feed Herman again with another batch of Herman Food. On the tenth day, use two cups of the Herman mixture for cooking, give one cup to a friend, feed the remaining cup with another batch of Herman Food and return to refrigerator to start the process again.

Norma Hemann (New Douglas)

HERMAN OATMEAL COOKIES

¾ cup brown sugar
6 tablespoons butter, softened
¼ cup vegetable shortening
1 cup Herman
½ teaspoon vanilla
1 cup flour
½ teaspoon baking soda

½ teaspoon cinnamon
¼ teaspoon ground cloves
¼ teaspoon allspice
½ teaspoon nutmeg
1½ cups rolled oats
½ cup chopped nuts
¾ cup chopped raisins

In large bowl of electric mixer, cream together sugar, butter and shortening until fluffy. Add Herman and vanilla and beat just until combined (mixture will look curdled). In another medium bowl, mix flour, baking soda, cinnamon, cloves, allspice and nutmeg. Add to Herman mixture, mixing until well combined. Fold in oats, nuts and raisins. Drop by teaspoonfuls onto lightly greased baking sheet and bake at 375° F. about 10 minutes, until lightly browned on the edges. Makes about 4 dozen cookies.

Norma Hemann (New Douglas)

HAWAIIAN HERMAN CAKE

1½ cups brown sugar
2 teaspoons cinnamon
¼ teaspoon ginger
½ cup chopped walnuts
¼ cup chopped macadamia
  nuts
½ cup bread crumbs
1 cup sugar
½ cup butter
½ cup vegetable shortening

2 eggs
1 teaspoon vanilla
3 cups flour
2 teaspoons baking powder
½ teaspoon salt
1 cup Herman
1 8½-ounce can crushed
  pineapple, well drained
¼ cup rum
½ cup melted butter

In medium bowl, combine brown sugar, cinnamon, ginger, walnuts, macadamia nuts and bread crumbs; mix well and set aside. In large bowl of electric mixer, cream together sugar, butter and vegetable shortening. Add eggs and vanilla and beat until light and fluffy. Add flour, baking powder, salt and Herman; beat until smooth. Spoon half the batter into a well-greased and floured 9x13-inch baking pan. Spoon half the reserved brown sugar mixture over the batter and sprinkle with pineapple. Smooth the remaining batter over the top and sprinkle with the remaining brown sugar mixture. Sprinkle with rum and pour melted butter over all. Bake at 375° F. 25 to 30 minutes, until cake is puffed and browned. Cool several minutes before serving, but serve warm. Makes about 12 to 15 servings.

Norma Hemann (New Douglas)

HERMAN BLUEBERRY PANCAKES

2 cups Herman
¼ cup vegetable oil
2 eggs
2 tablespoons sugar

1 teaspoon salt
1 teaspoon baking soda
½ cup fresh or frozen
  blueberries

In a large bowl, combine Herman, vegetable oil, eggs, sugar, salt and baking soda. Mix thoroughly with wooden spoon. Gently fold in blueberries. Heat a lightly greased griddle until a drop of water bounces on it. Pour about ¼ cup of the mixture per pancake on griddle and cook until browned, about 3 minutes per side. Handle pancakes carefully (they tend to break apart). Makes about 12 pancakes.

Norma Hemann (New Douglas)

HERMAN CRUMPETS

1½ cups Herman
1 cup warm water
⅓ cup non-fat dry milk
2 teaspoons salt

¼ cup vegetable oil
3 to 4 cups flour, divided
Cornmeal

In large bowl, combine Herman, water, dry milk, salt and oil; beat well, then beat in one cup of the flour. Cover bowl loosely and let stand in warm place for 3 to 6 hours. Stir in 2 cups of the remaining flour and mix well. Turn out on well-floured surface and knead lightly, adding more of the remaining flour when necessary to keep dough from sticking. (Dough will be stickier than ordinary bread dough.) Rinse out mixing bowl and grease with vegetable oil. Place dough in bowl; swirl dough in bowl so entire surface is oiled. Cover with plastic wrap and let rise in warm place until doubled in bulk, about 2 to 3 hours. Punch down dough and let rest, covered 30 minutes. Turn out dough on floured surface and roll to ½-inch thickness. Cut into 3-inch rounds with cookie cutter or empty tuna can. Sprinkle cookie sheets lightly with cornmeal; place dough patties about an inch apart on the sheets and sprinkle with more cornmeal. Let rise in warm place until puffy and light, about 30 to 60 minutes. Heat an ungreased skillet or griddle over medium heat. Carefully transfer patties to hot griddle with spatula. Bake until golden brown on each side, about 10 minutes. Cool on wire racks.

To serve: Tear crumpets in half by inserting a sharp fork into the middle of the crumpet all around the sides. Separate the halves and butter liberally. Toast under hot broiler until browned and butter is bubbly. Makes about 20 crumpets.

Norma Hemann (New Douglas)

HERMAN COFFEE CAKE

1 cup brown sugar
½ cup chopped nuts
¼ cup margarine, softened
2 cups plus 1 tablespoon
flour, divided
1 tablespoon plus 1 teaspoon
cinnamon, divided
2 cups Herman
1 cup sugar

⅔ cup vegetable oil
2 eggs
2 teaspoons baking powder
½ teaspoon salt
½ teaspoon baking soda
1 cup raisins
1 cup drained, crushed fruit
(pineapple, peaches, etc.)

To make topping:
In medium bowl, combine brown sugar, nuts, margarine, one table-spoon of the flour and one tablespoon of the cinnamon. Mix until well blended; set aside.

To make coffee cake:
In large bowl, combine the remaining 2 cups flour, remaining one teaspoon cinnamon, Herman, sugar, vegetable oil, eggs, baking powder, salt and baking soda. Beat until well combined. Fold in raisins and crushed fruit. Pour into well-greased and floured Bundt pan, large ring mold or 9x13-inch baking pan. Top with reserved topping. Bake at 350° F. 50 to 60 minutes, until cake tests done. Makes about 12 servings.

Norma Hemann (New Douglas)

ESCALLOPED PINEAPPLE

2 cups sugar
1 cup butter
3 eggs

1 #2 can crushed pineapple
¼ cup milk
6 slices fresh bread crumbs

Preheat oven to 300° F. Cream together sugar, butter and eggs. Add crushed pineapple, juice and all, milk and bread crumbs. Bake in a well greased casserole for 1 hour.
NOTE: This makes a large size casserole and it has a tendency to bake over if the casserole dish is too small.

Judy Ernst (New Douglas)

COLD SOAP

Dissolve 1 can Lewis Lye in 1 quart cold water and let stand until cold. Pour lye solution into:
5 pounds luke warm grease.

Mix

3 tablespoons borax	½ cup water
2 tablespoons sugar	1 teaspoon salt
¼ cup liquid ammonia	

Add to first part and stir until thick. Cut while warm. Pour lye into fat, never fat into lye.

Mrs. Don Wilkening (Edwardsville)

MOM'S HOME MADE SOAP

1 quart water	½ cup borax
1 can lye	½ cup ammonia
3 pounds grease	

Mix water and lye, add grease, borax and ammonia and stir well. Pour in pan. When set, cut into bars. Lay out to dry. The grease you can accumulate in a three pound Spry can. DO NOT use bacon grease.

Virginia Herrmann (Edwardsville)

ACCOMPANIMENTS AND MISCELLANEOUS

ACCOMPANIMENTS AND MISCELLANEOUS

MELTING POT

State Capitol Building
Springfield, Illinois

AMISH SUGAR COOKIES

1 cup granulated sugar
1 cup powdered sugar
1 cup margarine or butter
1 cup cooking oil
2 eggs

4¾ cups flour
1 teaspoon cream of tartar
½ tablespoon vanilla
1 tablespoon baking soda

Cream sugars and butter together. Add the eggs and cream again. Add oil and mix well. Add dry ingredients which have been sifted together. Drop by small teaspoonful on ungreased cookie sheet. Press down with fork dipped in sugar. Bake at 350° F. for 10 to 12 minutes. Makes 10 dozen cookies. Dough may be stored in refrigerator over night.

Verna Kasubke (New Douglas)

BEEF LOUISE

2½ pounds stew meat
2 cans cream of mushroom
  soup, undiluted
1 package dry onion soup mix

¾ cup Burgundy wine
1-2 teaspoons salt
½ teaspoon pepper

Cut stew meat into small pieces. Mix meat, mushroom soup, onion soup mix, wine, salt and pepper and place in casserole. Cover and bake 3 hours at 325° F. Serve over hot rice or noodles.

Kathryn Cook (Marine)

FRENCH OVEN BEEF STEW

2 pounds beef stew meat,
  1½ inch cubes
2 medium onions cut, ⅛ inch
  thick
2 stalks celery, cut into pieces
4 medium carrots, cut into
  pieces
1½-2 cups tomato juice

⅓ cup quick cooking tapioca
2 medium potatoes, ¼ inch
  cubes
1 tablespoon sugar
1 tablespoon salt
½ teaspoon basil
¼ teaspoon pepper

Combine beef, onion, celery, carrots, tomato juice, tapioca and seasonings in a 2½ quart casserole or roasting pan. Cover and bake at 300° F. for 2½ hours. Add potatoes to stew and cook uncovered for 1 hour. Stir occasionally.

Genevieve Heepke (Edwardsville)

QUICHE

1 pie shell, unbaked	1½ cups grated cheese
1 onion	1 tablespoon flour
2 eggs	Salt and pepper to taste
¾ cup of milk	⅛ teaspoon cayenne, optional
4 slices of bacon	⅛ teaspoon paprika, optional

Preheat oven to 350° F. Fry bacon and drain on paper towel. Pour off ½ the bacon fat and sauté the chopped onion in the rest. Beat eggs and add onion, seasonings and milk. Crumble in the bacon, add cheese mixed with flour. Pour into unbaked pie shell and bake for 40 to 45 minutes. Let stand 10 minutes before serving.

Suzanne Blattner (Madison)

VICHYSSOISE

4 leeks, white part only, sliced	1 quart chicken broth
1 medium onion, sliced	1 tablespoon salt
4 sprigs parsley, chopped	3 cups milk
4 small stalks celery, sliced	2 cups heavy cream, divided
½ cup unsalted butter	Few grains of nutmeg
5 medium potatoes, thinly sliced	Chopped chives

In a deep kettle, brown leeks, onion, parsley and celery in the butter. Add the potatoes, broth and salt. Boil 30 minutes or until very tender. Rub through a fine sieve or puree in an electric blender. Return pureed mixture to kettle; add the milk and 1 cup of cream. Bring to a boil, remove from heat. May be served hot or cold. Add remaining cup of cream and garnish with nutmeg and chives before serving.

Kay Losch (East Alton)

CREOLE BEANS

8 slices bacon	1 tablespoon onion soup mix
2 1-pound cans green beans, drained	1 pound can stewed tomatoes
	1 teaspoon sugar

Sauté bacon until crisp; drain on paper towel. Pour off all but 1 tablespoon of bacon drippings. Add drained beans and onion soup mix and heat thoroughly. Snip bacon into pieces and add half of bacon to beans and also add tomatoes and sugar. Top with remaining bacon. Place casserole in oven for 30 minutes at 300° F.

Genevieve Heepke (Edwardsville)

COQ AU VIN
Chicken Braised in Wine

2½ pounds broiler-fryer, cut up (or 3 chicken breasts, halved or 3 drumsticks and 3 thighs)
6 bacon slices, diced
⅔ cup sliced green onion
8 small white onions, peeled
½ pound whole mushrooms
1 clove garlic, crushed
1 teaspoon salt
¼ teaspoon pepper
½ teaspoon dried thyme leaves
8 small new potatoes, scrubbed
1 cup Burgundy wine
1 cup chicken broth
Chopped parsley

In large skillet, sauté diced bacon and green onions until bacon is crisp. Remove and drain on paper towel. Add chicken pieces to skillet and brown well on all sides. Remove the chicken when it has browned. Set aside. Put peeled onions, mushrooms and garlic in crock pot. Add browned chicken pieces, bacon, green onions, salt, pepper, thyme, potatoes and chicken broth. Cover and set on low for 8 to 10 hours. (High 3 to 4 hours) During last hour, add Burgundy and cook on high.

Mrs. Louis A. Schmidt (Edwardsville)

CREOLE SPICED STEWED OKRA

1½ pounds okra
3 large, firm ripe tomatoes, peeled and chopped
½ pound sliced bacon
1½ cups coarsely chopped onions
1 cup coarsely chopped green peppers
3 dried hot red chilies, each 2″ long
1 teaspoon salt

Wash okra under cold water; scrape to remove any surface fuzz. Cut off stems and slice crosswise into ½-inch rounds. Fry bacon over moderate heat until crisp. Transfer bacon to paper towels to drain, then crumble. Pour off all but about ¼ cup of fat in skillet; add the onions and green peppers. Stirring frequently, cook over moderate heat for 5 minutes, until vegetables are clear. Add okra and, still stirring from time to time, cook uncovered for 15 minutes. Add tomatoes, chilies and salt; reduce heat to low and simmer, tightly covered, for 10 minutes. Mound okra in heated serving bowl and sprinkle crumbled bacon on top. Serve at once. Yield 6 servings.

Kay Losch (East Alton)

FRENCH APPLE COBBLER

FILLING:

5 cups sliced apples	¼ teaspoon salt
¾ cup cane sugar	1 teaspoon vanilla
2 tablespoons flour	1 tablespoon soft butter
¼ teaspoon cinnamon	¼ cup water

Preheat oven to 375° F. Make filling by combining the filling ingredients. Turn into a 9x9x1¾ inch baking dish. Dot with butter.

BATTER:

½ cup flour	¼ teaspoon salt
½ cup sugar	2 tablespoons soft butter
½ teaspoon baking powder	1 egg, slightly beaten

Make batter by combining the batter ingredients and beat until smooth. Drop batter in 9 portions on apples, spacing evenly. Batter will spread during baking. Bake 35 to 40 minutes or until apples are tender and crust is golden brown. Serve with ice cream or Dream Whip if desired.

Mildred Prange (New Douglas)

KARTOFFELKOESSE
(Potato Dumplings)

6 medium potatoes	½ cup butter or drippings
2 eggs	¼ cup bread crumbs or ½ cup
1½ teaspoons salt	croutons
½ cup flour	

Boil potatoes, uncovered, with jackets until tender. Chill thoroughly for 12 hours. Peel and grate or rice. Add eggs, salt and flour. Beat the batter with a fork until it is fluffy. Roll it lightly into balls, the size of medium size potato, and drop them into gently boiling salted water for 10 minutes. Drain them well. Melt butter, stir in bread crumbs or croutons. Pour this over the dumplings. Some cooks prefer to put 1 crouton in the center of each dumpling. This recipe serves 6. Good served with beef roast and gravy.

Florence Dinwiddie (Roxana)

KRAUT KUCHEN
or
Butch's German Hamburgers

1 cup milk
2 tablespoons shortening
2 tablespoons sugar
1 teaspoon salt
1 package dry yeast

¼ cup lukewarm water
1 beaten egg
3½ cups flour (sometimes
   a little more)

CABBAGE FILLING:

1 pound ground beef
1 small head cabbage

2 onions chopped
Salt and pepper to taste

Scald the milk. Add shortening, sugar and salt. Cool. Add yeast softened in lukewarm water and egg beaten. Add flour to form soft dough. Mix and knead. Cover and let rise until double in bulk (about 1½ hours). Turn onto a floured board and roll out to ¼ inch thickness. Using five inch plate, make circles. Put cabbage and meat mixture on one side and fold over. Crimp well and brush with melted butter. Put on greased baking sheet and let rise 20 minutes. Bake in 375° F. oven for about 35 minutes.

CABBAGE MIXTURE:
Brown hamburger; add cabbage and onions. Cook together until cabbage is tender. We like ours with hot mustard.

Lillian Brokaw (Granite City)

KNEDLE
(German Dumpling)

Mix together:

2 teaspoons Spry
2 eggs

1½ cups cream of wheat,
   uncooked

Mix ingredients well. Place by teaspoonfuls into soup and let cook 10 minutes before serving. For use in soup when you don't have noodles to add.

Brenda Norwood Dusek (Collinsville)

447

KNEDLIKY ZE SZELIM
(Dumplings in Kraut)
(Czechoslovakian Dish)

2 pounds sauerkraut
1 tablespoon caraway seed
1 or 2 tablespoons brown
  sugar

4 or 5 tablespoons pork
grease

Heat kraut with brown sugar and caraway seed in pork grease.

DUMPLINGS:

2 large potatoes, cooked
  and mashed
2 cups flour
2 teaspoons salt

2 eggs
Dash pepper
1 teaspoon cream of wheat

Mix potatoes, flour, salt, eggs and pepper. Roll to ¾ inch thick, slice into ½ inch strips. Drop in boiling water, boil until dumpling floats to top. Drain and place in large casserole. Cover with sauerkraut mixture. Heat in 350° F. oven for 30 minutes. Good with pork and cucumbers in sour cream.

Brenda Norwood Dusek (Collinsville)

"DUTCH BABIES"

A different way to have eggs for breakfast.

PAN SIZE	BUTTER	EGGS	MILK AND FLOUR
2-3 quart	¼ cup	3	¾ cup each
3-4 quart	⅓ cup	4	1 cup each
4-4½ quart	½ cup	5	1¼ cups each
4½-5 quart	½ cup	6	1½ cups each

Salt to taste

Put butter into pan, set into 425° F. oven while mixing batter. Put eggs in blender at high speed for one minute. Turn blender on stir (low speed), gradually add milk. Then slowly add flour and salt. Continue stirring 30 seconds. Pour batter slowly into pan with melted butter. Bake until puffy and browned—20 to 25 minutes. Eat as is or with syrup.

Mrs. Leslie J. Cooper (Dorsey)

DEUTCHEN HUHN IN PILZSUCE
(Chicken Deutch Style)

12-ounces fresh mushrooms
(about 4 cups)
2 chicken breasts, skinned
and halved
1 teaspoon salt
1 teaspoon prepared mustard
¼ cup flour

3 tablespoons vegetable oil,
divided
¾ cup water
Pinch ground white pepper
½ cup sour cream
1 teaspoon flour
Paprika

Rinse and pat dry and slice mushrooms. Set aside. Sprinkle both sides of chicken with ½ teaspoon salt and spread with 1¼ teaspoons mustard. Coat with flour. In a large skillet, heat 2 tablespoons oil until hot. Brown chicken on both sides. Remove from pan, wipe out pan. Add mushrooms and sauté until golden, about 5 minutes. Combine water, white pepper and ½ teaspoon mustard. Stir and add chicken, spoon sauce over chicken. Bring to a boil; reduce heat and simmer until tender. Combine sour cream and flour and stir into mixture for 5 minutes.

Mary K. Willaredt (Granite City)

RICHARD'S CHRISTMAS PFEFFERNUESSE

½ cup butter or margarine,
melted
1 cup sugar
2 eggs
½ teaspoon grated lemon rind
½ teaspoon anise oil
2 cups sifted enriched all-
purpose flour

1½ teaspoons cinnamon
½ teaspoon cloves
½ teaspoon baking soda
½ cup finely chopped citron
1½ cups finely chopped
blanched almonds
Powdered sugar

Combine melted butter, sugar and eggs. Blend well. Add lemon rind and anise oil. Sift flour, cinnamon, cloves and soda together. Add to butter mixture. Blend. Add citron and almonds. Shape into small balls using one teaspoon of dough. Place on greased cookie sheets. Bake at 350° F. for 12 to 14 minutes. Coat with powdered sugar. Yield: approximately 12 dozen cookies. May be ripened by placing in a tight covered container.

Alberta Brandt (Worden)

DUTCH CHOCOLATE COOKIES

½ cup butter
1 cup sugar
1 egg
½ cup cocoa

1 cup flour
½ teaspoon baking soda
¼ teaspoon salt

Cream butter and sugar. Add egg and beat well. Sift flour with soda, salt and cocoa. Add to butter mixture. Roll mixture into balls about 1 inch in diameter. Dip tops in sugar and place on cookie sheet. Flatten slightly. Bake on top rack at 350° F. for 12 to 15 minutes. Makes 3 dozen.

Janice Bradley (Marine)

GREASE DEVILS-KEIGLES-DOUGHNUTS

4 cups flour
¼ cup sugar (for doughnuts
    use ½ cup sugar)
4 teaspoons baking powder
2 eggs

1 teaspoon salt
¼ teaspoon nutmeg
1 tablespoon shortening (lard)
Milk

Mix all ingredients and add enough milk to make an elastic and rubber-like dough, not too stiff for the grease devils and keigles. For the doughnuts, make stiff enough to roll. Drop thin dough into hot grease 400° F. Let cook until nice and brown. Can add different flavoring. Sprinkle with powdered sugar, after draining on brown paper bag.

Mrs. Lylah I. Hock (Cottage Hills)

ROSETTES

2 eggs
1 teaspoon sugar
¼ teaspoon salt

1 cup milk
1 cup flour
Powdered sugar

You will need a rosette iron for this recipe. Use a large skillet and heat oil for deep frying. Beat eggs slightly, add sugar, salt and milk. Stir in flour gradually and beat until smooth. Dip iron in hot oil, then into batter, but not letting batter come over top of the iron. Fry for at least 20 seconds, but not over 35 seconds. Remove from iron with a fork or clean cheese cloth. Sprinkle with powdered sugar. Allow to cool before serving.

Elsie Schrumpf (Highland)

HARTSHORN COOKIES

½ cup butter
1 cup sugar
2 to 3 cups flour
3 eggs

1 teaspoon hartshorn,
   dissolved in 2 teaspoons
   warm water
1 teaspoon anise oil

Combine all ingredients well. Keep dough warm if possible. Roll dough out. Cut out cookies. Bake at 350° F. for 15 minutes.

Linda Meyer (Staunton)

SPRINGERLE

2 eggs
1 cup sugar

¼ teaspoon anise extract
1½ cups sifted enriched flour

Beat eggs and sugar over hot (not boiling) water for ten minutes. Remove from heat and continue beating until cool. Add anise extract. Fold in flour to make a moderately stiff dough. Turn out on generously floured board or pastry cloth. Sprinkle top of dough generously with flour. Roll out gently to ¼ inch thickness. Press in design gently with springerle rolling pin or board. Brush off excess flour gently with a clean, dry pastry brush. Cut dough and place on baking sheets that have been greased and floured. Bake in slow oven, 300° F., for ten minutes. Turn off heat and allow cookie to remain in oven five minutes longer. Remove to cooling rack. Yield: Approximately five dozen small cookies. May be ripened. These will keep up to four weeks.

Rhoda Brandt (Worden)

CHICKEN PARMESAN

1½ cups Italian Progresso
   bread crumbs
½ cup Parmesan cheese
1 tablespoon salt

1 teaspoon pepper
6 chicken breasts, or 3 whole
   chickens
1 stick margarine or butter

Combine bread crumbs, cheese, salt and pepper. Dip chicken in melted butter and then into bread crumbs, coat heavily. Place the breasts, skin side up, in baking dish and bake at 350°F. for 30 to 35 minutes. Do not turn chicken. (Can be done a day ahead and refrigerate. Freezes well before or after baking. To reheat after thawed, bake in 325°F. oven until hot.)

Virginia Herrmann (Edwardsville)

ITALIAN SALAD

1 small head cauliflower,
separate into pieces
1 16-ounce can string beans,
drained
1 bunch sweet onions, cut
into bite size pieces
1 green pepper, cut lenthwise

1 box button tomatoes, sliced
in half
1 7-ounce can ripe olives,
drained
1 20-ounce package frozen
peas and carrots, thawed
1 cup celery, diced

DRESSING:

½ cup olive oil

¼ cup wine vinegar

Sprinkle in a dash of parsley flakes, garlic salt and celery salt. (These may be omitted if you wish.) Keep in refrigerator until time to serve. May be made a day ahead.

Jean Highlander (Edwardsville)

LASAGNA

1 8-ounce package lasagna
noodles (long ones)
1 pound ground beef
1 medium onion, minced
1 clove garlic, chopped
1 teaspoon parsley (can be
dried)
1 tablespoon whole basil
2 6-ounce cans tomato paste

2 cups water
½ teaspoon salt
½ teaspoon pepper
2 eggs
¾ pound cottage cheese
½ or ¾ pound Mozzarella
cheese
Grated Parmesan cheese

Brown ground beef until pink disappers, not hard. Add onion, garlic, parsley and basil. Add tomato paste, water, salt and pepper. Simmer *uncovered* at least 1½ hours. Add lasagna to 6 quarts boiling salted water. Cook until tender. Drain. Mix beaten eggs and cottage cheese together. Arrange lasagna in baking dish, 13x9x2 inches. Sprinkle grated Parmesan over top, then a layer of sauce, then cottage cheese. Begin again with lasagna, then Parmesan, then sauce and then cottage cheese, etc. Make 3 layers. Put the sliced Mozzarella cheese on top. Bake in moderate oven, 350° F., for about 30 minutes. Let stand out of oven 10 to 15 minutes before cutting into squares. This makes cutting and serving easier.

Madelyn Grotefendt (Marine)

ITALIAN BEEF

1 6-pound rump roast
3 large onions
1 teaspoon salt

¼ teaspoon coarse ground
black pepper

Place beef in roaster, half filled with water. Add salt, pepper and onion. Bake in moderate oven, covered, 350° F. Roast until tender. Take from oven. Remove from roaster, transferring to a container in which meat and seasoning can stand overnight. Next day remove fat. Slice beef very, very thin. Almost shave it. Strain liquid and add:

½ teaspoon garlic salt
½ teaspoon oregano
¼ teaspoon basil

½ teaspoon Italian seasoning
½ teaspoon seasoned salt
1 teaspoon Ac'cent

Bring all ingredients to a boil. Remove from stove. Place thinly sliced beef in layers in pan, sprinkling each with seasoning. Pour remaining liquid over to cover beef. Place in 350° F. oven for one hour. Serve warm on buns or hard bread and serve with small hot peppers.

Madelyn Grotefendt (Marine)

LASAGNA

1 6-ounce can tomato paste
2½ cans water
1 teaspoon garlic salt
2 tablespoons sugar
½ teaspoon Italian seasoning
½ teaspoon salt
½ teaspoon pepper
2 tablespoons butter
1 tablespoon vegetable
   shortening

¾ pound ground beef
½ cup chopped onion
1 16-ounce package lasagna
   noodles
2 cups cottage cheese
6 ounces Mozzarella cheese,
   shredded

For sauce, combine tomato paste, water, garlic salt, sugar and seasonings. Bring to boil. Set aside. In butter and shortening, brown ground beef and onion. Add meat to tomato mixture. Simmer 45 minutes. Prepare lasagna noodles as directed on package. Cover a 9x13 inch pan bottom with noodles, then add a layer of meat sauce, a layer of cottage cheese, a layer of Mozzarella cheese. Repeat the layers until pan is filled, ending with sauce on top. Bake at 350° F. for 30 minutes.

Mary Lou Sutton (Alton)

SHORTCUT LASAGNA

1 tablespoon vegetable oil
1½ pounds ground chuck
1 1-pound 12-ounce can whole
   tomatoes
1 8-ounce can tomato sauce
2 envelopes dehydrated
   spaghetti sauce mix
2 12-ounce cans cocktail
   vegetable juice

1 16-ounce package lasagna
   noodles
1 12-ounce carton cottage
   cheese
1 8-ounce package Mozzarella
   cheese, shredded
¼ cup grated Parmesan
   cheese
Chopped parsley

Heat oil in large skillet; add meat and cook, breaking up with wooden spoon. Stir in tomatoes, tomato sauce, sauce mix and vegetable juice. Bring to boiling; lower heat and simmer 10 minutes. Cover the bottom of an oiled 13x9x2 inch baking dish with a thin layer of meat sauce. Then add a layer each of uncooked noodles, cottage cheese and Mozzarella cheese. Repeat layers until all ingredients are used, ending with meat sauce. Cover casserole tightly with heavy-duty aluminum foil. Set on a jelly-roll pan. Bake in moderate oven 350° F. for 1 hour. Remove from oven; let stand 15 minutes. Sprinkle with Parmesan cheese and chopped parsley. Cut into squares to serve.

Beverly Dustmann (Dorsey)

CUBE STEAK PARMIGIANA

4 cube steaks
1 egg, beaten
½ cup Parmesan cheese
½ cup fine bread or cracker
   crumbs
⅓ cup salad oil
1 medium onion, minced
1 teaspoon salt

¼ teaspoon pepper
½ teaspoon sugar
½ teaspoon marjoram
1 15-ounce can tomato sauce
1 6-ounce can tomato paste
1 cup boiling water
½ pound shredded Mozzarella
   cheese

Carefully dip cube steak in egg; roll in Parmesan cheese and crumb mixture. Heat oil in skillet and brown steaks over medium heat on both sides until lightly browned. Put in shallow baking dish. In same skillet, cook onion until transparent. Stir in remaining ingredients except Mozzarella cheese. Heat until well blended. Pour ¾ of sauce over meat; top with Mozzarella cheese; add rest of sauce. Bake at 350°F. about 1 hour. Makes 4 servings.

Reita Sparrowk (Bethalto)

EGGPLANT PARMESAN DINNER

1½ pounds ground beef
1 large eggplant
3 eggs, beaten
2 cups dried bread crumbs
½ cup grated Parmesan
    Cheese

2 teaspoons Italian seasoning
1 pound cottage cheese
1 15-ounce can tomato sauce

Cook ground beef until pink is gone. Set aside. Pare eggplant, cut into ¼ inch thick slices. Dip each slice into eggs, then into crumbs. Sauté in skillet until golden on both sides. In large casserole, layer eggplant, ground beef, cottage, cheese, tomato sauce and seasoning. Sprinkle on Parmesan cheese. Repeat; topping last layer with tomato sauce and Parmesan cheese. Bake, 350° F. uncovered, ½ hour or until sauce is bubbly.

Mary Jane Gass (Granite City)

LITTLE PIZZAS

1 pound sausage
½ pound Velveeta cheese
1 tablespoon ketchup
1 tablespoon Worcestershire
    sauce

Salt to taste
Garlic to taste
1 large loaf party rye bread

Brown and drain sausage. Add ketchup, Worcestershire sauce, salt and garlic. Place over double boiler and add cheese until all is melted. Spread on individual rye slices and bake at 325° F. for 20 minutes. Makes approximately 30 "little pizzas." Serve warm.

Janine Cooper (Edwardsville)

PIZZA SQUARES

1 pound Velveeta cheese
1 pound hot sausage
1 6-ounce can tomato paste

Oregano
Garlic salt
2 loaves party rye bread

Cook sausage and drain. Melt cheese in double boiler, then add tomato paste, seasonings to taste and sausage. Simmer. Spread over rye bread. Bake at 350° F. for 10 minutes. Can also be frozen and baked later.

Donna Price (Granite City)

PIZZA BY THE YARD

1 unsliced loaf French bread
1 6-ounce can tomato paste
⅓ cup grated Parmesan
 cheese
¼ cup finely chopped green
 onion
¼ cup chopped pitted ripe
 olives
½ teaspoon dried oregano,
 crushed

¾ teaspoon salt
⅛ teaspoon pepper
1 pound ground beef
2 tomatoes, sliced
1 green pepper, cut in rings
4 ounces sharp processed
 American cheese
⅛ teaspoon pepper

Cut loaf in half lenghwise. Combine tomato paste, Parmesan cheese, onion, olives, oregano, salt and pepper. Add meat, mix well. Spread atop loaf halves. Place on baking sheet. Bake in 400° F. oven for 20 minutes. Remove from oven, top with tomato slices and green pepper rings. Sprinkle cheese atop tomatoes. Bake 5 minutes more. Serves 4 or 5.

Kathryn Cook (Marine)

PERKY PORKY PIZZA BAKE

½ cup milk
1 tablespoon sugar
¼ cup warm water
1 package dry yeast
2⅔ cups flour
⅓ cup shortening (liquid)
1 teaspoon salt
1 pound ground pork sausage
1 small onion, chopped

1 teaspoon oregano
½ teaspoon garlic salt
2 8-ounce cans tomato sauce
4 slices American cheese
1 4-ounce can sliced
 mushrooms, drained
¼ cup grated Parmesan
 cheese
4 slices Brick cheese

Preheat oven to 400° F. To make crust, scald milk and add sugar. Cool to lukewarm. Dissolve yeast in warm water. Then mix in milk-sugar, yeast, flour, shortening and salt. Knead dough. Roll ½ the dough to cover bottom and ½ way up sides of a greased 9x13 inch pan. Roll out remainder for top crust and put aside. Brown sausage, drain. Add onion, oregano, garlic salt and 2 cans tomato sauce. Line bottom crust with American cheese. Then layer meat mixture, mushrooms, then Brick cheese. Cover with top crust. Slit it, brush with oil and sprinkle with Parmesan cheese. Bake 20 to 25 minutes. Makes 6 to 8 servings.

Virginia Schuette (Staunton)

POLENTA PARMIGIANO

POLENTA:

1 tablespoon butter or margarine	1 cup yellow cornmeal
¼ cup chopped onion	1¼ teaspoons salt
3½ cups water, divided	½ cup grated Parmesan cheese

Melt butter in a 3 quart sauce pan over medium heat. Add onion and cook until tender. Add 2½ cups water and bring to a boil. In a mixing bowl, mix remaining 1 cup water, cornmeal and salt. Stir into boiling water. Stir constantly for 3 minutes or until mixture thickens. Cover and cook over low heat for 15 minutes. Remove from heat and stir in Parmesan cheese. Turn into a greased 15½x10½x1 inch pan. Cover and chill 1 hour.

SAUCE:

1 pound Italian sweet sausage	¼ teaspoon dried leaf thyme
½ cup chopped celery	⅛ teaspoon pepper
¼ cup chopped onion	1 pound zucchini, sliced
1 clove garlic, minced	1 cup shredded Mozzarella cheese
2 16-ounce cans tomatoes	
¼ teaspoon salt	

Remove casing from sausage. In large skillet brown sausage over medium heat. Stir in celery, onion and garlic. Cook until vegetables are tender. Stir in tomatoes, salt, thyme and pepper. Simmer uncovered for 20 minutes. Stir in zucchini slices and remove from heat.

To assemble casserole:
Cut polenta into 8 rectangles. Place 4 rectangles, overlapping slightly, on bottom of a greased 11¾x7½x2 inch baking dish. Top with half of the sauce. Repeat with polenta and sauce. Sprinkle Mozzarella over all. Bake at 350° F. for 45 minutes. Let stand 5 minutes before serving. Yield 8 servings.

Kay Losch (East Alton)

RAVIOLI

1½ cups flour (approximate)   ⅛ teaspoon salt
1 egg, slightly beaten   1 tablespoon cold water

Heap flour on bread board and form well, drop in beaten egg, salt and water; work into stiff dough, knead. Divide into two pieces. Roll into thin sheets, let rest.

FILLING:

1 cup cooked ground meat   1 teaspoon parsley, minced
2 tablespoons Parmesan   1 tablespoon butter
  cheese   4 ounces chopped cooked
1 egg, beaten   spinach
Salt and pepper to taste

Mix all ingredients, spread on one sheet of dough. Roll top sheet a little wider. Place over filling. Roll with ravioli maker or use pie crimper. Make squares about 1½ inches. Separate squares.

BOILED RAVIOLI:
Drop squares into boiling water, cook until they float to top; about 4 to 5 minutes. If they are gummy, let set in hot water a little longer. Carefully take from water, drain. Put on platter, cover with meat sauce.

BAKED RAVIOLI:
Boil ravioli as above, drain, place in baking dish, cover with meat sauce, sprinkle with Parmesan cheese, bake at 350° F. for 15 minutes.

TOASTED RAVIOLI:
Heat oil in deep-fat fryer or deep pot. Dip uncooked ravioli in milk, roll in bread crumbs. Deep fry in hot oil. They will rise to top of oil when done. Turn squares as they cook to an even doneness.

Helen Miller (Granite City)

CANESHOUNE
Italian Easter Bread

FILLING:

12 eggs
2 medium mashed potatoes,
  if desired
½ pound plus 1 cup cooked
  rice (approximately 2½ cups
  uncooked)

1 pound grated Romano
  cheese
1¼ teaspoons baking soda
1 teaspoon pepper

Spread cooked rice on sink top to dry a little. Then mix rice and all ingredients and set aside. (Consistency should be like thick cream.)

DOUGH:

5½ cups sifted flour
3 eggs
Dash pepper (or two)
1½ teaspoons salt

¼ cup Mazola or olive oil
1½ teaspoons shortening
¾ cup water
1 egg, beaten

Knead dough until not too soft or not too rubbery. Roll dough to ⅛ inch thickness. Cut in circles 8 to 10 inches around. (Cover dough and circles when not using.) Put 2 heaping tablespoons of filling in the middle of each circle, fold over until edges meet, using egg to glue edges and seal with fork. Place on cookie sheet and brush tops with beaten egg. Bake 1 hour at 350° to 400° F.

Brenda Norwood Dusek (Collinsville)

SPAGHETTI

1 large onion, chopped
3 large celery stalks
3 garlic buds
1 stick butter
2 pounds ground beef
Salt and pepper to taste
2 4-ounce cans tomato sauce

1 6-ounce can tomato paste
1 4-ounce can mushrooms
⅛ teaspoon rosemary
⅛ teaspoon oregano
⅛ teaspoon marjoram
1 10-ounce package spaghetti

Melt butter in pan, sauté chopped onion, celery and garlic. Do not brown. Brown ground beef, drain fat, add tomato sauce and paste. Add celery and onion mixture, then seasonings. Simmer for 2 hours. Cook 1 package of spaghetti until tender and serve over meat sauce. Serves 4. Sauce may be made ahead of time and frozen for later use.

Cindy Hemann (New Douglas)

HOT ITALIAN BEEF SANDWICH

3 or 4 pound roast
3 large onions
1 teaspoon salt
1 teaspoon onion salt
1 teaspoon garlic salt
1 teaspoon oregano

½ teaspoon basil
1 teaspoon Italian seasoning
1 teaspoon seasoned salt
2 teaspoons Ac'cent
Poor boy buns or hamburger
buns

Place roast, chopped onions and salt in a covered roaster half full of water. Cook until meat pulls apart easily. Approximately four hours at 350° F. While meat is warm, pull apart and remove excess bone and fat. Place meat in a medium size baking dish. Add remaining seasoning to beef juice and bring to a boil. Pour juice over meat. Bake at 350° F. for 35 minutes. Serve on warm poor boy buns, hamburger or hot dog buns. Serves 12. (In pulling the meat apart, I use two forks to get a shredded result. Meat will be juicy and flavorful.)

Cindy Hemann (New Douglas)

STROMBOLI SANDWICHES

1 pound ground beef
1 tablespoon finely chopped
  onion
½ cup tomato sauce
½ cup catsup
2 tablespoons Parmesan
  cheese

½ teaspoon garlic powder
½ teaspoon oregano
6 slices Mozzarella cheese
6 Kaiser rolls

Brown beef and onion. Add tomato sauce, cheese, catsup, garlic and oregano. Cook 20 minutes. Split rolls and spread with garlic spread (recipe below). Spread with meat sauce. Top with Mozzarella cheese. Wrap each in foil. Bake at 350° F. for 15 minutes.

GARLIC SPREAD:

2 tablespoons softened butter
¼ teaspoon garlic salt

½ teaspoon paprika

Mix together well.

Carol Russell (Bethalto)

460

SPAGHETTI DINNER

1 pound ground beef
½ cup chopped onion
½ cup chopped green pepper
1 10-ounce can tomato soup
1 15-ounce can tomato sauce
1 teaspoon garlic salt
2 teaspoons Italian herb
  seasoning

Pepper and salt to taste
1 tablespoon sugar
1 4-ounce can mushroom
  pieces
1 pound long spaghetti,
  cooked according to
  directions on package

Cook ground beef until pink is gone. Add onion and peppers; cook until onions are tender. Add soup and sauce; heat thoroughly. Add seasonings and simmer about 5 minutes. Add mushroom pieces last. Meanwhile, cook spaghetti according to package directions. Drain. Arrange cooked spaghetti on plates. Pour hot sauce over spaghetti and serve with grated Parmesan cheese.

Mary Jane Gass (Granite City)

MIKE'S GREEK VEGETABLE STEW

½ pound okra, sliced
  lengthwise
1 cup water

1 cup vinegar
¾ pound eggplant, diced
1 pound zucchini, diced

Soak okra for 2 hours in a solution of water and vinegar.

SAUCE:

4 tomatoes, peeled and
  chopped
3 ribs celery, chopped
1 green pepper, chopped
1 medium onion, chopped

1 clove garlic, minced
Parsley to taste
2 tablespoons sugar
Salt and pepper to taste
2 tablespoons olive oil

Combine tomatoes, celery, pepper, onion, garlic, parsley, sugar, salt and pepper. Simmer 15 minutes, set aside. Drain okra; rinse under cold running water until slickness is gone. Add okra, eggplant and zucchini to prepared sauce; cook until vegetables are tender; add oil. Can be used as main or side dish.

Carolyn Losch (East Alton)

HAWAIIAN CAKE

1 18½-ounce package yellow
cake mix
1 5½-ounce large package
instant vanilla pudding mix
1 cup cold milk
1 8-ounce package cream
cheese, softened
1 9-ounce container frozen
whipped topping, thawed

1 20-ounce can crushed
pineapple, well drained
½ cup chopped pecans
½ cup flaked coconut
½ cup Maraschino cherries,
chopped and drained

Preheat oven to 350°F. Prepare cake mix according to package directions. Pour batter into a greased 10x15 inch jelly roll pan. Bake 15 to 20 minutes or until cake tests done. Cool in pan. When cooled, blend pudding mix with milk by hand. Blend in well softened cream cheese until smooth. Fold in whipped topping. Be sure to move quickly as it may get stiff. Spread pudding mixture on top of cooled cake. Spread drained pineapple over pudding. Sprinkle with chopped cherries, nuts and then coconut. Refrigerate until ready to cut. Serves 15 to 18.

Mrs. George P. Eckert (Collinsville)

HAWAIIAN WEDDING CAKE

1 yellow cake mix (butter
batter preferred)
1 8-ounce package cream
cheese
½ cup milk
1 large package instant
vanilla pudding

2½ cups milk
1 large can crushed
pineapple, well drained
1 9-ounce container Cool
Whip
Coconut, maraschino
cherries, walnuts, chopped

Bake cake in 15½x10½x1 inch foil pan or cookie sheet. Bake for 20 minutes. Mix cream cheese and milk. Set aside. Make instant vanilla pudding with milk as directed on package. Add cheese mixture to pudding mixture. Beat well. Spread this mixture over cooled cake. Spread pineapple on next, then Cool Whip over cheese mixture. Sprinkle with coconut, cherries and walnuts. Keep refrigerated.

Peggy Torrence (Highland)

HAWAIIAN DREAM CAKE

1 package yellow cake mix
1 8-ounce package cream
  cheese
1 3-ounce package vanilla
  instant pudding
1 cup cold milk

1 20-ounce can crushed
  pineapple, drained (reserve
  liquid)
1 cup coconut
1 cup pecans
1 container Cool Whip

Mix yellow cake according to directions, substituting pineapple juice for part of liquid. Bake in 15x11x1 inch pan which has been greased and floured. Cool. For icing, beat softened cream cheese, pudding mix and cold milk. Fold in pineapple. Put on cake and cover with Cool Whip, coconut and pecans.

Ruth Brave (Granite City)

GAZPACHO SALAD

2 cups peeled, chopped
  tomatoes
½ cup chopped cucumbers
½ cup chopped celery

¼ cup chopped green peppers
2 tablespoons chopped onions
½ cup vinegar and oil salad
  dressing

Mix all ingredients together; let marinate in the salad dressing several hours. Drain portion to be served. Will keep in tightly covered jar several days in refrigerator.

Kay Losch (East Alton)

TACOS

2 cups flour
1 teaspoon salt
1 teaspoon baking powder

1½ tablespoons Crisco
¾ cup tepid water

Blend dry ingredients and Crisco until it resembles coarse corn meal. Add water, mix. Divide into 12 balls. Roll on slightly floured board until thin as possible. Heat iron skillet with 1 inch deep fat. Fry taco until lightly browned. Fold over slightly as you fry them.

FILLING:
Shredded lettuce, chopped tomatoes, refried beans or cooked ground beef. Onions and radishes sliced thin. Use any or all of the above. Sprinkle with grated cheese. Spoon on taco sauce.

Helen Miller (Granite City)

CLEAR GAZPACHO
(Cold Soup)

4 cups regular-strength
chicken broth, chilled
4 medium-sized tomatoes,
chopped
2 tablespoons olive oil or
salad oil
6-8 tablespoons fresh lime
juice (about 3 limes)
Salt to taste

½ teaspoon seasoned pepper
1 small red onion, finely
chopped
1 or 2 green bell peppers,
finely chopped
1 or 2 stalks celery, finely
chopped
Lime slices and watercress
sprigs for garnish (optional)

Remove any fat from broth and discard. Mix with tomatoes (including juices), pepper, oil, lime juice (taste for tartness desired), and salt. Chill thoroughly. Serve from a tureen or bowl, ladling into dishes and offering individual containers of onion, green pepper, and celery to add according to personal preference. Garnish bowls with lime slices and watercress. Makes 4 to 6 servings.

Kay Losch (East Alton)

TACO CASSEROLE

1 pound ground beef,
browned with:
1 onion
1 teaspoon chili powder

1 teaspoon salt
¼ teaspoon pepper
Pour off grease and set aside

Butter 6 tortillas and cut into strips.

1 7-ounce can olives
1 15-ounce can tomato sauce

2 cups shredded Cheddar
cheese
⅔ cup water

In a buttered casserole, put the tortillas in alternate layers with the meat and other ingredients. Pour water around the edges to the bottom of the casserole. Top with cheese and bake at 400°F. for 40 minutes.

Peggy Torrence (Highland)

CHILI CON QUESO
Chili Cheese Dip

Use electric range, skillet or chafing dish. Use low temperature. Yield 1¾ cups. Freezes well.

1 cup American cheese
½ cup Cheddar cheese
¼ cup cream or evaporated
 milk
⅛ teaspoon garlic powder
1 medium, fresh, chopped
 tomato

1 or more fresh or frozen or
 canned green chili peppers,
 chopped
Tostados
Tortillas

Melt both cheeses together on low heat of electric surface unit. When melted, add cream, stirring constantly. Add chopped tomato, green chili and garlic, stir to blend all. Add more cream if desired. Serve warm in electric skillet or chafing dish with Tostados, crisp fried, Tortillas.

Brenda Norwood Dusek (Collinsville)

EL RANCHO CASSEROLE

1 pound ground beef
1 cup chopped onion
1 7-ounce package elbow
 macaroni
1 1-pound 12-ounce can
 tomatoes or 3½ cups
 tomatoes
1½ cups whole kernel corn,
 undrained (12-ounce can)

½ pound Velveeta cheese,
 cubed
½ cup water
1 tablespoon chili powder
1 teaspoon salt
¼ teaspoon pepper

Brown meat; drain. Add onions and cook until tender. Stir in remaining ingredients. Cover and simmer, stirring occasionally, 30 to 35 minutes. Makes 6 to 8 servings.

Diane Dustmann (Dorsey)

465

MEXICAN HAMBURGERS

1 pound ground beef
1 tablespoon butter
Salt and pepper
1 onion, finely minced
Small pieces of green pepper,
  finely minced
2-3 stalks celery, chopped

1 tablespoon sugar
1 tablespoon prepared
  mustard
1 tablespoon vinegar
1 teaspoon salt
1 cup catsup

Brown beef in butter. Salt and pepper to taste. Add onion, green pepper and celery. Simmer until onion is tender. Add sugar, mustard, vinegar and catsup. Simmer one half hour. Makes 6 sandwiches.

Norma Meyer (Edwardsville)

SKILLET SPANISH RICE

¼ cup Wesson, pure vegetable
  oil
1 cup raw regular rice
1 medium onion, thinly sliced
½ medium green peper,
  chopped
1 pound ground beef

2 8-ounce cans Hunts tomato
  sauce
1¾ cups hot water
1 teaspoon prepared mustard,
  optional
1 teaspoon salt
¼ teaspoon pepper

Heat Wesson in large skillet. Add rice and brown lightly, then add onion, green pepper and beef. Stir over high heat until meat is lightly browned. Add remaining ingredients. Mix well; bring quickly to boil. Cover tightly; simmer for 25 minutes. Makes four servings.

Diane Dustmann (Dorsey)

SCANDINAVIAN COOKIES

½ cup butter
¼ cup brown sugar
1 egg, separated

1 cup sifted flour
½ cup chopped nuts
Jelly or white icing

Cream butter until soft. Blend in sugar. Add egg yolk, beating until light. Blend in flour. Roll dough into small balls (1 inch diameter). Dip in whipped egg white and roll in chopped nuts. Place on greased cookie sheet and make a depression in center. Bake 5 minutes in slow oven, 300° F. Remove from oven and press down centers again. Continue baking 1 minute longer. Cool slightly and fill centers with jelly or plain white icing. Yield 1 dozen cookies.

Sharon Schlaefer (St. Jacob)

HAMBURGER HACIENDA

1 pound hamburger, browned and drained
2 cups tomatoes
1 cup chopped onion
1 cup chopped green pepper

1 cup uncooked macaroni-n-cheese from one package Kraft macaroni-n-cheese dinner

Mix all the above ingredients together. Cover and simmer for 20 minutes.

Alice Stille (Alhambra)

FLAN

1 13½-ounce can evaporated milk
1 teaspoon vanilla

4 eggs
⅞ cup sugar, divided

Put ½ cup sugar into a deep baking pan and place over heat. Stir constantly until sugar melts and turns golden brown. Remove from heat and tip pan back and forth until it is entirely coated with caramelized sugar. Beat eggs well, add milk, remaining sugar (6 tablespoons) and vanilla. Beat until sugar dissolves, then put custard into caramelized-coated pan. Cover custard; place pan in a larger pan containing 1 inch of hot water and bake at 350° F. for 1 hour. While still hot, turn on serving platter.

Kay Losch (East Alton)

BEEF STROGANOFF

¼ pound butter
1 large onion, chopped
2 pounds round steak
Flour
Salt
Pepper

Ac'cent
3 beef boullon cubes
3 cups boiling water
1 4-ounce can mushrooms
1 8-ounce carton sour cream

Sauté onions in butter. Cut round steak into strips and then into 1½ inch pieces. Put flour, salt, pepper and Ac'cent into a plastic bag and shake meat until coated. Brown meat in butter. Add water and boullion cubes to make a thin gravy. Cook meat slowly until tender (approximately half hour). Add canned mushrooms and the sour cream just until heated. Do not cook. Good served over rice or noodles.

Mrs. Wilma Becker (Moro)

CHICKEN PAPRIKASH

3-4 pound chicken
2 teaspoons salt
¼ cup shortening
2 small onions, chopped
1½ tablespoons paprika

⅛ teaspoon ground red
  pepper, optional
1½ cups hot water
½ pint sour cream

Wash, clean and cut chicken in serving pieces. Salt and flour the pieces and brown in hot shortening. Add onions and paprika. Sauté until onions are a golden brown. (If you like the gravy hot, add the ground red pepper now). Add the hot water. Cover and let simmer for one hour. About five minutes before serving, mix in the sour cream (must be room temperature). Serve with noodles, dumplings or mashed potatoes.

Helen Eich (Edwardsville)

SCANDINAVIAN FRUIT SUPE

2 cups dried fruit (prunes and
  packaged mixed dried fruit)
½ cup raisins
1 stick cinnamon
2 tablespoons quick cooking
  Tapioca

6 cups liquid (water or fruit
  juice drained from canned
  fruit
1 lemon, cut in thin slices
¼ cup sugar
¼ teaspoon salt

Combine dried fruits, cinnamon stick and liquid. Bring to a boil. Reduce heat and simmer about 30 minutes or until fruit is tender. Add remaining ingredients. Bring to boil. Reduce heat and simmer 15 minutes longer. Serve warm or cold for dessert, breakfast, as an appetizer or snack. Will keep up to two weeks stored in a covered bowl in the refrigerator.

Mrs. George Eckert (Collinsville)

KASHA

To go with beef roast.
Kasha is roasted buckwheat kernels.

3 cups water   **½ cup Kasha**
2 beef bouillon cubes

Bring above water and bouillon to a boil. Pour half cup Kasha into boiling liquid. Continuing cooking for ten to twelve minutes. Stir occasionally. Serve hot with a pat of butter or sauce from roast.

VARIATION: Can be eaten as a breakfast substitue for Cream of Wheat or Oatmeal.

Mildred Urban (Highland)

SUKIYAKI WITH NOODLES AND SESAME SEEDS

1 10-ounce package fresh
  spinach
½ cup beef broth, made with
  ½ cup boiling water and 1
  beef bouillon cube
½ cup soy sauce
¼ cup dry sherry wine
4 teaspoons sugar
1 teaspoon vegetable oil
2 tablespoons sesame seeds
2 tablespoons vegetable oil

1 bunch green onions cut into
  2 inch lengths (about ¾ cup)
½ pound fresh mushrooms,
  sliced thin (about 3 cups)
1 pound chinese celery
  cabbage, cut into 1 inch
  slices (about 5 cups)
1 tablespoon cornstarch
3 cups cooked vermicelli or
  thin spaghetti (½ pound
  uncooked)

Remove and discard tough stems from spinach, wash several times, drain. In a measuring cup combine the beef broth, soy sauce, sherry and sugar. In a large skillet or wok, heat the vegetable oil over moderate heat; add sesame seed and cook until lightly toasted. Remove seeds to a paper towel to drain. Add the 2 tablespoons vegetable oil to skillet, increase heat to moderately high and add green onions; stir-fry 3 minutes. Add mushrooms, stir-fry 1 minute longer. Add cabbage and ½ cup of soy-sherry mixture and stir over high heat 1 minute. Then cover and cook 1 minute longer, until cabbage is crisp-tender. Mix cornstarch with remaining soy-sherry mixture, stir into vegetables in skillet. Reduce heat slightly, when sauce begins to thicken, stir in spinach and vermicelli. Cover and cook about 3 minutes, stirring until spinach wilts and noodles are hot. Sprinkle with sesame seeds and serve.

Helen Miller (Granite City)

CHINESE FRIED WALNUTS

6 cups water
4 cups English walnuts
½ cup sugar

Salad oil
Salt

In four quart saucepan over high heat, bring water to boil. Add walnuts, heat to boiling and cook one minute. Rinse walnuts under hot water in sieve and allow to drain. In large bowl, mix warm walnuts with sugar. Let stand five minutes to dissolve sugar. In saucepan or deep fryer, heat one inch salad oil to 350° F. With slotted spoon, add about one half of walnuts. Fry five minutes, stirring often. Remove to sieve to drain. Sprinkle lightly with salt and toss to keep from sticking. Cool on paper towels. Fry and prepare remaining walnuts in same manner. NOTE: not good with pecans.

Ruth Brave (Granite City)
Esther Zimmer

CHINESE LETTUCE SALAD

¾ cup chopped celery
1½ heads lettuce, chopped
1 can bean sprouts, drained
½ cup chopped onion
⅛ cup sesame seed
1 small package slivered
  almonds

1 3-ounce can Chow Mein
  noodles
3 or 4 chicken breasts, fried,
  skinned and cut up to small
  pieces

DRESSING:

4 tablespoons vinegar
½ cup oil
4 tablespoons sugar

2 teaspoons salt
3 teaspoons Ac'cent
½ teaspoon pepper

Toss the first six ingredients together until well mixed. Blend all dressing ingredients. Dribble dressing over lettuce and mix well until lettuce is coated. Sprinkle Chow Mein noodles on top and add pieces of chicken, or spoon lettuce into individual dishes and top with Chow Mein noodles and chicken.

Sharon Schlaefer (St. Jacob)

CHICKEN CANTONESE

1 quart chicken broth
3 cups thinly sliced celery
2 cups diced onion
2 cups green pepper chunks
½ cup cornstarch
½ cup water
1 4-ounce can water
  chestnuts, drained

1 4-ounce can mushrooms,
  undrained
½ cup soy sauce
3 cups cooked chicken in bite-
  size chunks

Cook chicken in salted water until done. Remove chicken. In 1 quart of broth parboil celery, onion and green pepper for *5 minutes*. Remove skin and bones and dice cooked chicken. Dissolve cornstarch in water. Add to vegetables and heat. When thickened, add water chestnuts, mushrooms, soy sauce and diced chicken. Simmer only enough to heat the last ingredients added. Serve over hot rice. Garnish with strips of pimento.

Ruth Brave (Granite City)

CHOP SUEY CHOW MEIN

½ pound diced pork
½ pound diced beef
½ pound diced veal
1 cup water, or chicken stock
1 cup onions, sliced or diced,
  large pieces

3 cups celery, sliced in 1 inch
  pieces
1 teaspoon salt
¼ teaspoon pepper

Brown meat thoroughly in pressure pan. Add remaining ingredients. Cover pressure pan, cook at 10 pounds of pressure for 15 minutes, or ½ hour without pressure or until meat is tender. Cool, remove gauge and add:

1 #2 can Chop Suey
  vegetables or bean sprouts

6 tablespoons soy sauce
3 tablespoons dark molasses

Stir until thick. Serve with hot cooked rice and Chow Mein noodles which have been warmed in oven.
NOTE: ¾ pound of pork and ¾ pound of beef may be used in place of the veal.

Florence Rapp (Edwardsville)

ORIENTAL BEAN SPROUT SALAD

1 16-ounce can bean sprouts, drained
1 can chestnuts, sliced and drained
1 16-ounce can French style green beans, drained
1 green pepper, sliced lengthwise
1 red pepper, sliced lengthwise
1 small onion, sliced and separate rings and leave whole
1 small jar pimento (optional)
1 cup sliced celery

DRESSING:

1 cup sugar
¾ cup vinegar
OR

¼ cup wine vinegar
½ cup lemon juice
1 cup sugar

Serve cold. May be made a day ahead.

Jean Highlander (Edwardsville)

SWEET SOUR PORK

1 pound boneless pork, cut into 1 inch cubes
1 egg
¼ cup flour
1 tablespoon cornstarch
¼ cup chicken broth
½ teaspoon salt
Cooking oil
1 green pepper, cut into 1 inch cubes
½ cup carrots, sliced (not too thin)
1 clove garlic
2 tablespoons oil
1 cup chicken broth
½ cup sugar
⅓ cup wine vinegar
2 tablespoons soy sauce
¼ cup water
2 tablespoons cornstarch

Trim excess fat from pork. In a bowl, add egg, cornstarch, flour, chicken broth, and salt. Beat. Dip pork cubes into batter and deep fry in the cooking oil. Drain. In skillet, cook peppers, carrots and garlic in 2 tablespoons oil until tender. Stir in broth, sugar, vinegar and soy sauce. Bring to boil, boil 1 minute. Blend in water and cornstarch, stir into vegetables. Cook until thickened and bubbly. Stir in pork cubes. Serve on cooked rice or chinese noodles. Serves 6.

Helen Miller (Granite City)

BEEF CHOP SUEY

1 pound beef, cut into small
  cubes
3 tablespoons cooking oil
½ teaspoon pepper
2 teaspoons salt
2½ tablespoons soy sauce
3 cups celery, cut into 1 inch
  pieces
2 large onions, cut into 1 inch
  pieces
1 tablespoon bead molasses
2 cups boiling water with 2
  bouillon cubes
1 can bean sprouts, drained
3 tablespoons cornstarch

Heat oil, add beef, salt and pepper, cook until tender. Stir in soy sauce, celery, onions, molasses and water with bouillon cubes. Bring to boil, stir frequently until vegetables are tender. Add bean sprouts, cook 3 minutes. Mix cornstarch and ¼ cup water. Add to hot mixture, stir until thickened. Serve on hot rice or chinese noodles. Serves 4 to 6.

Helen Miller (Granite City)

MELTING POT

INDEX

The Women's Committee had been operational only two years when construction began on a new Farm Bureau building. The Oak tree plantings have grown along with us.

V. I. F.

Appetizers

Beverages

Soup

Dairy

Salads

Salad Dressings

Breads

Vegetables

Beef

Ground Beef

Pork

Poultry

Seafood

How Men Cook

Children's

Leisure Cooking

Crock Pot

Candy

Canning

Accompaniments

Melting Pot

INDEX

Please send _____ copies of **Cookbook 25 Years**

@ $17.95 (U.S.) each $_____

Plus postage/handling @ $3.50 each $_____

Texas residents add sales tax @ $1.30 each $_____

Check or Credit Card (Canada-credit card only)   TOTAL $_____

Charge to my _____ Master Card or Visa Card

Account #_____

Expiration Date_____

Signature_____

MAIL, CALL OR EMAIL:
Cookbook Resources
541 Doubletree Drive
Highland Village, TX 75077
972/317-0245
carla@cookbookresources.com

NAME_____

ADDRESS_____

CITY_____ST_____ZIP_____PHONE_____

Please send _____ copies of **Cookbook 25 Years**

@ $17.95 (U.S.) each $_____

Plus postage/handling @ $3.50 each $_____

Texas residents add sales tax @ $1.30 each $_____

Check or Credit Card (Canada-credit card only)   TOTAL $_____

Charge to my _____ Master Card or Visa Card

Account #_____

Expiration Date_____

Signature_____

MAIL, CALL OR EMAIL:
Cookbook Resources
541 Doubletree Drive
Highland Village, TX 75077
972/317-0245
carla@cookbookresources.com

NAME_____

ADDRESS_____

CITY_____ST_____ZIP_____PHONE_____
